# AUSTRALIAN
# FASHION
## *Unstitched*

# AUSTRALIAN
# FASHION
## *Unstitched*

### THE
### LAST
### 60
### YEARS

Bonnie **ENGLISH** & Liliana **POMAZAN**

**CAMBRIDGE**
UNIVERSITY PRESS

CAMBRIDGE UNIVERSITY PRESS
Cambridge, New York, Melbourne, Madrid, Cape Town, Singapore,
São Paulo, Delhi, Dubai, Tokyo

Cambridge University Press
477 Williamstown Road, Port Melbourne, VIC 3207, Australia

Published in the United States of America by Cambridge University Press, New York

www.cambridge.org
Information on this title: www.cambridge.org/9780521756495

First published 2010

Designed & typeset by Adrian Saunders
Printed in China by Printplus

*A catalogue record for this publication is available from the British Library*

*National Library of Australia Cataloguing in Publication data*
English, Bonnie.
    Australian fashion unstitched : the last 60 years / Bonnie English, Liliana Pomazan.
    9780521756495 (pbk.)
    Includes index.
    Fashion–Australia–History.
    Fashion design–Australia–History.
    Fashion designers–Australia–History.
    Pomazan, Liliana.
746.920994

ISBN 978-0-521-75649-5 Paperback

*This book is dedicated with love to our fathers,*
*Bruce and Virgilio*

# Contents

# Contributors

**Craig Douglas** lectures in art theory and curatorship at the Queensland College of Art, Griffith University, Brisbane. Dr Douglas has curated a number of exhibitions, including *Tokyo Vogue* (1999) with Bonnie English. His current research focuses on fashion exhibitions in public art museums from 2000 to 2010.

**Bonnie English** is Associate Professor, Queensland College of Art, Griffith University, Brisbane. She has written several fashion books, including *A Cultural History of Fashion in the 20th Century* (2007), *Little Book of Big Ideas: Fashion* (2009) and *Japanese Fashion Designers: Issey Miyake, Rei Kawakubo & Yohji Yamamoto* (to be published in 2011).

**Jo-Anne Kellock** is the Executive Director of the Council of Textile and Fashion Industries of Australia Limited, the peak body for the Textiles, Clothing and Footwear sector. Over the years her work has embraced key projects, including the *Launch of Size Aus* project and Australia-wide research into clothing size standards. She has been awarded the 2002 IBM National Awards, Outstanding Women in Non-Traditional Areas of Work and in 2003 the *AusIndustry COMET*, development grant for pre-production technology.

**Roger Leong** is the Curator of International Fashion and Textiles at the National Gallery of Victoria, Melbourne. His exhibitions include *Dressed to Kill: 100 Years of Fashion*, *From Russia with Love: Costumes for the Ballets Russes*, *Black in Fashion: Mourning to Night* and *Persuasion: Fashion in the Age of Jane Austen*.

**Louise Mitchell** is a textile and dress specialist and former Curator of Decorative Arts and Design at the Powerhouse Museum in Sydney. Her exhibitions and publications include *Christian Dior: The Magic of Fashion*, *Stepping Out: Three Centuries of Shoes* and *The Cutting Edge: Fashion from Japan*. She has contributed to numerous publications.

**Daniel Palmer** is Senior Lecturer in the Theory Department of the Faculty of Art & Design at Monash University. Dr Palmer publications include *Twelve Australian Photoartists* (2009), co-authored with Blair French, and *Photogenic: Essays/Photography/CCP 2000–2004* (2005).

**Liliana Pomazan** is Senior Lecturer in the Fashion Program of the Royal Melbourne Institute of Technology University, Melbourne. Her expertise lies in the areas of Parisian haute couture and fashion design of the twentieth to twenty-first centuries and recent forms of contemporary Australian fashion practice. Her publications include *Punch Out: Material by Product* (2005).

**Kate Rhodes** is Editor of *Artichoke*, an architecture and design magazine, and Adjunct Curator, Object: Australian Centre for Craft and Design. Kate has worked as a curator at the National Design Centre and Craft Victoria and was formerly Assistant Curator of Photography and Contemporary Art at the National Gallery of Victoria.

**Christine Schmidt** is Fashion and Television History Researcher, Creative Industries, Queensland University of Technology. Dr Schmidt's doctoral thesis traced the career of the modern swimsuit, showing how a peripheral nation, Australia, influenced the design direction of the swimsuit to create a distinctly Australian niche in global fashion. As a fashion and concept consultant for the Australian National Maritime Museum travelling exhibition, *Exposed: The Story of Swimwear*, she developed the Woollen Mermaids project, an inter-institutional and fashion industry collaboration.

**Katie Somerville** is the Curator of Australian Fashion and Textiles at the National Gallery of Victoria, Melbourne. Her exhibitions include *Swish: Fashionable Melbourne of the 1950s*, *Akira Isogawa: Printemps-Eté*, *Pins & Needles: Textile and Technique from the Australian Collection*, *Martin Grant, Paris* and *Together Alone: Australian and New Zealand Fashion*.

**Danielle Whitfield** is Curator, Australian Fashion and Textiles at the National Gallery of Victoria. Her recent exhibitions include Katie Pye, *Clothes* *for Modern Lovers* and *Black in Fashion: Mourning to Night*. She has also written for the *Berg Encyclopaedia of World Fashion* (forthcoming 2010).

**Liz Williamson** is Senior Lecturer, Head and Textiles Coordinator at the School of Design Studies, College of Fine Arts, University of New South Wales, Sydney and an internationally respected textile artist. In 2008, Liz was selected as a *Living Treasure: Masters of Australian Craft* by Object Gallery and the Australian Craft Design Centres Network, acknowledging her contribution to the industry through education, advocacy and as a practising artist.

# Thanks to our sponsors

Griffith
UNIVERSITY

Queensland
College of Art

RMIT
UNIVERSITY

Architecture+Design

Design Research Institute

MONASH University
Art & Design

COUNCIL OF **TEXTILE & FASHION**
INDUSTRIES OF AUSTRALIA LIMITED

# Acknowledgements

We would like to extend a very special thanks to RMIT University, Melbourne, Griffith University, Brisbane, Monash University, Melbourne and the Council of Textile & Fashion Industries Australia Ltd (TFIA) for their generous support for this research project. We are delighted and honoured to have had the opportunity to produce Cambridge University Press' first fashion publication in Australia.

There are a number of special people we would like to thank. First, we are immensely indebted to Cambridge's Publishing Manager Debbie Lee, who mentored us with great enthusiasm, encouragement and support. We thank Paulina de Laveaux for her vision and contribution to the initial direction and shaping of the book and to Sue Jarvis and Frances Wade for their expert copyediting. We would like to acknowledge our remarkable team of contributing writers, Louise Mitchell, Dr Daniel Palmer and Kate Rhodes, Liz Williamson, Dr Craig Douglas, Dr Christine Schmidt, Roger Leong and Katie Somerville, Danielle Whitfield and Jo-Anne Kellock, whose knowledge and expertise in their specific fields have not only enriched the book but have also provided fascinating studies to inspire readers from all walks of life. They have painstakingly secured beautiful visuals to complement their writing and to enhance the aesthetic appeal of the publication. Extending our sincere gratitude to the many designers and photographers who have graciously given permission for their images to be reproduced – we wish to express our admiration for your well-earned success and contribution to the Australian fashion industry.

As co-editors and great friends, we have enjoyed working together, mutually supporting and encouraging each other through the writing and editing process of the book. As academic colleagues, we have worked enthusiastically towards our common goal of making a worthwhile contribution to Australian fashion education. We take great pride in this achievement.

Bonnie's personal acknowledgements: I greatly appreciate the continuing professional support of Professor Paul Cleveland, Director and Associate Professor Ross Woodrow, Deputy-Director Research and Postgraduate Studies, Queensland College of Art, Griffith University for my research endeavours. My family and friends, my colleagues and my students who have shown such unwavering support, interest and enthusiasm over the years have kept my (late night) lights burning.

Liliana's personal acknowledgements: I am highly indebted to my colleagues at RMIT University: Professor Richard Blythe (Head of School: Architecture and Design), Associate Professor SueAnne Ware (Director of Research: School of Architecture and Design and Research Leader: Design Research Institute Urban Liveability Program) and Mick Peel (Program Director, Fashion) for their generous support of the project. Sincere thanks to Alex Syndikas for his photographic expertise and assistance with several of Beril Jents' images. Special thanks to my colleagues and friends in the Fashion, Architecture and Landscape Architecture Programs for their insight, encouragement and support: Michael Howard, Sue Thomas, Karen Webster, Jo Cramer, Denise Sprynskyj, Peter Boyd, Diana Klein, Jan McIllree, Peter Allan, Denise Solley, Robyn Healy, Janette Gavin, Anne-Marie Nankivell and Winnie Ha. As always, I wish to thank my family and friends – I am truly blessed.

# AUSTRALIAN FASHION UNSTITCHED

*Bonnie English*

**1.1** Jimmy Pike, Desert Designs, *Jila Waterhole*, 1983. Indigenous textile print (original is text pen on paper). Courtesy Desert Designs.

**I**N THE YEARS immediately following World War II, glamorous fashion shows from Paris were brought to our major cities, attracting large audiences and bringing European styling to our consciousness. It was at this point that the word 'couturier' became a part of the Australian vernacular. Now, several generations later, young emerging Australian designers, proud in their own heritage, are in their turn offering Australian fashion to the world. Since those early postwar days, cutting-edge Australian swimwear, Indigenous-inspired textiles and our innovative versions of global trends have infiltrated the international marketplace and placed Australian design 'on the map'. The journey has been a long one. In *Australian Fashion Unstitched* this fascinating story is told from the diverse points of view of people who study, write, teach and curate in the field of fashion design. Placing this subject within our nation's social, cultural and historical context, these writers will inform, fascinate and amuse all readers who have a love of fashion and a respect for history.

Valerie Steele, one of today's most prolific fashion authors, writes: 'It is crucial to analyse the culture of fashion from several perspectives, not limiting ourselves to a narrative account of the creations of "the great designers".' In recent years, scholars and costume curators have increasingly realised that fashion must be placed firmly within its cultural and historical context (2000: 1).

The twelve chapters that follow discuss key developments in Australian fashion over the last sixty years. The chapters make reference to specific themes that are fundamental to the postwar growth of the Australian fashion industry, including the rise of a cosmopolitan dress culture; the emergence of local couture design and the influence of Parisian haute couture upon Australian designers; the interaction of fashion photography with fashion journal publications; and the establishment of Sydney and Melbourne as the two main fashion manufacturing centres. By looking at Australian fashion from a sociological, historical and aesthetic perspective, the reader will soon gain an understanding of why new fashion directions emerge.

Key issues are addressed, including the way in which the rise of a beach culture impacted upon the success of Australian swimwear, both at home and abroad; why a strong cultural interrelationship existed between Australian fashion and textile design and the visual and performing arts; and what role major museums and art galleries played in the presentation, promotion and display of fashion.

The last chapters explore the emergence of a mainstream commercial industry that reflected international directions; examine the positioning of contemporary Australian designers within the global arena, discussing how they framed unique Australian fashion directions; and assess whether current Australian avant-garde fashion design is at the cutting edge of global innovation and enterprise. Finally, a report summary documents the business of Australian fashion and the last chapter, 'Fashion Frontiers', considers what the future may hold for the rise of the independent designer and the impact of advanced and future technologies. In general terms, the chapters follow a loose chronological development so that the book can be used effectively both as a textbook and as a reference work, as well as having considerable appeal to the general reader.

Considering the breadth and depth of over 200 years of Australian history, relatively little attention has been paid to the history of fashion here. From early times, the fashion industry was built on the fortitude and moral fibre of the émigré machinists and sewers, the backbone of this burgeoning industry, who were instrumental in the production process. It relied on the craft of local dressmakers and milliners, who created individualised, custom-made garments for their customers, and the drapery shops that supplied the fabric, sewing implements and patterns. Ready-to-wear clothing was distributed by small family businesses initially and then by department stores, which not only provided a venue for the parades and spectacles of the fashionable garments, but also distributed the goods to every corner of this vast country through their mail order services.

We owe a great deal to the fashion entrepreneurs who fostered the growth of an industry hinged on Australia's major domestic textile manufacturers, which in turn drew upon the primary wool and cotton growers, as well as upon the research and development technology laboratories that produced human-made synthetic fabrics. We applaud the seminal writers and researchers who have documented the evolution of fashion in Australia. While few in number, they have produced outstanding publications from which we have drawn much of our knowledge in this field of research.

Significantly, this book offers an insightful evaluation of the fashion industry – an industry that is essential to the well-being of the Australian economy. In historical terms, the cities of Sydney and Melbourne have been the main contenders in the evolution of the fashion industry because, while individual designers may originate in other major cities, manufacture, production and distribution have been centred in these two main locations.

As editors, we deliberately chose a diversity of experts in the various fashion disciplines: Australia's leading curators of state galleries and museums, whose market audience is the general public; highly-esteemed practitioners in the field; emerging researchers offering new primary material to an extremely limited research area; academics with a proven international research profile who are still actively teaching practice-based undergraduate students; and leading influential business representatives, directly involved in liaising with members of the industry. *Australian Fashion Unstitched* contains innovative and seminal material never published before in this collective format. This publication provides a far-reaching, highly informative overview of each fashion discipline as well as a balanced, 'real world' interpretation of the evolution of Australian fashion over the past sixty years.

The study of fashion can be approached using a number of different methodologies, from object-based dress histories relying on primary source investigations relating to production, technology and distribution; through to traditional historical and designer case study documentation; to social and economic histories that can encompass issues dealing with material culture and consumption theories; to cultural studies that place fashion within a visual and performing arts context. *Australian Fashion Unstitched*

**1.2** MATERIALBYPRODUCT, *Curtain Dress*, S/S 2009
Photo: Sue Grdunc. Courtesy MATERIALBYPRODUCT

incorporates all of these approaches, each one particular to a chapter, and provides an expansive and encompassing synopsis of the evolution of fashion in Australia. According to the Textile and Fashion Industry Association (TFIA) representatives, this summary approach is fully endorsed and seen as critical to the fundamental education of future fashion design students.

Furthermore, this study provides the most comprehensive view of contemporary design and designers ever published in an academic format. While the book can only focus on key designers, photographers and textile artists, these selective case studies have been positioned within a social and cultural setting that highlights other major events. They underline the influence and impact of international design upon Australian design and designers and point to new global concerns and developments. An informed discussion, such as this, of the significance and contribution of contemporary Australian designers over the past twenty years, contextualised within an academic framework, is long overdue.

## Chapter overviews

The first few chapters consider the 'boom years' of Australian 1950s fashion, which were inspired by Christian Dior's New Look creations as promoted by *Vogue Australia*, the *Australian Women's Weekly* magazine and the French Fashion Parades (an idea of Frank Packer's), which were presented in major department stores across the country. More than twenty thousand copies of these hourglass-silhouetted garments were made in Australia and large stores like Myer's and David Jones distributed them to Australian women in both urban and rural areas. This consumerist phenomenon highlights the importance of the fashion industry to postwar economies. The significant contribution of the Australian Wool Board[1] to fostering interest in fashion's stylistic developments over the last six decades is acknowledged. The re-emergence of 'glamour' after the austerity of the war years, which inspired designers to create a sumptuous array of extravagant satin and lace evening gowns that appealed to young and old alike, is documented.

Chapter 2 begins our story with the woman who was hailed by the 1950s media as Australia's first *haute couturière*. Sydney's Beril Jents set the benchmark for original, exquisitely made couture garments and was feted by the media, both nationally and internationally. Her clientele included stars of the stage and screen, such as Dame Margot Fonteyn, Elizabeth Taylor, Eartha Kitt, Lorrae Desmond, Bettina Welch and Evie Hayes, as well as members of high society and the sartorial elite. Chapter 3 describes in detail how Jents, through her designs, fabrics and methods of construction, stood at the forefront of a locally developed aesthetic in Australia.

For decades, while fashion photographers were producing advertising images for the glossy pages of leading fashion magazines, including Australian *Vogue*, *Harper's Bazaar* and *marie claire* as well as high-circulation newspapers across the country, fashion journalists – in particular the savvy writers of the *Women's Weekly* – served as a beacon for Australian women. The *Weekly* covered all of the key social events with much aplomb, providing detailed descriptions of what was worn to celebrity occasions and, more importantly, fostering national talent among Australia's designers, photographers and journalists. Interestingly, today's magazines express, as their aims, to be 'entertaining and inspirational, thought provoking and challenging' and 'stimulating reading for the intelligent, thinking woman'. Fashion features not only tell a good 'yarn', but reference celebrity interviews, art, culture and ideas. The role of the fashion photographer in marketing Australian fashion over the past six decades is highlighted in Chapter 4, where outstanding talents such as Athol Schmith, Henry Talbot, Helmut Newton, Laurence Le Guay, Fabio Ongarato and Justin Edward John Smith are featured.

The middle chapters consider how fashion and textiles became an art form in the 1960s and 1970s, and how classic hallmark fashion enterprises resulted in the 1980s. Famous fashion personalities such as Jenny Kee, Linda Jackson and Katie Pye became household names, and showed how fashion and art practice could be linked. As Chapter 5 shows, many other designers turned fashion into a 'living' art form, and applied artistic methodologies to fabric rather than to canvas. The combination of national pride and popular cultural images saw the emergence of the lovable Blinky Bill, the ubiquitous gumleaf and the vibrant waratah flower as key icons in fashion imagery, coupled with the emergence of Indigenous patterns and colours in textile design. Fashion also became a postmodernist tool to comment on social and political issues, allowing designers to have a visual voice in society.

Chapter 6 highlights the major role played by the Australian wool industry in supporting and sustaining clothing production for well over a century. This development underpinned the growth of the knitting and spinning mills, which in turn established a thriving national textile industry. After World War II, textile design studios such as Prestige Ltd, Alcorso and Tasmania Silk & Textile Printers developed unique fashion fabric designs for the Australian market while others, including Francis Bourke and Hoad, served the craft and furnishing industries. Indigenous textile design studios

**1.3** Rebecca Paterson,
*Culture Bites,* 2006

Photo: Brad Hick, Six 6 Photography,
L'Orèal Melbourne Fashion Festival.
Courtesy Rebecca Paterson

proliferated across Australia, and designer-printed and hand-painted fabrics and clothing that captured the brilliance of Aboriginal motifs were produced by firms such as Desert Designs (Fremantle), Designer Aboriginals (Bronwyn Bancroft), Tiwi Designs (Utopia) and Balarinji (Sydney).

The importance of fashion and the visual and performing arts in the cultural sphere, underlined by the growing connection between fashion and the museum, is explored in Chapter 7. Celebrating the material culture of Australia as a nation has become an important part of the spectacle of fashion. Through the mechanisms of collections, displays and exhibitions, key fashion exhibitions held over the past thirty years at major institutions such as the Australian National Gallery, the National Gallery of Victoria and the Powerhouse Museum are discussed.

One of the most successful fashion business enterprises was based on the shaping of the modern Australian swimsuit from a one-piece garment immortalised by Annette Kellerman in her international swimming exploits to its eventual incorporation into global high fashion. Chapter 8 reveals how the two-piece bikini became synonymous with Surfer's Paradise and designer Paula Stafford, and how 'designer' swimwear emerged from the studios of Brian Rochford, Watersun, Sunseeker, Seafolly and Jets. High styling was merged with functionality to produce both leisure and competitive garments. Swimwear is now considered high-fashion apparel, yet it did not emerge from the catwalks of Paris. It has developed from influences from Australia, California and more recently Brazil – locations not traditionally associated with international fashion. Australia has been a launching pad for a number of international swimwear and surfwear companies, from iconic brands like Speedo, Quiksilver, Mambo and Billabong through to a new breed of contemporary swimsuit designers who tap into fashion trends while maintaining an Australian handwriting, exemplified by the labels of Zimmermann and Tigerlily.

Mainstream fashion is contextualised in Chapter 9. It explains how, since the 1960s, American and particularly British design has played a vital part in fashioning Australian sportswear, business wear and evening wear. Specifically, it traces the impact of youth culture upon emerging 1960s designers such as Prue Acton and John and Merivale Hemmes, and the influence of British ready-to-wear designers, London's Carnaby Street and the subcultural streetwear styling epitomised by San Francisco's hippie movement. In 1981, designer Trish Fitzsimon commented: 'The tyranny of distance actually works in our favour. We're all influenced by overseas fashion, but only by the best of it.' The casual lifestyle of the 1970s inspired designers such as Adele Palmer of JAG to extend the creative possibilities of denim and to interpret international trends in sportswear, especially from America, for the local market.

The 1980s saw the emergence of an independent culture of fashion, closely aligned with the energetic club and music scenes, Punk and New Wave trends and the intersection of art, design and music and draws attention to designers Sara Thorn and Bruce Slorach (ABYSS STUDIO), Leigh Bowery and Richard Tyler. Chapter 10 makes reference to mainstream designers working both in major cities across Australia and at international locations. Collette Dinnigan was the first Australian to be invited by the Paris Chambre Syndicale to present a full-scale ready-to-wear parade in 1995. Akira Isogawa, who received the inaugural Australian Fashion Laureate Award in 2007, and Martin Grant, working in Paris since 1992, regularly show their work at Paris Fashion Week. Lisa Ho, Wayne Cooper, Carla Zampatti and Nicola Finetti, Bettina Liano, Michelle Jank, Sass & Bide, Easton Pearson and Ksubi, among others, have received international attention. This chapter shows how their work reflects both national and global trends and competes with that of other outstanding designers worldwide.

Chapter 11 examines how designers, often starting from small non-commercial workrooms, adopt an experimental design approach based on exploring new techniques and concepts, working with ideas as well as cloth to challenge traditional practices that have emerged in the twenty-first century. Since the 1990s, multicultural influences – in particular, Japanese design – have impacted upon Australia's avant-garde designers. In terms of the deconstruction of fabric, surface patterning and finishing techniques and the reconstruction of form, they question the notion of dress in today's society. Emerging designers, including Susan Dimasi and Chantal Kirby (MATERIALBYPRODUCT), Peter Boyd and Denise Sprynskyj (S!X) and the Gwendolynne and Romance Was Born labels, are also making their mark in this challenging sector of the fashion industry. Ethical design issues such as sustainability and eco-fashion are considered in the context of Lisa Gorman, a young emerging designer.

In Chapter 12, *Australian Fashion Unstitched* highlights the business of fashion by summarising how major Fashion Weeks held in most of the capital cities showcase the work of both established and emerging fashion designers and businesses, and how the Australian Textile and Fashion Industry Association (TFIA) monitors industry and trade policies, supports

**1.4** S!X, *Untitled*, Spring/
Summer 2008

Photo: Thuy Vy. Courtesy S!X

education and training, and promotes Australian fashion to the world. It outlines the growth of new consumption patterns linked to global economic markets and subsequent changes in current marketing strategies. This chapter also notes new directions in manufacturing led by technology, and makes reference to the emergence of designer diffusion lines and fashion syndicates – all strategies that have deliberately been put in place to ensure that the industry stands firm and progresses to face the challenges of the future.

Finally, Chapter 13 considers the future of fashion in Australia in terms of globalisation and the impact of future technologies and new styling. It records the prophecies of a range of industry practitioners, journalists, designers and academics regarding what they think the future may hold.

*Australian Fashion Unstitched* provides a framework for the senior high school student, the TAFE fashion student and the university undergraduate student to view developmental trends and analyse the new directions and identities that have characterised Australian fashion over the past sixty years. It outlines the ways in which fashion and textile designers, photographers, writers and curators have responded to international trends and describes a new-found sense of national identity, a social layering of old and new cultures, and a need to forge new paths through innovation and experimental vision. Collectively, these writings show that fashion manifests itself according to ethical, social, political and environmental ideas and intersecting perspectives. Underpinning each chapter is the notion that the strength of Australian design lies in its diversity, its enterprise and the tenacity of its designers to succeed in this challenging and exciting industry. Finally, we hope that *Australian Fashion Unstitched: The Last 60 Years* will inspire the reader to want to learn more about the history of the Australian fashion industry.

## Note

1 The Australian Wool Board became the Australian Wool Bureau in 1953, then the Australian Wool Board again in 1963, and then the Australian Wool Corporation in 1973.

## References

Joel, A. (1984), *Best Dressed: 200 Years of Fashion in Australia*, Sydney: Collins.

—— (1998), *Parade: The Story of Fashion in Australia*, Sydney: Harper Collins.

Mackay, E. (1985), *Australian Fashion Design*, Sydney: Kevin Weldon & Associates.

Maynard, M. (1994), *Fashioned from Penury: Dress as Cultural Practice in Colonial Australia*, Melbourne: Cambridge University Press.

—— (2001), *Out of Line: Australian Women and Style*, Sydney: UNSW Press.

—— (forthcoming), *Making and Retailing Exclusive Dress in Australia*, Oxford: Berg.

Steele, V. (2000), *Fifty Years of Fashion: New Look to Now*, New Haven, CT: Yale University Press.

# THE FABULOUS FIFTIES

## GLAMOUR AND STYLE

*Louise Mitchell*

**2.1** Athol Shmith, *Untitled*, model Madame Chambrelent, 1949
Courtesy National Gallery of Victoria and Michael Shmith

'**T**O ME, THE FIFTIES is the most beautiful period of this century,' claimed the designer Hall Ludlow in an interview with *Vogue Australia* in 1991 (von Alderstein 1991: 156). 'The most glamorous era was the fifties,' echoed the designer Beril Jents in her autobiography (Jents 1993: 75). For many, these recollections by leading fashion designers run counter to a commonplace view that the postwar period was an era of conservative and dreary conformity. However, in fashion it was a time of formality and new-found femininity and glamour after wartime austerity. It was also a time when Australian women followed the dictates of fashion by wearing extravagant ball gowns, swish cocktail dresses, elegant tailored suits and feminine day dresses, complemented with carefully selected accessories.

Interest in fashion was intense in the immediate postwar years and into the 1950s. Influences came from Britain, America and most importantly France – specifically Paris. Traditional cultural links with Britain were emphasised during the Queen's coronation in 1953 and her tour of Australia in the following year. American fashion had already gained a hold during the interwar years with the popularity of Hollywood films and screen stars. The development of American sportswear and mass production methods also impacted on local fashions. The strongest influence on the high end of Australian fashion, however, came from France and the most influential designer was Christian Dior, whose New Look of 1947 proved a defining moment for changes in the look of fashion. As the exaggerated styles introduced by Dior in the late 1940s settled into something more practical, a dress with a softly gathered or flared skirt and cinched waist became the dominant look throughout the 1950s.

Paris couture not only changed the look of fashion; the very structure of fashion changed as couture was transformed through its licensing system from a small-scale atelier system to a global corporate one. Australian consumers were introduced to Paris couture through the buyers and press, who were quick to bring back the latest fashions through relentless media coverage, fashion parades and models of couture. Paris couture was held up as the epitome of style and quality, which local dressmakers and manufacturers strove to copy either as precisely as possible or with variations to suit local conditions and taste. Parisian couture complemented the formality in fashion during the postwar period.

A major difference in fashion during the 1950s from that of nowadays was dress codes specifying 'appropriate' attire for time and place. For a start, during the day a well-turned-out woman was expected to wear carefully selected gloves, shoes, umbrella and a hat. Throughout the decade, fashionable middle-class women wore a hat almost every day, and to be seen without a hat was to appear 'naked' and inappropriately attired. It was also a period when a fashionable woman was obliged to change her clothing a number of times throughout the day, according to time and place. Cocktail dresses were appropriate for early evening but not after 8.00 p.m.; a dinner dress needed to be of certain fabric; a hostess could go hatless and gloveless but her guests should not; a ball dress should be worn with matching high-heeled shoes and long white gloves. Cocktail parties were a popular form of entertaining and the cocktail dress was less formal than the ball gown or dinner dress. A staple in the 1950s wardrobe was the long, often strapless evening dress.

These rules, which seem so Victorian today, were taken quite seriously in the postwar period, although they started to relax towards the end of the 1950s. However, as late as 1958, the Australian fashion magazine *Flair* advised women that it was 'non-U' (non-upper-class) to:

> wear a suit without a hat. Wear no stockings in town. Wear too many petticoats at any time. Wear no gloves when formally dressed. Wear black shoes with anything but black. (*Flair*, January 1958: 16)

The don'ts included:

> high heels with slacks, the hat-but-no-gloves, the gloves-but-no-

stockings. The too-much jewellery and the dressy hat with the tailored suit. (*Flair,* January 1958: 51)

The upshot of formality in fashion was the boost it gave the fashion industry. Smart suits, elegant accessories, complex foundation garments, cocktail and dinner dresses, and elaborate ball gowns were essential items in the wardrobes of Australia's fashionable women. Shopping and looking one's best was an expensive and time-consuming business. For the elite, elaborate formal clothes were needed to participate in the lively social scene witnessed in Australia in the postwar period. A never-ending round of race meetings, balls, fashion parades, charity events, lunches and afternoon receptions provided women with opportunities to be seen and admired in fashionable attire. The era's social set, their activities and their clothing were all relentlessly reported upon in newspapers and magazines.

After World War II, Australia lost little time in renewing its interest in Paris couture. The role of the couturier had emerged in Paris during the second half of the nineteenth century and haute couture – custom dressmaking – had been formalised with the foundation in 1868 of the Chambre Syndicale de la Couture Parisienne, which provided its members with a strict set of formal criteria for operation, thus protecting its reputation. Couture was stamped on the international consciousness as typically French, and standards of creativity and skill set by Parisian couturiers in the first half of the twentieth century reinforced Paris' role as the undisputed centre of fashion. By World War II, it was understood that fashions bearing a Parisian couturier's name were the quintessence of excellent design and fabrication.

Although couture was seemingly exclusive and apparently catered to a wealthy minority, in the postwar years Parisian couturiers increasingly sold their designs to the mass market and developed a system of licensing, which had first been introduced in the interwar years to protect designers from copyists. The traditional role of the couture house, and a requirement of the haute couture establishment, was to produce made-to-measure designs for private clients. The second role of the couture house was to meet the needs of the commercial buyer. Couture became a complex and paradoxical business, as a couture house specialised in custom-order trade but was compelled to produce thousands of repetitions (Palmer 2007: 63–83). International buyers, most often from department stores, paid a deposit for the right to view a couturier's collection. Once a collection was seen, a buyer could purchase a garment – known as the model – with the right to take it back to their home

**2.2** Rowe Street, c. 1950

Photo: Kerry Dundas. Courtesy Mitchell Library, State Library of NSW, Sydney

**2.3** Henriette Lamotte, hat, 1954

Photo: Marinco Kojdanovski. Courtesy Powerhouse Museum, Sydney

country and have it copied. Sometimes buyers would purchase toiles – the design made up in unbleached cotton – of the model along with information about the material and trimmings to complete the garment. In this way, thousands of copies of Paris haute couture were made throughout the world, including in Australia.

Throughout the postwar years, Australians were exposed to Parisian couture through the combined promotional efforts of couture houses, local media and department stores. As early as 1946 the *Australian Women's Weekly*, Australia's leading magazine, decided to bring Paris fashions to Australia in a display of glamour and luxury after the lean wartime years. The *Weekly*'s London correspondent and its Sydney-based fashion editor were dispatched to Paris, where they met with leading designers. Garments and accessories were selected, and French mannequins recruited to wear them, from leading couture houses such as Worth, Fath, Lelong, Balmain, Carven, Patou and Molyneux. In partnership with the Sydney department store David Jones, the *Weekly*'s first French Fashion Parade was launched at a gala event reported as one of the most glamorous occasions of the year, and was later seen by enthusiastic crowds in Sydney, Melbourne, Adelaide and Brisbane (Mitchell 1994: 42).

The aim of the *Women's Weekly* French Fashion Parades, held annually from 1946 to 1949, was to garner consumer interest in fashion and stimulate local production. The *Weekly*'s second French Fashion Parade included garments by Dior, who had become famous seemingly overnight following the launch of his couture house in Paris on 12 February 1947 with a collection that became known as the New Look. The change in the look of women's clothing in the immediate postwar years can be attributed directly to Christian Dior's famous collection. Dresses and suits in Dior's New Look collection were characterised by the use of metres of fabric made into full skirts, tight bodices and a cinched waist, thus creating an exaggerated and curvaceous female form. Full skirts had made an appearance in the late 1930s, but during the war clothing restrictions had resulted in a simple silhouette with square shoulders and a knee-length, narrow skirt. In his autobiography, Dior wrote:

> In December 1946, as a result of the war and uniforms, women still looked and dressed like Amazons. But I designed clothes for flower-like women, with rounded shoulders, full feminine busts, and handspan waists above enormous spreading skirts. (Dior 1958: 21)

Dior had captured a new mood in fashion, which was characterised by a return to femininity and romance.

Christian Dior agreed to show his 1948 Autumn/Winter collection for David Jones in Sydney in what was billed as the first-ever parade of New Look clothes outside of Paris. Dior lent himself to the occasion and claimed in an interview with the *Sydney Morning Herald*'s European correspondent that Australia was the right country for his clothes, as:

> living in the sunshine of a comparatively new country unscathed by war, Australians have a cleaner, brighter outlook and are more receptive to new ideas than the tired people of European countries. (Foster 1948: 5)

During the ensuing years, Australia's department stores competed to bring out the best of international fashion with parades of couture and ready-to-wear fashion not only from France but from the United States, Ireland, Italy and Germany. International couture brought to Australia attracted enormous media coverage and, in turn, stimulated local fashion industries such as modelling and photography. The New Look required a small waist, immaculate grooming and an aristocratic *soignée*. One of the most memorable images of the postwar period is a fashion photograph by Athol Shmith, who was commissioned to photograph New Look clothes for Myer's in Melbourne. In the photograph of Patricia (Tuckwell) Shmith wearing Dior's New Look (see Figure 4.1), the contrived glamour, sophistication and opulence of Paris couture is immediately apparent. Other photographers to capture the fashionable image of the era include Bruno Benini and Helmut Newton. Parades and photography gave models considerable exposure, and women such as Diane Masters, Judy Barraclough, Maggie Tabberer and June Dally-Watkins enjoyed high-profile careers as models and public identities.

Special occasions such as the Queen's coronation in 1953 and the Royal Tour 1954 also provided a stimulus for interest and spending on fashion. The Melbourne department store George's invited leading British designer Peter Russell to show and design a collection of 'Coronation' gowns suitable for Australian women to wear for the occasion (Somerville 2004). The young Queen was much admired for her elegant taste, and her clothing was much scrutinised in the local media. During the 1954 tour, her wardrobe featured a restrained version of current Paris fashions, notably Dior's New Look, made for her by leading British couturiers Norman Hartnell and Hardy Amies.

The young Queen provided a model of sensible and elegant dressing, a foil to Paris extremes. Concomitant with a local deference to Parisian

**2.4** Printed cotton day dresses made in Australia. From left to right the dresses are labelled Ridley's, McDowell's Fashions and Michael Asmar

Photo: Marinco Kojdanovski. Courtesy Powerhouse Museum, Sydney

couture, the rhetoric in advertising and editorials insisted Australian women required a modified version of exaggerated Parisian styles: something more practical and comfortable that suited their more informal lifestyles. Local manufacturers repeatedly advertised that their products followed the latest styles but were suited to 'sensible' Australian women.

For more practical clothes, Australia could look to American sportswear for inspiration. There was an obvious similarity in American climate and lifestyle. America had pioneered standardisation in ready-made fashion and its industry had developed in the early twentieth century to a point where it rivalled European fashion by the outbreak of World War II and partially eclipsed Paris during the war. American fashion was admired for its commitment to making attractive ready-to-wear and affordable fashion realistic for women of all classes. Largely independent from the grand style of French couture, American designers – the most influential of whom was Claire McCardell – modernised dress by rationalising it and bringing versatility into fashion. American fashion was simple, practical and accessible, and ease of care was important; therefore, fabrics that could be washed and pressed at home were used. Casual and informal coordinates that were easy to wear best suited Australian conditions. Therefore, during the 1950s, Australian manufacturers began to produce unpretentious slacks, playsuits and cotton sun-dresses to cater for the market for more informal clothes. These clothes were sold as alternatives to Parisian styles and gained more currency as the formality of dress relaxed towards the end of the decade.

Another important part of fashion production during the 1950s was home dressmaking. Most women were able to sew, and most had the dressmaking skills to make their own clothes. The home dressmaker worked from Butterick, Simplicity, McCall's and Vogue dressmaking patterns, or from patterns published in or available through newspapers and magazines. Fabrics were purchased from large specialty stores or from department stores where whole floors were devoted to the needs of the home dressmaker. One of the ways fashion looked forward was in the development and widespread use of the synthetic textiles available on the market. Synthetics had been used as fashion fabrics since the 1920s, but during the 1950s they came of age. Embraced by the whole range of fashion producers, from the couturier to the home dressmaker, synthetic textiles were praised for washability and crease resistance. Month after month, week after week in magazines and newspapers, there were features and advertisements showing these new fabrics. The main types used were nylon, polyester and acetates. New treatments for textiles were also developed, such as glazes and coatings that were applied to natural fabrics – principally cotton – which made them easier to care for.

Although many women could sew their own clothes, increasingly in the postwar period Australian women bought ready-made garments, and there was a proliferation of wholesale manufacturers that catered to middle-of-the-road taste. Although stylistically there was an emphasis on conformity during the period, with Paris more often than not dictating style, there was a growing rhetoric that stressed the merits of Australian fashion. It was a time of great confidence for the Australian fashion industry, which was vigorously promoted through industry and government initiatives. The boom in prosperity led to increased consumption, which allowed clothing manufacturers to flourish and provided opportunities for talented designers and dressmakers, milliners, photographers, models and stylists. This was particularly evident in Sydney and Melbourne.

During the 1950s, Melbourne became the most important centre of fashion in Australia. Collins Street and the neighbouring Flinders Lane led the Australian fashion industry. Flinders Lane was a hub of fashion manufacturing dominated by Jewish workers, many of whom were newly arrived immigrants. In the postwar period there were over 600 clothing firms in Flinders Lane, and the number of people employed in manufacturing grew by 100 000 (Epstein 2001).

Flinders Lane manufacturers included Elegance, Leroy, Charlotte of Fifth Avenue, Samos French Modes, Hartnell of Melbourne, Saba of California, Margeaux Hayes, Park Avenue Gowns, Henry Haskin, Ninette Creations, Champs Elysées, Paris Gowns, London Fashions, Parisienne Models and Los Angeles Fashion (Rosenthal 2005). The practice of adopting English, French or American names reflects the influences on local fashion at the time. An attempt to create fashion with a distinctively Australian flavour was made by Leroy, one of the largest manufacturers. In 1954, the House of Leroy teamed up with Claudio Alcorso of Silk and Textile Printers in Hobart to hold the Leroy Alcorso Textile Competition. In a bid to improve the quality of printed textiles in the fashion industry, the competition aimed to produce a printed fabric with an Australian theme to be made up into dresses. Leroy went on to produce a version from one of the submitted textile designs, which was fashioned into a cotton dress with a princess line and a flounced skirt that sold 20 000 copies throughout Australia (Rosenthal 2005: 21).

Other initiatives that supported manufacturers included the establishment of the Australian Designers' Guild and the Gown of the Year Award. Inaugurated in 1953, the first Gown of the Year Award was won by Du Barri Gowns with Florence Raymond as the designer. Hilda Corbett and Dulcie Harbour for Myer Emporium won it the following year, Hall Ludlow in 1955 and 1959 for Prestige Ltd, Henry Haskin in 1956, and Hartnell of Melbourne in 1958. Initiatives such as the Gown of the Year Award gave the local industry credibility and designers a new-found visibility. Another important government initiative was the promotion of wool. The Australian Wool Board was reconstituted under its new name, the Australian Wool Bureau (1953–63), and was responsible for a range of promotional events aimed at stimulating the use of wool in the fashion trade and at increasing public interest in Australian fashions (Black 2009).

Since the mid 1800s, Collins Street had been the city's fashion precinct (Joel 1984: 33), and in the postwar period the upper end became known as the 'Paris end'. A tree-lined boulevard with broad footpaths, small exclusive shops and a number of cafes, it was the most glamorous and fashionable destination in Melbourne – and indeed Australia – during the 1950s. It was a place to shop, to be seen and to be entertained. It was also the home of some of Australia's leading photographers of the day, who had studios that serviced the thriving fashion business. Dominating Collins Street was the up-market department store George's, which was perhaps the most iconic store of the era, setting new standards of marketing and presentation of luxurious fashion. It was the first to hold in-house mannequin parades and its window displays were particularly memorable. The store's in-house dressmaking department specialised in couture copies from France and England (Somerville 2004).

Although most women obtained their clothes from department stores and retailers of manufactured fashion, the designers working within these businesses were largely anonymous. Only the handful of exclusive custom-made dressmakers and designers patronised by the wealthy elite were recorded and are remembered more vividly today.

Dominating the exclusive end of Melbourne fashion was Le Louvre, which was founded by Lillian Wightman (1903–92). As a teenager, Wightman had worked as a salesgirl for Melbourne's premier dressmaking establishment, GHV Thomas, before starting her own business in a terrace house at 74 Collins Street, where it continues to operate today. Although she had never travelled outside Australia, Wightman had a vision of a Paris salon, which she created in her new premises with inspired confidence. Influenced by the decorator Elsie de Wolfe, Wightman created a meeting-place for wealthy society women that was original and flamboyant, with gold carpet and gilt mirrors, a valuable collection of furniture and animal skins on the sofa (Whitfield 2006a: 117).

Wightman believed that 'everything beautiful is made in Paris and everyone wants it' (Perkin 1986: 26). Although she rarely travelled to Europe (an exception was a trip to Paris, where she met the French couturier Coco Chanel), Wightman – like the owners and operators of many Australian department stores and dressmaking establishments – purchased toiles and models from representatives in Paris and had them copied in her workroom. During the 1950s, the heyday of Le Louvre, Wightman had thirty seamstresses, many of them immigrant Italians, working in Le Louvre's back room (Whitfield 2006a: 117). Le Louvre specialised in weddings, trousseaux and other special occasions. Its success during the 1950s is credited to Wightman's ability to deliver to her clients a modified couture version of the latest looks from Paris. Her own designs, again strongly inspired by French fashion, also reflected her taste for flamboyance: her signature was an ocelot print which was made up for dresses, coats, handbags and scarves (Joel 1998: 81).

Also located at the Paris end of Collins Street was Hall Ludlow (1919–2003), who began his career in New Zealand with Trilby Yates, an Auckland designer, before immigrating to Australia in the late 1940s. He established a salon in Melbourne in 1948, which he decorated with pearl-grey walls, heavy satin drapes, lustrous mirrors and chandeliers (Lim 1994: 10). Inspired by Paris, Ludlow's parades were accompanied by a commentary delivered in both English and French (von Alderstein 1991: 157–8).

Although inspired by Paris, Ludlow was an original designer. He did not travel to Paris to buy models for copying, but looked to Paris to keep abreast of trends. He was particularly inspired by Balenciaga, the Spanish-born, Paris-based couturier, who was renowned for his tailoring and clothes that expressed a formality and avant-garde approach. Ludlow's meticulous workmanship and his ability with clients were quickly recognised by Melbourne's fashionable elite. A dress that won the Gown of the Year Award in 1959 was made of white Australian wool skilfully cut and shaped. The dramatic silhouette was nipped in at the waist with a skirt shaped below the knee with layers of fringed and pintucked bands. A tour-de-force in design and technical skill, the dress has been described as a defining moment in local design (Healy 2005) (see Figure 2.5).

Another salon at the Paris end of Collins Street that catered for custom-made dressmaking was La Petite, founded by Pat and Neil Rodgers in 1940. Specialising in sumptuous evening wear, La Petite's specialty was embroidery. Evening gowns covered with beading and embroidery were a feature of couture fashion during the 1950s and suited formal occasions in grand settings such as the opera or state events. Dresses selected for embroidery were usually of simple cut and reliant on embellished surface detail to bring them to life. Parisian haute couture was supported by as many as forty specialist embroidery ateliers dotted around the city, which

**2.5** Athol Shmith, *Diane Masters, Wearing a Hall Ludlow Dress, Gown of the Year*, 1959

© The Estate of Athol Shmith.
Licensed by Kalli Rofe Contemporary Art

could produce elaborate embellished textiles for the couture houses (Wilcox 2007: 136). Within La Petite's workroom, imitations of current Paris styles were carefully sewn, embroidered and lavishly covered with glass beads and sequins. Each gown took a minimum of forty hours of specialist work (Harris 1995).

Collins Street was also the best place to go for millinery, either to the in-house millinery salon of George's or to the smaller exclusive salons established by Thomas Harrison, Thomas Beale and Ann Austin. The postwar period was exceptional for the production of millinery. Within the conformity of fashion of the period, hats provided a point of interest and milliners exercised a degree of imagination and autonomy denied to dressmakers. Hats came in a variety of shapes from turbans, to broad-brimmed hats that complemented the New Look's silhouette, to close-fitting caps for slim-fitting suits. They were designed with an outfit in mind. At the beginning of the twentieth century, individual milliners turned the simple hat shop into an exclusive space that enhanced their signature styles. This 'salon' environment, similar to that of exclusive dressmaking salons, offered the customer an intimate place to view, try and buy elegantly displayed hats.

Thomas Harrison (1897–1981), Melbourne's leading milliner, moved his salon to 163 Collins Street in 1931 and saw his clients in a grand space furnished in the Louis XV style. Harrison's salon stocked the latest models by leading French milliners such as Jean Barthet and by the London milliner Aage Thaarup. Harrison's clients were many of Australia's wealthy elite, but he also produced hats for charity events, parades and dressmakers, particularly for Lillian Wightman's salon Le Louvre. Workmanship, whimsical effect and originality were the hallmarks of Harrison's hats, as shown in a retrospective of his work held at the National Gallery of Victoria in 2006 (Whitfield 2006b).

Sydney also boasted a number of designers and milliners who were able to make names for themselves as talented designers and dressmakers. Department shopping was dominated by the David Jones store, where the sixth floor provided in-house designers and workrooms for the production of copies of couture. However, if they had the means, fashionable women in Sydney went to Germaine Rocher, the city's most celebrated couturier. Germaine Rocher established her couture business in Sydney in about 1934, shortly after immigrating from Europe (Leong 1997: 211). As early as 1936, Rocher's elegant dresses were advertised in the art-conscious magazine *The*

*Home*, and by the 1950s her reputation for creating couture garments similar to, and as good as, couture garments commissioned in Paris was well and truly established. At her Paris salon-like premises in the Trust Building in Sydney's King Street, clients were ushered along a marble corridor into rooms painted in grey and decorated with gilt chairs, cabinets and mirrors (Stokes 1972: n.p.). Slim, elegant and impeccably groomed, Rocher herself was considered the epitome of French style with her typically Gallic gestures, although her origins were Russian (Leong 1997).

To cater to the demands of her clients, Rocher flew to Paris twice a year to keep abreast of fashion and to buy fabric, buttons and trims along with original models and toiles (*Vogue* 1963: 24–5). Twice a year, society women – most from Sydney but some flying interstate – attended fashion parades in the Rocher salon, where they viewed not only Germaine Rocher originals but also gowns made from the toiles of the major Paris designers. For example, in 1957 Rocher showed eighty outfits, forty-eight of them from Paris couture houses including Dior and Balenciaga, and thirty-two originals (*The Sun*, 25 August 1957). To produce these parades and run the ensuing business, Rocher ran a workshop of sixty dressmakers. Rocher's clothing was unobtrusive and subdued, relying on quality cloth, perfect fit and finishing.

A more flamboyant designer who established her reputation during the postwar years was Beril Jents (1918–). Born in Bondi and self-taught as a dressmaker, Jents started working in her teens and by the early 1950s had established a salon in the St James Building. Although she did not travel or import couture models, Jents was sufficiently influenced by Dior to adopt his method of introducing a new line with each collection (Jents 1993: 86).

Jents was someone who understood the Sydney society of the time. According to her, local society was divided into the racing fraternity, the society establishment and the new moneyed Europeans. Her exuberant nature was seen in her theatrical parades, reported on enthusiastically in the press, and in her clothes made for Sydney society – which were more often than not brightly coloured and elaborately embellished. The most elaborate dresses she ever produced in her long career were made for society weddings during the 1950s (Jents 1993: 63–103).

Zita Waine was another European émigré who established a business in Sydney's Double Bay, operated along couture lines. Waine was from Romania and worked for the Parisian couturier Jacques Fath before immigrating to Australia in 1949. Zita Couture was noted for its fine copies of Parisian couture models and the salon was given a fresh, sophisticated look with

**2.6** Germaine Rocher,
*evening dress, silk chiffon*

Photo: Marinco Kojdanovski. Courtesy
Powerhouse Museum, Sydney

décor by the leading interior designer Marion Hall Best and a mural by the artist Elaine Haxton (Leong 1997: 218).

Frank Mitchell was hailed as one of Australia's most promising young designers in the early 1950s. Mitchell (1920–99) was the son of a sea merchant and a dressmaker, who moved from his home town of Newcastle to Sydney to study painting at the Julian Ashton School (*People* 1954: 40). In 1949, he took a studio in a house at Woolloomooloo and started designing and making clothes. A man of considerable personal appeal, Mitchell had a flair for publicity and his parades, held in the courtyard of the bohemian house he shared with an eclectic crew of artists, intrigued the press. As a result of favourable press coverage he was able to open an establishment, Frank Mitchell Gowns, on New South Head Road in Edgecliff, which became popular with the fashion press and with society women who enjoyed the unorthodox and informal nature of his shop (Barrowclough 1996: 15). He made a limited range of off-the-peg clothes, but for the most part his clothes were made-to-measure garments that are remembered for their informality and glamour. He was supported in his career by the mannequin June Dally-Watkins, who wore a wardrobe by Mitchell when she travelled to the United States to promote her fledgling mannequin school.

As with Rocher, Sydney society was entranced with the Frenchwoman Henriette Lamotte (d. 1979), who became the city's best-known milliner as well as Germaine Rocher's preferred hat-maker. A combination of flair, personality and French mannerisms made Henriette Lamotte's salon popular among Sydney's smart set during the 1950s. One fashion editor recorded the atmosphere of Lamotte's intimate salon showings: '[She] always manages to create what her Australian customers regard as a thrillingly genuine Parisian atmosphere' (*Smith's Weekly* 1950: 28). Lamotte established a salon in Rowe Street, Sydney's little slice of Bohemia which was noted for its mix of cafes, bars, theatres and shops (see Figure 2.2). Lamotte learnt millinery in Paris in the Faubourg St Honoré, immigrated to Sydney and set up a millinery salon in 1938 with her husband, the Count d'Espinay. As well as importing models from Paris by famous milliners such as Paulette and Gilbert Orcel, Lamotte created many original hats that were notable for their whimsical detailing. Other noted milliners working in Sydney during this period included the McDougal brothers, the Vienna-born Stella Frankel, Madge Wainwright of Brasch's and Margot McRae.

Brisbane, Adelaide and Perth also supported fashionable designers and dressmakers. Adelaide's exclusive dressmaker was Angela Hambourg, who ran a business from North Terrace and became well known for her beading, embroidery and appliqué. Gwen Gillam was Brisbane's number one dressmaker, and she is remembered for her appliqué evening dresses and elegant day suits. The smart set in Brisbane had their clothes made by Gillam and their hats by Kevin Gibney, Brisbane's leading milliner. In Perth, Neil Hunsley opened a salon in the late 1950s after a start in theatre design. Provincial centres in Australia were regularly visited by leading dressmakers from Melbourne and Sydney. Le Louvre's Lillian Wightman and the milliner Thomas Harrison would travel to Adelaide by train to sell couture copies to the wives of wealthy businessmen and squatters (Whitfield 2006b: 117). Germaine Rocher also regularly travelled interstate to promote her business.

Growing in strength during the 1950s was the conviction that Australia had the capacity to produce manufactured ready-made clothing of style and quality. In 1957 *Flair* magazine's fashion correspondent, Leigh Robson, travelled overseas and took with her a wardrobe of Australian outfits to prove that the local industry was as good as any in the world. Her selected wardrobe was a mix of sportswear coordinates and couture-style formality. Supplied by leading manufacturers, Robson's Australian wardrobe consisted of a Stell-Ricks of Melbourne coat, an 'Everglaze' cotton knit dress, a Lillibet swimsuit that teamed with a four-piece 'Signature' playsuit, slacks from Sportscraft, a red satin dinner dress from E. Lucas – an adaptation of a French model – an organza evening dress with a theatre coat from Margeaux from Melbourne; shirtwaisted floral dresses in drip-dry cottons from Ninette Creations and a cotton sheath dress and jacket by Eyecatcher made in Tennyson cotton. Robson claimed her clothes were much admired and applauded wherever she went, because 'here in Australia . . . we have gay, glamorous fashions, as inexpensive and as well made, as anywhere in the world.' (Robson 1957: 35)

Within the promotion of fashion by the government, manufacturers, retailers and the media, there was an acknowledgement that comfortable, practical fashions geared to a casual way of life would suit Australian women. The practice of couture and copying reached its heyday in the 1950s and, while it provided a standard to which local manufacturers could aspire and which they could emulate, it also provided a climate for change and recognition of a local production and identity in fashion.

# References

Barrowclough, N. (1996), 'Absolutely Frank', *Sydney Morning Herald, Good Weekend*, 30 November, p. 15.

Black, P. (forthcoming March 2010), 'The wool industry in Australia', in Margaret Maynard (ed.), *Australia, New Zealand and the Pacific Islands, The Berg Encyclopedia of World Dress and Fashion*, Oxford: Berg.

Crombie, I. (989), *Athol Shmith*, Melbourne: Schwartz.

Dior, C. (1957), *Dior by Dior*, London: Dior.

Epstein, A. (2001), *Schmatte Business: Jews in the Garment Trade, exhibition brochure*, Sydney: Jewish Museum of Australia.

Foster, E. (1948), 'New Look: Dior calls us representative', *Sydney Morning Herald*, 27 April, p. 5.

Harris, C. (1995), 'Unforgettable frocks', *Progress Press*, 12 December.

Healy, R. (2005), *Dressed to the Eyes: The Fashions of Hall Ludlow*, Melbourne: RMIT Press.

Jents, B. (1993), *Little Ol' Beryl from Bondi*, Sydney: Pan Macmillan.

Joel, A. (1984), *Best Dressed: 200 Years of Fashion in Australia*, Sydney: Collins.

—— (1998), *Parade: The Story of Fashion in Australia*, Sydney: Harper Collins.

Leong, R. (1997), 'Sydney's most fashionable Europeans', in R. Butler (ed.), *The Europeans: Emigré Artists in Australia 1930–1960*, Canberra: National Gallery of Australia.

—— (forthcoming Mar 2010), 'Making and retailing exclusive dress in Australia', in M. Maynard (ed.), *Australia, New Zealand and the Pacific Islands, The Berg Encyclopedia of World Dress and Fashion*, Oxford: Berg.

Lim, A. (1994), 'Master of the dress circle', *The Australian, Weekend Review*, 8–9 October, p. 10.

Loxley, A. (1996), *Belles of the Ball: 60 Years of the Black and White Committee*, Sydney: State Library of New South Wales.

Maynard, M. (2001), *Out of Line: Australian Women and Style*, Sydney: UNSW Press.

Mitchell, L. (1994), 'Christian Dior and postwar Australia', in L. Mitchell et al., *Christian Dior: The Magic of Fashion*, exhibition catalogue, Sydney: Powerhouse Museum.

Palmer, A. (2007), 'Inside Paris Haute Couture', in C. Wilcox (ed.), *The Golden Age of Couture: Paris and London 1947–57*, London: Victoria and Albert Publishing.

Parsons, B. (1994), 'Reflections of a glamorous man', *Age Tempo*, n.d.

People (1954), anon., 'An artist becomes a dressmaker', *People*, 20 October, n.p.

Perkins, C. e (1986), 'Lil of Le Louvre', *Sydney Morning Herald, Good Weekend*, 18 April 1986.

Permezel, B. (1993), *A Crucible of Creative Fashion Talent: Australian Gown of the Year, 1953–1993*, Melbourne: Shop Distributive and Allied Employees Association.

Robson, L. (1957), 'My Australian wardrobe', *Flair*, November, pp. 34–35.

Rosenthal, L.S. (2005), *Schmattes: Stories of Fabulous Frocks, Funky Fashion and Flinders Lane*, Melbourne: Lesley Sharon Rosenthal.

Sheridan, S. (2002), *Who was that Woman? The Australian Women's Weekly in the Postwar Years*, Sydney: UNSW Press.

Slater, R. (1989), 'Flinders Lane . . . memory lane: history of clothing manufacturing in Melbourne', *Australian Jewish Historical Society Journal* 10(7), p. 10.

*Smith's Weekly* (1950), 'Our hat dictators', 18 February, p. 28.

Somerville, K. and Whitfield, D. (2004), *Swish: Fashionable Melbourne of the 1950s*, Melbourne: National Gallery of Victoria.

Steele, V. (1997), *Fifty Years of Fashion: New Look to Now*, New Haven: Yale University Press.

Stokes, W. (1972), 'The end of an era for Madame Rocher', *Sydney Morning Herald*, 18 April 1972, n.p.

Van Wyk, S. (2006), *The Paris End: Photography, Fashion and Glamour*, Melbourne: National Gallery of Victoria.

*Vogue Australia* (1963), 'Haute couture, Sydney: Germaine Rocher', June/July, pp. 24–25.

von Alderstein, M. (1991), 'Hall Ludlow', *Vogue Australia*, March, pp. 157–8.

White, J. (1989), , Scone, NSW: The Seven Press.

Whitfield, D. (2006a), 'La mode Francaise Australian style', in S. van Wyk (ed.), *The Paris End: Photography, Fashion and Glamour*, Melbourne: National Gallery of Victoria, pp. 105–13.

—— (2006b), *Thomas Harrison, Milliner*, Melbourne: National Gallery of Victoria.

Wilcox, C. (2007), *The Golden Age of Couture: Paris and London 1947–57*, London: Victoria and Albert Publishing.

Winkworth, K. (1993), 'Followers of fashion: dress in the fifties', in J. O'Callaghan (ed.), *The Australian Dream: Design of the Fifties*, Sydney: Powerhouse Publishing, pp. 59–73.

# BERIL JENTS

## AUSTRALIAN *HAUTE COUTURE*

*Liliana Pomazan*

**3.1** Beril Jents in her home in Woollahra NSW, 2006
Photo: Liliana Pomazan. Courtesy Liliana Pomazan

*Though there are many others who might also claim the title of haute couture, none can compare with Miss Jents, for every high fashion model that leaves her Sydney salon can truly be called a unique Australian design . . . her ideas about style and fashion are Australian. Perhaps this is one of the reasons for her success. (Glenys Bell, fashion journalist, 1972)*

**I**N BELL'S ARTICLE, entitled 'Alone at the top of haute couture', Beril Jents (1918–) is cited as being the only one left with the skill for top quality in custom-made clothing in the early 1970s. Bell highlights that Jents:

makes not only the dressiest clothes in Sydney, she probably makes the dressiest clothes in the country, since she is the sole survivor of haute couture in Australia. Not that you would say Miss Jents is merely surviving. She is highly successful, and is looking forward to another winning collection when she presents her winter season models in Sydney. (Bell 1972)

From the early 1950s onwards, Beril Jents has been widely acknowledged as the first Australian Queen of Haute Couture,[1] even though she never considered herself as such. She recalls:

I never set out to make haute couture . . . I was just determined to make the very best clothes. Every time I got a bit more successful I just moved to better premises and my clothes got more in demand and attracted more attention. It was the press which first started talking about my Haute Couture clothes. I'd never presumed to talk about them that way myself. (Tellick 1975)

This accolade to Jents was repeated by the media in Sydney as hundreds of articles featuring her original designs appeared in the papers and advertisements of the period (Rayner 1998). She kept many articles similar to this in her scrapbook,[2] dating from the 1930s to the 1980s, which confirm her status as an exceptional Australian haute couturière who did not copy Parisian styles but rather invented her own: '. . . the garments she makes are haute couture by world standards, and they are her own exclusive designs. She does not copy anyone or anything' (Tellick 1975). In fact, most of the fashion *cognoscienti* of the day believed that Jents created many of the most glamorous and original haute couture ensembles in Australia's history.

Reportedly, she made clothes that suited her lifestyle, which was very similar to that of her clients. She explained: 'I think that our way of life is much simpler than the European life' (Bell 1972). Jents felt that women often made errors in judgement when purchasing couture or high-end, ready-to-wear garments from Paris because they were generally far too elaborate for the casual Australian lifestyle. Instead, she designed modern, high-quality garments with a classic timelessness, as attested by so many younger clientele wearing vintage Beril Jents clothing. She had a faithful clientele that she retained for decades, such as Sydney socialites Betty McInerney and Molly McSweeney. It is interesting that she did not need to advertise her work; she gained high-profile clients by both word of mouth and by regular reports of her collections in the press.

Jents came from humble beginnings, but with talent, drive and imagination her small fashion practice soared to dizzying heights and the success of these decades came from a great dedication to her craft and a determination to excel within this highly competitive arena. At a very young age she felt compelled to help her mother, Alice Strudwick, with her dressmaking after school in order to make ends meet. Strudwick was a skilled dressmaker and passed on these skills to her daughter. Like her mother, Jents shared the strong Australian work ethic that was typical of both men and women of her generation. Her dynamic spirit and bold character were shaped by her poor circumstances and a fervent desire for a better life; however, dressmaking for her was not only a necessity but became the great passion of her life.

Jents' source of motivation to become a fashion designer emanated from the rarified glamour associated with Hollywood films and its stars in the 1930s. The psychological impact of Hollywood was intensified during these years, as Australians were still suffering from the Great Depression and 29 per cent of Australians were unemployed (Australian Government 2007: para. 1). The 'silver screen' provided an escape from reality and had a major impact upon many impressionable young women of the day. For Jents, the film *Letty Lynton* of 1932 and the highly acclaimed costume designer

Adrian's famous evening dress for Joan Crawford's character became a turning point in her life. This beautiful white cotton organdie gown, with very large ruffled sleeves, was documented as one of the most influential dresses in the history of fashion; when it was reproduced commercially in America it sold over one million copies and was distributed by many stores, including Macy's New York (Walker 1974).

For young Jents, the seed was thus sown for a future career in fashion. She replicated the Letty Lynton dress and later, in 1993, reminisced about her adolescent dream of making beautiful clothes in the future:

> I was fascinated by photographs of . . . Letty Lynton, whom my mother told me was so famous the dress [Joan Crawford's character wore] was named after her. I copied it . . . It was ankle length, in a sky-blue organdie fabric that wasn't in the best condition but was the best I could scrounge. The shape was fitted to the body to below the hipline, where it softly shaped out towards the hem. Flared, hand-rolled frills were ruffled all over the skirt and on the huge puff sleeves. The Saturday after I finished it, I wore it out for a walk along the main street in Charing Cross. I felt beautiful in it, though I must have looked a scream. Nevertheless, it planted in my mind another seed for the future, to go on and create glamorous clothes. (Jents 1993: 24–25)

From this key moment in time, Jents left school and secured an apprenticeship with the well-known French dressmaker Madame Gallet, who had great confidence in her ability and talent. Over the next two years, she diligently applied herself to learning the craft of high dressmaking. Gallet taught her the techniques, especially cutting without a pattern, and instilled in her the main principles of fine dressmaking:

> As well as the finer points of cutting, Madame taught me about quality – how to appreciate and flow with the cloth, how to distinguish the pure from the artificial. But even more important was her advice that the greatest ingredient for this craft was common sense. Thanks to her knowledge and expertise, I was on my way to becoming a dress designer. (Jents 1993: 30)

When Madame Gallet abruptly closed her business in 1934 and returned to France, Jents was forced to make a decision about the direction her career would take next. At only sixteen years of age she had gained a maturity and knowledge of fine pattern-cutting and dressmaking far beyond her years. Bravely, she initially opened her own fashion practice in 1934 in Charing Cross, Waverley. As her practice grew quickly, she soon moved into a larger studio on the corner of Newland Street, Bondi Junction. During the next ten years she further refined her techniques and honed her skills by producing innovative made-to-measure garments that required a high level of expertise, such as the perfection of her sharply tailored suits and draped evening gowns of the period.

In the 1990s, as testimony to Jents' specialised tailoring and dressmaking expertise, the Sydney-based fashion designer Carla Zampatti (1942–) asked her to teach her design assistants how to cut, drape and fit tailored garments. She was consistently noted for the impeccable manner in which she cut and constructed sleeves in jackets (Foster 2006). In direct contrast to her exceptional tailoring, she also had a natural aptitude for draping on the stand, or directly on the body. In particular, garments cut on the straight grain of the fabric were regularly embellished with clever pattern-cutting features, then realised in the draping method, clearly evident in Jents' garments dating from the late 1930s to the postwar years. Her day dresses, suits and ball gowns were meticulously constructed, inspired by her great admiration for the work of the 'virtuoso of drapery', the Parisian haute couturière Madame Grès (1903–93) (Jents 2006b).

Significantly, when the Beril Jents label was formally registered in 1944, her studio was located in King's Cross, the bohemian and artistic hub of Sydney, and these unconventional surroundings encouraged her to challenge traditional norms. Like Coco Chanel (1883–1971), she was not afraid to masculinise women's clothing, especially during the war years when women were involved in so many non-traditional activities. She designed extravagant and innovative garments during this time, including her homage to the zoot suit for women, replete with a watch chain. For Jents, the suit signified freedom and power dressing for women. However, the suit was seen as an outrageous ensemble even for the bohemian community living in King's Cross, because pants suits for women were not common. She explained:

> Amongst my earliest designs were peg-bottom trousers, which I introduced to Australia in 1944. I got the idea from a picture in a magazine of black American men wearing zoot suits. When I adapted this style for women, I even kept the fly-front – possibly the first time this had been done in the world. It was quite daring . . . One day I walked through King's Cross wearing a pair of these trousers . . . People turned to look at me and I felt terrific. (Jents 1993: 38)

In America, the zoot suit was a signifier of racial pride and rebellion.

> [It] emerged in the mid-1930s but made its greatest impact during the war when it was worn by African-American and Mexican-American youths as an emblem of their ethnic pride and alienation from mainstream society. (Mendes and de la Haye 1999: 123)

Throughout this dire period, 'zoot suiters' created enormous hostility in society because of the lavish amount of fabric required to create the suit, which was in direct defiance of government restrictions.[3] In Jents' case she used prewar fabric to construct the pants suit, which used several metres of fabric and was fully tailored. This meant that, like its American counterpart, it was considered an extravagant luxury item of dress in the mid-1940s. Similar in silhouette, Jents' female rendition was faithful to the oversized proportions of the ensemble. Trousers were typically high-waisted, very wide in the leg then tapering to a tight cuff and the coat was box-shaped with wide lapels and padded shoulders. The front of the wool jacket featured large checks with the back and sleeves constructed from solid-coloured fabric. The day that Jents wore the suit to her workroom, she was stopped in the street by a client who asked to buy the garment that she was wearing! As this quickly became a regular occurrence for her, she explained:

> I began to leave back-ups in the shop for me to wear home. Indeed, many outfits were sold literally off my back to the bookmakers' and punters' wives, who never seemed to mind that I had worn them. (Jents 1993: 40)

Interestingly, Jents created clothing for wealthy women in King's Cross and she discovered years later that many of them, such as Nellie Cameron, were mistresses of underworld figures, and highly paid prostitutes, as well as wealthy socialites and many of the 'racing crowd', as she would call them. During this period, she exhibited her first of many fashion shows at the Roosevelt Nightclub in King's Cross; it was both a great success and an important learning experience for her.

Jents continued to delight her clientele during the difficult war and postwar years by using her fertile imagination. She created clothing by employing 'ingenious recycling . . . to meet the demand for European styling and lavish couture despite shortages of fashion news, materials and trims' (Riley 1997).

Arguably, considering Jents' prolific career, there were two key collections – the Potato Sack (1947) and the Pan Am (1948) collections –

which highlighted her exceptional ability to consider alternative design methodologies. Significantly, her collection entitled the Potato Sack in particular showcased her leadership in developing a local fashion aesthetic in Australia. In her own words, she highlights her ingenuity and adaptable design expertise:

> During the War you couldn't really find any materials – the only actual cloth you could find was a moss crepe, a rather coarse looking crepe but it was lovely material because it didn't crease and . . . it was a synthetic. (Jents 2007)

Necessity inspired her to transform an existing non-fashion material into one that was incorporated into her Potato Sack couture garments. When asked whether this was a distinctly Australian design, Jents replied:

> Yes, they were very me, very Australian! I had never seen anyone do anything like that before. I used to buy big potato sacks and soak them in the bath and then boil them in the copper and then they come up to rather a nice [fabric], like very coarse linen and then I would sew them into . . . A-line full skirts and bead them, embroider them with straw work. I would buy the straw that they made hats out of and wind the straw around into patterns. They were very colourful . . . they were skirts mostly, and they had little boned strapless tops of perhaps a patterned material or something that went with the skirt. (Jents 2007)

Again, just as Coco Chanel used jersey – the poor person's material – for her first post World War I collection, Jents, more radically, chose to use hessian fabric pieces taken from several potato sacks purchased from the local greengrocer. World War II fabric restrictions did not hamper her creativity. According to Joel (1998: 156), 'inventiveness was synonymous with Beril's name.' On her many trips to the beaches of Sydney and Queensland, she collected a multitude of shells of varying shapes and sizes. She designed patterns on the skirts, which were realised in raffia embroidery and highlighted with shell beading. She drilled holes into the selected shells and heavily decorated the skirts with them. Mutely coloured shells ranging from whites and pinks to soft browns were chosen. To complement the hessian fabric and shells, she used colour-dyed raffia palm leaf embroidered on the skirts in large decorative stitches, similar to those which basket makers would use. Halter-neck, cross-over tops were made of silk purchased years before at David Jones' fabric department. The tops were waist-length and fitted firmly to the body, tied by long sashes bowed at the waist on the left. In

**3.2** Beril Jents, striped linen suit, Pan Am collection, 1948

Courtesy Beril Jents

an interview, Jents said that the coloured petticoats matched the raffia and that they 'were worth a lot of money because they were pure silk and there were about twelve inch [30 centimetre] frills of each colour on the bottom' (Jents 2007). The skirts were mid-calf in length and could easily be worn as evening wear. The length, of course, was dictated by Christian Dior's influential and highly copied New Look collection of 1947 (Mitchell 1996).

Jents' collection was enormously successful because it had a glamour and freshness rarely seen in other collections of Australian designers at the time. Other Sydney-based fashion designers – or couturiers, as they preferred to be addressed – such as the renowned Madame Paulette Pellier (est. 1920s–1940s) and Madame Germaine Rocher (est. 1935–1971)[4] were known to copy Parisian models for their collections. Madame Rocher, for example, visited and contacted Parisian haute couture houses for the purpose of purchasing licensed toiles, which she later reproduced in Australia (Foster 2006). Jents' Potato Sack collection was purchased in its entirety by the formidable Sheila Scotter, the then fashion buyer for the grand department store George's of Collins Street, Melbourne (Joel 1998: 156) and later *Vogue Australia*'s editor-in-chief. Throughout the latter part of the twentieth century, Scotter was considered a commanding authority on fashion and an arbiter of good taste.

Again, Jents continued to trial non-traditional materials in her work when she playfully designed her Tea Towel collection (c. 1948), in which the pieces were informed and constructed from kitchen tea towels. The brightly coloured collection was unique, and gained high praise from her ever-increasing and broad-ranging clientele for its quirky newness and wittiness. She also experimented with textile surface patterns to add excitement to her collections because of the lack of variety in available fabrics.[5] Jents employed various methods of printing on fabric, especially silkscreen printing, with the assistance of her friend, the artist Russ Woodward. She already had knowledge of the printing processes from a stint working as a young girl at the printing firm of Hollander and Govett.[6] She produced several collections using original screen-prints, and she pointed out: 'This fashion became popular again in the seventies, when it was revived by Linda Jackson and Jenny Kee' (Jents 1993: 48).

Frank Packer owned the leading fashion magazine of the 1940s, *The Australian Women's Weekly*, of which his sister-in-law Mary Hordern[7] was the fashion editor from 1946 to 1957. It is important to note that, as early as 1946, *The Australian Women's Weekly* was sponsoring the highly anticipated French Fashion Parades – one year before Christian Dior's New Look took the world by storm. According to Roger Leong:

> The *Australian Women's Weekly*'s French Fashion Parades were the most spectacular fashion events of the 1940s. Organisation of these parades fell to the *Weekly*'s reporter Mary Hordern who developed the project with Madame Chambrelent, directrice at the House of Worth in Paris. There were four tours starting in 1946 until 1949 selected from the most fashionable Parisian haute couture houses, milliners and shoe designers. (Leong 2010)

As she gained recognition as an avant-garde designer and an expert pattern-cutter, Jents frequently was asked by women from Sydney's high society to reproduce Dior's haute couture styles.[8] These women – including Hordern herself – envisaged themselves wearing the kinds of suits and evening gowns that swept down the catwalks in Paris. With her outstanding skills in pattern-cutting and construction she was able to reproduce a Dior to their specific body measurements. For one of the French fashion parades, Hordern implored her to reproduce Dior's famous Peg Skirt, which she desperately wanted to wear, but ironically it was the only garment she could not purchase in Paris. Jents studied the design and felt she could make it with ease. She added, 'Mary Hordern was thrilled with it' and 'I had a lot of staff start with me to learn how to do that Peg Skirt' (Jents 2006a). Because Hordern was a major media celebrity, Jents gained enormous recognition in Sydney because of her dressmaking ability and expertise, but the Peg Skirt made her famous. Needless to say, her clientele grew exponentially, as did the number of people she employed to meet the growing demand for a Jents original. She described the Peg Skirt as follows:

> The peg skirt was thirteen inches [33 centimetres] from the ground, irrespective of what heels you had on or what height you were and it had trouser pleats at the waist. The waist was nineteen inches [48 centimetres], a very small waist! Then the trouser pleats came out from that but pressed very flat over the hips but rounded because it had a slight padding inside the skirt. Then it tapered right down into the knees and . . . hobbled down to the hem. It had a Christian Dior split at the back, and it was called Christian Dior because he was the first one who ever put a split in a skirt at the back. (Rayner 1998)

Fashion historians have noted that Paris lost its foothold as the sole arbiter of taste in fashion during the World War II years when French fashion imports were restricted in Australia and the United States. This was significant, as it forced both American and Australian designers to stand alone, establishing and strengthening their own industries (Maynard 2001). The years in between were dominated instead by American fashions, especially those of the avant-garde Modernist designers: Claire McCardell, Bonnie Cashin, Elizabeth Hawes, Tina Leser, Vera Maxwell, Emily Wilkins and other women who liberated American fashion from the dictates of Parisian haute couture (Martin 1998).

In a similar Modernist vein, Jents' Pan Am collection attracted great media attention as she once again demonstrated her sartorial expertise as a leading contemporary designer of the period. As the title of the collection suggests, the garments were designed for air travel with Pan American Airways. Jents was invited to collaborate in a joint project with the company to create a collection of lightweight travel garments for Pan Am's launch of the Strato-Clipper aeroplane. She created a comprehensive wardrobe suitable for a range of climates, weighing the standard 88 pounds (about 40 kilograms) allowed for baggage (Jents 1993: 55). The collection was easy-care and produced from linen and cotton lace fabrics in mix-and-match

**3.3** Beril Jents, white silk and tulle, hand-beaded in jet evening gown, Pan Am collection, model June Mallet, 1948

Courtesy Beril Jents

styles. Garments such as shorts, strapless bustier tops, skirts, day dresses, suits and stoles could be layered for different times of the day, comfort and suitability for a range of climates. Jents' Modernist collection was in keeping with the American designers' vision for the modern twentieth-century woman. She employed the milliner Madge Wainwright[9] to create versatile hats, with each one able to be worn in two or three different ways, adding to the innovative modular concept. For example, one of the large sunhats had a detachable crownless brim which, when removed, revealed a beaded late-afternoon skull cap. The culmination of Pan Am's advertising campaign occurred when the famous Australian actress Bettina Welch, 'Sydney's most-sought-after fashion compere' (*Sydney Morning Herald*, 14 September 1949) introduced Jents' ensembles to guests on the new aeroplane while flying at 20 000 feet (about six kilometres) above the city: this was probably the first fashion show to be held in flight anywhere in the world (Jents 1993: 45).

Jents included other ensembles from her collections that year to complement the black-and-white Pan Am garments. The in-flight fashion show ended in traditional style with a luxurious elegant gown created in white tulle, silk and individually hand-encrusted black jet beads decorating the top of the strapless dress, then cascading into individual beads down to the hipline. Her *coup d'état* ball gown emulated the exaggerated proportions of the New Look: a handspan waist and a skirt so full with panniers at the hips that it would have looked commonplace within a Rococo setting. The silhouette of the gown was the antithesis of the minimalist aesthetic of the Pan Am collection, since Jents recognised that the splash of glamour was a final requisite for all fashion parades during this New Look era. Constructed in a similar mode to Dior's evening gowns of 1949, Jents' bodice fitted like a glove and the skirt was exaggeratedly full. The gown was constructed from many metres of tulle fabric, silk lining and an underskirt superstructure made of heavy horsehair interfacing supporting the amplified hipspan.

By the time she produced her Pan Am collection, Jents' practice and international reputation had grown substantially.[10] In 1949 Norman Hartnell (1901–79), renowned designer to the Queen, wrote her a letter of recognition of her fine practice:

Norman Hartnell wrote me a very nice letter, saying that he had employed two of my girls in his workroom in London and that they were the best seamstresses he had ever met and how well trained they were. I was very flattered and that was the late Forties when he was making for the Queen. (Jents 2006b)

**3.4** Beril Jents, wool coat, 1958

Courtesy Beril Jents

As Jents' cutting techniques were held in such high regard, many (Australian) experienced pattern-cutters sought employment in her company to be further trained by the designer herself (Jents 1993: 55).

    At the age of thirty-two, Jents was followed by her loyal clientele to her new grand salon in the Old St James Building[11] in Sydney's city centre, where she employed over thirty employees. Arguably, she had enjoyed a meteoric rise in her evolution from a competent dressmaker to a designer of high fashion during the early 1950s. Clients came from around Australia, but most were from Melbourne and Brisbane (Jents 2006a). It was at this time that the media enthusiastically acclaimed Jents as being 'Australia's Queen of Haute Couture'.[12] Her only counterpart in this area was the talented and eminent Melbourne-based couturier Hall Ludlow (1919–2003). Like Jents, he based his made-to-measure practice on the creation of independent designs. However, Ludlow was a Cristóbal Balenciaga (1895–1972) devotee, and the great designer's influence may be seen in Ludlow's collections of the period, especially in his heavily textured and structured grand coats and evening wear. Ludlow always spoke of the 1950s as 'the days of real haute couture . . . when people would come in and lay down £500 or £1000 and say, "Tell me when it's done"' (Joel 1998: 180).

Her salon was now highly prestigious and held great cachet for affluent women. Author Valerie Lawson wrote of the impact and popularity of Jents' designs as 'the wives of the trotting crowd came into town from their homes in Penrith, dressed to kill in exotica from designer Beril Jents' (Lawson 1990: 203). A large proportion of Jents' time was taken up designing and producing evening and bridal wear for the young daughters of high society. Some of her finest pieces may be seen in garments created for Nola Dekyvere, Iris Moore, Yvonne Nelson, Betty McInerney, Molly McSweeney, Fayette Haigh, Betty Dawes and Zara St Claire, to name a few. One of her lifelong clients was Sydney socialite Betty McInerney, who became famous for her fashionable style and elegance and was frequently photographed by the press. Jents' bridal gown (1952) for McInerney, now in the collection of the Powerhouse Museum, is described as being a '*pièce de resistance* of Sydney couturier Beril Jents who designed for many wealthy socialites and visiting celebrities from the late nineteen forties for many years' (Powerhouse Museum 2003). She acknowledged that the gown was her most technically challenging dress because of the elaborate design of the skirt:

> It was the most complex gown I had ever made. I felt I had built rather than created this dress! The hand-made silk satin roses which spilled all over the peplum were so heavy we had to build a frame of twisted wire and chiffon in the shape of a half-moon to take the weight. (Powerhouse Museum 2003)

Jents' couture garments continued to be in high demand and consequently her client list grew rapidly, eventually numbering in the hundreds. The list was made up of local, national and international women, including international stars of stage and screen such as Janet Gaynor, June Allison, Elizabeth Taylor, Eartha Kitt, Winifred Atwell and Dame Margot Fonteyn. These women ordered made-to-measure gowns on their visits to Australia

(Rayner 1999). For example, when Elizabeth Taylor visited Jents' salon with third husband Mike Todd[13] in a whirlwind trip in 1957, he purchased a pastel pink silk chiffon empire-line gown for his wife (Jents 1993: 108). A favourite client was the celebrated American pianist Winifred Atwell. Atwell ordered numerous Jents gowns because she adored the theatricality associated

**3.5** Beril Jents, cocktail dress, c. 1956

Courtesy Beril Jents

**3.6** Beril Jents, evening gown, c. 1952

Courtesy Beril Jents

with the designs and the comfortable fit of the garments. The renowned American singer Eartha Kitt ordered several made-to-measure, tight-fitting and sexually appealing evening dresses to appear on stage at the Silver Spade Room at the Chevron Hotel in King's Cross. Kitt was so impressed with the beauty, finish and particularly the perfect fit of the dresses that she immediately ordered more dresses to wear on stage. When Dame Margot Fonteyn organised for her to fly to Melbourne to design gowns for her, Jents had to instruct all of her thirty staff to work on these dresses exclusively because Fonteyn needed them immediately to wear to functions in Australia and overseas.

Interestingly, in terms of theatrical costume design, Jents was regularly commissioned to design costumes for the leading theatrical plays of her era, including *The Reluctant Debutante*, *Call Me Madame*, *Double Image*, *Nude With Violin*, *Simon and Laura*, *Dear Delinquent* and *There's a Girl in My Soup*. She engaged in numerous collaborations with actors, playwrights and directors, often travelling interstate for design briefings and fittings. Very often, well-known actors had fittings in her workrooms – to the delight of her regular clientele. An older Jents reminisced that: 'Clients were often surprised by theatrical scenes re-enacted in the salon so that I could perfect costumes I'd designed' (Jents 1993: 80). She collaborated with notable actors and directors of the stage, such as Noël Coward, Sir Robert Helpmann, Evie Hayes, Rene Paul, Rona Newton-John and Bettina Welch, approaching the design development of the costumes in the same manner as she did her fashion design process.

At the height of her practice in March 1957, she was thrilled to be invited to represent Australia in an international fashion show in New York. In the invitation she was acknowledged by the Americans as 'the pre-eminent Australian fashion designer'.[14] Leslie Cunningham, the fashion consultant organising the event,[15] believed that Jents' work would create 'great excitement' at the parade. The invitation was worded:

> Dear Beril Jents: We would like to invite you, Australia's foremost designer, to join a small group of the outstanding designers of the world taking part in our first international show of designer fashions. This extravagant production to honor the fashion genius of half a dozen nations will be presented April 25, 1957, in the Grand Ballroom of the Waldorf-Astoria in New York . . . We would like very much to have Australia represented at this great fashion event in New York. So far, Norman Hartnell has accepted for England, Givenchy for France, Rodriguez for Spain, Schuberth

for Italy, Rita Tillett for Mexico, George Oka for Japan, etc. Each of these prominent designers will submit three original creations most typical of their particular genius.

When Beril Jents retired in 1986, her career had spanned a remarkable six decades. Jents' exceptional *oeuvre* is a result of her life's love and passion for the craft of best dressmaking practice and an unyielding dedication to her work. Her well-designed and expertly constructed couture pieces continue to be appreciated throughout the world, as her garments are here in Australia. Jents has had a resurgence in popularity and a whole new generation of women has been wearing vintage pieces since the late 1990s. In 2006, for example, the Australian biannual international fashion magazine *SummerWinter* (which aims to target Generation Y) confirmed her high standing as an icon of Australian haute couture:

> Australia isn't famous for its glittering fashion history, but the story of our style extends a lot further . . . rediscovering the exquisite craftsmanship of Beril's work is exciting because it hints at all the incredible stories and personalities that have slipped just beyond our reach. (Scully 2006: 53)

While very little has been published about the life and work of Beril Jents, she stands at the forefront of a locally developed couture aesthetic in Australia. In retrospect, her substantial contribution to the Australian fashion industry as a leader in the field can no longer be ignored. Her works present a tapestry as aesthetically rich as any in the Australian fashion industry.

## Notes

1   In an interview for *Verbatim* on ABC Radio National entitled 'Beril Jents: Australia's Queen of Haute Couture of 1998', Jents recalled her crowning by the Sydney press as Australia's first haute couturier. Nevertheless, the use of the term 'haute couture' or just 'couture' is incorrect here in Australia, as well as in many overseas countries including America, Britain and Canada. This appropriated term has been used to mean any fashion designer working in a high-end, made-to-measure practice. The French have legislated and protected the term in the twentieth century through the Chambre Syndicale de la Couture Parisienne. This organisation became a federation in 1973: Fédération Française de la Couture, du Prêt-à-Porter des Couturiers et des Créateurs de Mode (French Federation of Fashion and of Ready-to-Wear of Couturiers and Fashion Designers). However, the criteria for being classed as a couturier were correctly used in this case: Jents did employ at least twenty

people (she had over thirty) in her workroom and presented at least fifty original designs twice yearly to the press (Rayner 1998).

2 Jents has kept a large scrapbook archive of her newspaper and magazine clippings that span her entire working life. She has short handwritten notes accompanying them, and the scrapbook includes personal photographs, letters and postcards. This valuable archive presents a detailed overview of her work from the 1930s through to the 1990s. However, it is missing quite a few details here and there regarding newspaper or magazine names, dates and page numbers. Interestingly, Jents designed for the times, and the scrapbook shows a developmental progression and a reflection of styles and ideas that represent an invaluable resource in many ways. She has bequeathed her scrapbook to the Powerhouse Museum in Sydney.

3 Famous 'zoot suiters' included the jazz musicians Dizzy Gillespie and Louis Armstrong, as well as the young Malcolm X (Mendes and de la Haye 1999: 125).

4 Russian-born Madame Germaine Rocher was born Vera Fels and lived in France with her husband Charles before immigrating to Australia. Joel states that 'Madame Rocher was a formidable woman of impeccable taste and exacting eye. She looked for line and finish above all else' (Joel 1998: 114).

5 In the mid-1940s Jents found that the only fabric available to her was moss crêpe, a human-made rayon fabric emulating the properties of silk.

6 Jents worked as a trainee lithographic artist for the firm Hollander and Govett in Sydney for several months before she accepted the apprenticeship with Madame Gallet.

7 In 1946 Mary Hordern, fashion editor of the *Australian Women's Weekly*, brought elegant and luxurious couture to Australia from the leading French design houses. Hordern understood that women in Australia craved glamorous clothes after years of wartime constraints on fashion. She organised extensive parades of the latest collections from the leading Parisian haute couturiers, except for Christian Dior because of his licensing obligations with David Jones. The lavish fashion parades were showcased in Sydney, Melbourne and Adelaide. The parades sold out immediately and ensured high sales of the magazine.

8 Olwyn Jacklin, former model to Norman Hartnell and a fashion buyer, asked Jents to reproduce Christian Dior's New Look collection first for herself and then later for the fashion store Curzon's. However, she did not put her name on the reproductions, so when Sydney's elite purchased the garments they presumed they were made in Paris, not by a local designer.

9 In Jents' scrapbook, marked under the date c. 26 March 1952 (written in her own handwriting), a newspaper cutting regarding her show 'An American in Paris', which was a sellout for the New South Wales Institute of Deaf, Dumb and Blind Children, is a small section devoted to Sydney-based milliner Madge Wainwright. It states: 'Also at the Parade . . . were hats to dream about, by Wainwright. This clever designer has captured the art of creating hats for every occasion. From a simple black felt with fluted brim to the adorable little jewelled cocktail chapeaus, Wainwright's hats are individual

and charming. Her collection of autumn and winter hats has just been opened, and are available this week at Brasch Pty Ltd, 1 Oxford Street, in their model department.'

10 The initial number of two sewing machines grew to twelve machines in her workroom, which measured 121 square metres.

11 The elegant and grand St James Building, 109 Elizabeth Street, Sydney was demolished and a new one built in its place.

12 Jents was so delighted with this extraordinary acknowledgement of her work that she now included the French term on her signage: Beril Jents Haute Couture.

13 Mike Todd was in Australia to promote his film *Around the World in 80 Days*.

14 Invitation from the Silhouette Corporation, New York, 1957.

15 All the designers were asked to send nine sketches of morning, afternoon and evening ensembles by 15 March; considering the letter was sent on the 8 March, this was a very tight timeline and somehow the post made the deadlines. As a further incentive, the designers were told that publicity resulting from the parade was over half a million dollars – an extraordinary amount for a fashion parade. An interesting turn of events occurred as news of this spread like wildfire. In Sydney, the clever Madame Rocher quickly sent her own designs to the parade's organisers, stressing that she too was a top Australian couturière and also offering to pay her own travel expenses to attend the event, which she did (Jents 1993).

## References

Bell, G. (1972), 'Alone at the top of haute couture', *The National Times*, 6–11 March.

Department of Health and Ageing (2007), 'Memories of the Great Depression: 1930s', Living History Archive, Canberra, <www.seniors.gov.au/internet/seniors/publishing.nsf/Content/Living+History+ Archived+Topic-The+Great+Depression>.

Foster, L. (2006), interview by L. Pomazan, Sydney.

Hamilton, H. (1986), 'The Jents set', *Harper's Bazaar*, July.

Jents, B. (1993), *Little Ol' Beryl from Bondi*, Sydney: Macmillan.

—— (2006a), interview by L. Pomazan, Sydney.

—— (2006b), interview by L. Pomazan, Sydney.

—— (2007), interview by L. Pomazan, Sydney.

Joel, A. (1984), *Best Dressed: 200 Years of Fashion in Australia*, Sydney: Collins.

—— (1998), *Parade: The Story of Fashion in Australia*, Sydney: Harper Collins.

Lawson, V. (1990), *Connie Sweetheart: The Story of Connie Robertson*, Melbourne: Heinemann.

Leong, R. (2010), 'Making and retailing exclusive dress in Australia', in M. Maynard (ed.), *Volume 7: Australia, New Zealand and the Pacific Islands*, part of J.B. Eicher (ed.), *Berg Encyclopaedia of World Dress and Fashion*, London: Berg.

Martin, R. (1998), *American Ingenuity: Sportswear 1930s–1970s*, exhibition catalogue, New York: Metropolitan Museum of Art.

Martin, R. and Koda, H. (1996), *Christian Dior*, exhibition catalogue, New York: Metropolitan Museum of Art.

Martyn, R. (1976), *The Look: Australian Women in their Fashion*, Sydney: Cassell.

Maynard, M. (2001), *Out of Line: Australian Women and Style*, Sydney: UNSW Press.

Mendes, V. and de la Haye, A. (1999), *20th Century Fashion*, London: Thames and Hudson.

Mitchell, L. (1996), *Christian Dior: The Magic of Fashion*, exhibition catalogue, Sydney: Powerhouse Museum.

Powerhouse Museum (2003), *Wedding Outfits and Photographs: 1952*, Powerhouse Museum Collection, Sydney, <www.powerhousemuseum.com/collection/database/?irn=12131>.

Rayner, M. (1998), 'Beril Jents: Australian Queen of Haute Couture', interview for *Verbatim*, ABC Radio National, Melbourne, 16 February 2006.

Riley, M. (1997), *The Australian Women's Diary 1998*, in K. Stackhouse (ed.), Sydney: Doubleday.

Scully, J. (2006), 'Revolution', *SummerWinter*, p. 4.

*Sydney Morning Herald* (1949), 'Flights of fashion', 14 September.

Tellick, Peggy (1975), 'A down to earth Queen of Couture', *The National Times*, Sydney, September.

Walker, A. (1974), *Stardom: The Hollywood Phenomenon*, London: Penguin.

# ENVISIONING INDEPENDENCE

## FASHION PHOTOGRAPHY IN AUSTRALIA

*Daniel Palmer and Kate Rhodes*

**4.1** Athol Shmith, *Fashion Illustration (Model Patricia Shmith)*, 1949
Courtesy National Gallery of Victoria, Melbourne

**T**HIS CHAPTER OFFERS an account of the significant developments and themes in Australian fashion photography, focusing on the postwar period. Beginning with a brief history of earlier developments that set the foundations for the heyday of Australian fashion photography in the 1950s and 1960s, we look at local nuances and international influences in the role of photography in marketing Australian fashion and style. Given that fashion photography – a genre of image-making whose primary purpose is to sell clothing, either directly for sale or as part of a broader advertising promotion – is closely linked to the rise of the modern print media of newspapers and magazines and, more recently the internet, we pay close attention to the significance of local publications. The chapter proposes that a sense of isolation and distance, as well as the particular qualities of the Australian landscape, have given shape to what is unique about Australian fashion photography. At the same time, we note that nationalistic imagery – insofar as it exists in fashion photography – has been on the decline since its peak in the 1970s.

Fashion photography in Australia, following a pattern developed in France, Britain and the United States, grew out of society and glamour portraiture, which in turn descended from *carte-de-visite* portraits and postcards of theatrical performers and other celebrities widely distributed from the 1860s. Such portraiture inspired sartorial imitation, and in this sense images of Australian theatrical celebrities in the late nineteenth and early twentieth centuries constitute an important archive of Australian 'proto-fashion photography' (Palmer 2005). The use of photography in fashion journalism occasionally appeared in the late nineteenth century in colonial society newspapers. In the main, however, print advertisements for department stores selling clothes in Australia remained hand-drawn rather than photographic until at least the second decade of the twentieth century (Maynard 2001). Although a degree of obscurity still surrounds the early history of Australian fashion photography, its gestation occurs in the years between Australian Federation (1901) and the outbreak of World War I – a period marked by social progress and an economic boom, coinciding with significant growth in the retail industry and the rapid rise of brand-mobilising stores such as David Jones and Myer.

Australian fashion photography was consolidated in the 1920s in the pages of the high-quality Sydney-based journal *The Home*. A taste-making magazine in the international style of American and British *Vogue*, *Harper's Bazaar* and *Tatler*, *The Home* published images and essays on modern, applied and decorative arts alongside fashion and patronised local art photographers. The involvement of these art photographers, both as 'amateur' Pictorialists and as commercial illustrators, was crucial to defining its overall look. Along with a new nationalist taste in graphic design, interior design and fashion itself, the publisher of *The Home*, Sydney Ure Smith, understood the expressive potential of photography as a modern medium, and the possibility that a photographer might adopt a unique, personal style was increasingly being recognised. Credited photographic fashion work, in which a photographer is privileged as a creative figure, appeared from the first issue in 1920. Indeed, the editorial promoted its 'special photographic service to record the latest and best achievements in dress that commerce has been able to make available for Australian wardrobes'. *The Home's* photographic style was initially set by its first official photographer, Harold Cazneaux (1878–1953), a well-known Sydney-based Pictorialist. Ruth Hollick (1883–1977) also provided portraits of society women in the most glamorous attire of the day.

Despite the onset of the Depression, the 1930s saw a rapid growth in commercial photographic studios. While women had featured prominently as glamour portraitists, men soon dominated the emerging profession of 'fashion photographer', along with an imported Modernist photographic aesthetic. Russell Roberts (1904–99), Max Dupain (1911–92) and Athol Shmith (1914–90) all frequently worked on fashion commissions for *The Home* in the mid 1930s. As exponents of the so-called 'New Photography', news of which trickled into Australia via European magazines, their work was of particular interest to advertising clients who quickly realised that bold compositions and sharp and often unusual angles as well as dramatic lighting would make for innovative product presentations. This fact, combined with innovations in printing technologies and artificial studio lighting along with the rise in local magazine publishing, meant that fashion photography in the 1930s had become a viable profession in Australia's two largest cities, Melbourne and Sydney. For most photographers, however, fashion was only one of several genres in which they worked.

A consummate entrepreneur, Russell Roberts had a Sydney-based studio that was the largest and most successful of its kind in Australia at that time. Along with traditional studio glamour work, Roberts' studio brought a modern and more naturalistic approach to fashion, including movement, inspired by location shots from Europe. He also pioneered the production of colour fashion photographs in the early 1930s and played a vital role early in the careers of some of Australia's most influential photographers, including Max Dupain and German émigré Hans Hasenpflug (1907–77).

By 1935, Dupain was cast as the leader of avant-garde photography when a portfolio of his Modernist still-lifes and nudes was published in the esteemed journal *Art in Australia* (Newton 1988: 111). An apprentice of Cecil Bostock (1884–1939) – well known for his fashion work for David Jones – Dupain deployed both the dramatic lighting and geometry of Modernist advertising and some of the contorted spaces and odd conjunctions of Surrealism, revealing his early enthusiasm for the work of Man Ray. Most of Dupain's best-known fashion work, however, is relatively sombre: static, studio-based tableaux of women and clothes. Dupain left fashion entirely after the 1940s in favour of architectural and documentary photography; the experience of war led him to focus on what he called 'clear statements of actuality' and abandon the 'cosmetic lie of fashion photography or advertising illustration' (*Australia's Culture Portal*, n.d.).

Athol Shmith is today recognised as the greatest pioneer of modern Australian fashion photography. He began to take fashion photographs in Melbourne in the 1930s at a time when the profession of fashion modelling was still in its infancy – establishing his reputation by using non-professional models from upper-class Melbourne families – and continued to be a leader in fashion photography through to the 1960s (Crombie 1989). By the 1940s, Shmith's high-profile Collins Street studio had established a reputation for elegant fashion photography that incorporated the conventions of Modernist photographic practice and seductive Hollywood glamour portraiture. Hasenpflug worked briefly for Athol Shmith's studio in Melbourne after 1937, and Shmith held the Melbourne contract for Russell Roberts' studio. With the end of wartime austerities, Shmith's photographic business expanded considerably and, as smart new fashions were produced, he won long-standing contracts to photograph both for couture houses (such as Le Louvre) and department stores.

In 1948, Shmith was commissioned by Myer Melbourne to photograph a group of Parisian models brought by the department store to Australia to parade Christian Dior's New Look fashions. *Fashion Illustration (Model Patricia Shmith)*, 1949, is a classically elegant Shmith image, showing the clean lines of Dior's dresses to excellent effect. As Isobel Crombie observes:

> A reference to internationalism is neatly suggested by Shmith who has the model (Patricia [Tuckwell] Shmith) hold an illustration of another model posed in a baroque French interior. However, unlike the lush illustration, this photograph has a pared-down quality that draws the viewer's attention to the distinctively angular lines and nipped-in waistline of the garment. This photograph is a wonderful example of Shmith's trademark skill with lighting which helps create a vibrant fashion photograph of this stylish, postwar woman. (Crombie 2004)

Shmith's innovative and stylish work, well represented in art museum collections and published histories, embodies Melbourne's sense of itself as a stylish and classical city. Thus *The Haunted Ballroom*, c. 1949–52, shot in a ruin, offers a parallel to Cecil Beaton's fashion photography, taken a few years earlier amidst war ruins in Britain. An image at Melbourne's Botanical Gardens, *Fashion Illustration (Model Ann Chapman)*, 1961, typifies Shmith's grasp of elegance, carefully linking the model in a feathered gown with a real swan on a lake, their necks both gently arched. In general, Shmith preferred simple postures and graceful backdrops, favouring European aristocratic looks.

Responding to the altered social, political and economic conditions of the 1950s, Bruno Benini (1925–2001) also created a style of photography that conveyed an image of opulence and sophistication, following the end of the era of rationed commodities when women's fashion was more utilitarian and austere. Benini was himself the child of Italian migrants who moved to Australia when he was ten years old. He trained as an industrial chemist before starting out in the fashion industry as a model for Shmith. Along

with Melbourne's other leading fashion photographers of the 1950s, Benini positioned his female mannequins as glamour icons while simultaneously creating a new ideal of femininity, responsive to the evolving fashion industry. In the ensuing decade of economic strength and stability, fashion was again celebrated as a visible symbol of wealth and social standing. Beauty was associated with feminine 'ideals' of chic elegance and luxury.

Benini's work has a strong graphic sense, often involving an interplay between the model and architecture or sculpture. In many respects, the brilliance and intrigue of Benini's photography during the 1950s lay within his use of unexpected locations to create a deliberate ambiguity. For example, he shot one of his most famous photographs, *Fashion Illustration (Model Catherine Patchell, National Gallery of Victoria)*, 1956, in front of Giambattista Tiepolo's *The Banquet of Cleopatra*, 1743–44, at the National Gallery of Victoria. Meanwhile, *Fashion Illustration (Model Janet Dawson), Eastern Markets, Melbourne*, 1957, was taken outside a dingy soup kitchen as a means of augmenting the impression of sensuous luxury through stark contrasts. In this photograph, adapting the conventions of Hollywood film stills, Benini constructed a Cinderella-like fantasy, a demure style of sensual frailty in an opulent silk gown (Messenger 2004).

Laurence Le Guay (1917–91) also delighted in cheeky and unexpected scenarios, but represented a more bohemian approach to fashion that was ultimately to define Australian fashion photography in the 1960s. Following a period making surrealist anti-war montages in the 1930s and then as an official photographer in World War II, Le Guay established a magazine called *Contemporary Photography* in 1946, which focused on the role of documentary photography in exposing and redressing the social ills besetting postwar Australia. The magazine also published fashion photographs and works of commercial photo-illustration from the burgeoning class of professional photographers. Ever versatile, in 1947 Le Guay entered into a partnership with John Nisbett in a studio that specialised in fashion and commercial illustration. A well-known fashion image from 1948 reveals his talent for crossing boundaries; it shows a fashion model striking a pose with a basket of flowers against a slum backdrop, a looming Dickensian building under dark grey skies. As if plucked from a country idyll and dropped into this urban setting, the model seems deliberately at odds with her surroundings.

**4.2** Bruno Benini, *Fashion Illustration (Model Janet Dawson)*, Eastern Markets, Melbourne, 1957
Courtesy National Gallery of Victoria, Melbourne and Hazel Benini

Le Guay developed an energetic style, using all manner of daring outdoor locations and even posed fashion models with garbage collectors. *Fashion Queue with Masked Child*, 1960, reveals Le Guay's skill at directing a fashion moment on the street. A highly choreographed and playful image of tall fashion models and everyday travellers waiting for a bus, it was produced in the same year as the similar comical *Girl in White Swimsuit with Underwater Divers*, 1960, set on a theatrical rocky beach. As a rule, Sydney photographers have always been 'rather more informal' than their Melbourne counterparts, and – for obvious climatic reasons – have tended to 'gravitate to beach and leisurewear' (Maynard 2006: 10). However, as Margaret Maynard suggests, even as 'the combination of documentary, humor and fashion' in these curious images could be said to possess a 'characteristic Australian quirkiness', there is still little in Le Guay's work that could be said to be uniquely 'Australian' (Maynard 2006: 11–12). Nevertheless, in 1959 Le Guay seems to have been the first Australian photographer to venture into the centre of the continent to photograph a fashion model against the vast backdrop of Ayers Rock (Uluru) (Maynard 2001: 108). Many others have followed. By this time, Le Guay was at the height of his powers, fully in touch with the Australian zeitgeist. Later, in the 1960s, his images even took on a space-age theme; he produced a number of psychedelic fish-eye photographs on sand dunes, shot into the sun, to advertise jeans and bikinis.

The postwar period had seen Australia's fashion industry come of age. By the 1950s – a time of affluence following the constraints of the war years – fashion advertising and illustration work had become a major specialist industry for photographers and their growing teams of collaborators. A professional models' association was formed and standardised remuneration rates were instituted. This was the era of grand Collins Street studios in Melbourne and major clients such as Myer, as chain department stores benefited from the upsurge in production of consumer goods following World War II. As well as those mentioned here, other important fashion photographers of the time included Ray Leighton, Geoffrey Lee, Rob Hillier, Geoffrey Powell and Norman Ikin. It was, by all accounts, the heyday of Australian fashion. But as photography curator and historian Gael Newton has observed, the individual photographer's control over design and approach was increasingly subject to direction from specialised advertising departments. Agencies tended to be in awe of overseas trends in fashion photography and wanted Australian photographers simply to produce local versions (Newton 1988: 130).

Britain remained the model from which Australian fashion editors took their cues. An Australian supplement for British *Vogue* was first published in 1955, leading to an independent Australian edition of the Condé Nast publication in 1959. As Maynard has observed, *Vogue Australia* imported Rosemary Cooper from London as editor and the magazine embodied a ladylike tone, projecting itself as 'an arbiter of taste for the well-heeled, well travelled, slightly mature woman' (Maynard 2006: 7):

> Its first issue patronisingly offered to sift, select and explain fashion to Australians, for it inferred fashion was the same all over the world. Another article in the same issue, 'Fashion for Two Hemispheres' argues fashion is not about geography but mood and taste. While acknowledging Australian women were less formal than the British and regional urban styles existed, it advises what mattered was the 'international rightness of style', in other words that which was un-Australian. (Maynard 2006: 7)

Nevertheless, the local publication *Flair* magazine (1956–1973) also began promoting Australian fashion exports and suggested in 1959 that Australian women were developing their own fashion 'look' that was as 'indigenous to Australia as the tweeds of England, and the "white collar" fashions of America, are to their respective countries' (Maynard 2006: 8).

It was in this context that a young Helmut Newton (1920–2004) first established himself as a fashion photographer. Newton arrived in Australia in 1940, after fleeing Nazi Germany via Singapore. After a period of internment at the Tatura detention camp and then a stint in the Australian army, Newton began working as a photographer in Melbourne, taking up the profession from his earlier training in a fashionable Berlin salon as a teenager in the 1930s. Changing his name from Neustadter to Newton in 1946, by the mid 1950s he had built up a reputation as one of Australia's leading fashion photographers, with his work regularly appearing in *Flair* and *Vogue Australia* – the country's two magazines exclusively devoted to fashion. Even though he retrospectively claimed that most of his pictures of this period were 'dreadful' (Newton 2003: 168), Newton's Australian photographs already demonstrate a characteristic technical precision and a breezy appreciation of coolly beautiful women. He used urban environments imaginatively – road signs appear often, adding both a light-hearted, optimistic view of the city and geometric drama. He even photographed a model jumping from a helicopter. His Australian images make maximum use of bright outdoor settings: the beach, lush gardens or picturesque ghost towns such as Walhalla. Occasionally there is a touch of noir – such as one photograph from 1960 of a demure fur-clad celebrity model and personality Maggie Tabberer being protected by gangsters in trench coats with mob-style machine guns. Here there is even a hint of the dark erotic mood, and narrative, that was later to become Newton's distinctive contribution; the woman stands comfortably between the two men, gloved hand resting upon the weapon and with eyebrows raised as if the photographer's flash is an imposition.

Newton's ambition went well beyond Australia, however. As he describes in his autobiography, after an unhappy period seconded in London working for *British Vogue* in 1957, he fell in love with Paris. Despite his success, and although by this time married to an Australian actress – June Browne, who later also worked as a photographer under the pseudonym Alice Spring – he eventually determined to leave Australia for Paris permanently in 1961 and never returned. Describing his state of mind, he wrote:

> **Australia was not a country where a photographer could make a great career. You can only make a great career in fashion photography in Paris or New York. You can't go anywhere else. (Newton 2003: 168)**

Newton, of course, went on to become one of the most significant international names in fashion photography of the 1960s and 1970s. His influence in Australia continued through the work of his studio partner Henry Talbot (1920–99). Yet another émigré artist with a talent for making images of fashion, Talbot arrived in Australia in 1940 aboard the infamous *Dunera* – an overcrowded ship of European 'enemy aliens'. He had previously studied graphic design at the Reimann School in Berlin before emigrating to England just prior to the outbreak of war. After establishing a reputation working for some of the leading Melbourne photographic studios of the day, in 1956 Newton, with whom he formed a friendship during the war, invited him into partnership. The Melbourne studio of Newton and Talbot was a great success, securing a vast number of advertising clients including the Australian Wool Board, Prestige and Hilton Hosiery, Kayser and Sportscraft. (When Newton left in 1961, their studio on Bourke Street had ten employees.) In 1958, Talbot was awarded the prestigious *Australian Fashion News* award for Fashion Photographer of the Year (van Wyk 2004).

The fresh, modern look of Talbot's work – linking contemporary fashion and popular culture – came to reflect the emerging youth culture and widespread social changes that characterised the 1960s.[1] It was a time in Australia in which fashion photographers gained a new confidence. Elegance, high-key glamour and the idealised society portraits of the previous era were no longer the main currency. Instead, a form of fantastic documentary was now in vogue, reflected by Le Guay in Sydney. Colour and outdoor images spoke to women seeking a broader vision of life than family and home (Maynard 2001: 106). Even Shmith – ever the nimble professional – worked increasingly outside the studio at this time. Shmith's *Fashion Illustration for Le Louvre*, 1960, depicts a model in a chic strapless dress, fingers mid-click. With elbow learning on a wooden packing crate with the words 'Melbourne' and 'Made in France' stencilled on the side, it suggests the newly imported dress has just been put on for the shot. The setting also reflects a contemporary everyday feel: the model stands on a grease-stained concrete floor surrounded by rubbish and cigarette butts.

Although the exoticism of an overseas shoot became more common in the 1960s, as Australian fashion was gaining international credibility and overseas air travel became more prevalent, local colour was also possible. Talbot's *Fashion Illustration for Maglia Knitwear Advertisement*, 1969, is a typical image of the period, with its outlaws and youthful women in colourful mini-dresses and masculine-style pants suits, in a playful setting suggesting a B-grade Western heist on a train carriage. It can be seen as part of an emerging nationalism in advertising imagery at the time; the Australian Wool Board specifically encouraged Australian scenes for promotions, and numerous advertisements based on wool garments were photographed in rural environments (Maynard 2006: 12). Talbot's linking of contemporary fashion and popular culture typified the exuberant spirit of the times. Playing with gender and authority, his images precisely echoed the new freedom of the Baby Boomer generation.

With an increased interest in and demand for higher-quality colour processing, the exuberant fashion photography of this period was best exemplified by the images found in *POL* (1968–85) – later revived as *Pol Oxygen* (2002–08) – a more broadly defined design magazine. Modelled on the revolutionary British magazine *NOVA*, *POL* gave unprecedented creative autonomy to individual innovators such as Wesley Stacey and Grant Mudford (both better known for their documentary work) as well as Brett Hilder, Dieter Muller, Rennie Ellis and John Lethbridge. Fashion photography here often crossed over into social commentary. Staff photographers were closely involved in editing their photographs and choosing their layout, a level of involvement highly unusual before that time or since. Part of the first wave of desktop publishing, POL reflected a changing Australia that had been radicalised by the 1960s. Computers, Letraset, four-colour printing and other technological advances created new freedoms for art directors, designers and photographers (Sayers 2003: 3). POL defined itself in part through its use of these techniques to achieve innovative layouts that demanded attention.

POL featured a quirky sense of humour and a liberated sense of sexuality. Born as the women's movement was emerging, POL's editors understood the importance of reflecting these updated values. Feminist writer Germaine Greer was one of many occasional guest editors – a major step for a magazine within an industry built in large part on the objectification of women. Significantly, POL also reflected a growing body of Australian fashion design that was itself flamboyant and androgynous, with extremely loose, non-gendered cuts or tailored masculine shapes for women. In the pages of POL, women lost the haughty look pioneered by Shmith. Indeed, part of POL's appeal was its gender neutrality, with articles appealing to both men and women, in considerable contrast to the more conservative *Australian Women's Weekly* and *Vogue Australia* (McFarlane, quoted in Sayers 2003: 4). In short, POL was part of a wave of transformation in Australian image-making and the belief that original photographs could be made here and that they would be relevant to a local audience. In 1980, the flamboyant former premier of South Australia, Don Dunstan, even took over as editor for a few issues, offering an ironic manifesto:

> POL delights in excellence, individuality, creativity and zest for life. We chronicle Australia's maturity. We pursue the causes of the good. Australians of the world unite and read POL – you have nothing to lose but your cultural cringe. . . . POL is therefore a valuable mirror to Australia during the decades that saw a new national culture of self-belief. (Sayers 2003: 4)

POL pioneered the publication of fashion images created by artists and sometimes also used non-professional models. Artist and sometime fashion photographer John Lethbridge marked another kind of transmutation from gallery to magazine, and during the 1970s was involved with installation art and performance. (He photographed Marina Abromovic and Ulay on their visit to Australia.) While many of Lethbridge's peers in the visual arts found his interest in fashion photography unusual and even anti-intellectual (Rhodes 2007: 24), he was attracted to the freedom that POL encouraged,

**4.3** John Lethbridge, *Fashion Spread*, 1979, POL, September 1979 in Solar Flair
Courtesy John Lethbridge

saying that the 'more edgy your pictures were the more [the editors] wanted to run with them' (McFarlane 2003: 11). Later, in the early 1980s, Lethbridge teamed up with Sydney designer Katie Pye and, while many of these highly staged photographs were deliberately unpublished – created simply for the designer and the pleasure of making images – some of the wildly theatrical shots appeared in *POL* (Rhodes 2007). At the time, it was really the only Australian publishing platform that happily sat on the fringe as an independent barometer of fashion and fashion photography.

A deep-seated romanticism underpinned the 1970s emphasis on thrift-store fashion – with its nostalgia for garments of an indeterminate past – counter-cultural styles and environmental concerns (Maynard 2001: 110). This was a period in tune with a new cultural nationalism in Australia which was most obvious in the newly re-energised Australian film industry; thus Uluru and Alice Springs became fashionable backdrops. Unsurprisingly, given the country's coast-hugging population, the beach has long been the key backdrop for Australian fashion photography. However, from the 1970s onwards, Australian fashion photography exhibited a more general obsession with nature. In the emphatically nationalistic 1970s and early 1980s, so-called Australiana styles became popular in fashion as well. The garments produced by Jenny Kee and Linda Jackson, who ran their Flamingo Park boutique in Sydney's Strand Arcade, were structured in large part around local and Indigenous motifs, flora and fauna.

A new wave of magazines followed in the late 1970s and 1980s. Although short-lived, the monthly *Rag Times* (1977–81), produced in a newspaper format, mobilised readers with its high-impact content. Informal, offbeat and streetwise – guided by an idealistic manifesto based around personal liberty – it also attracted many of *POL*'s regular photographers, including Peter McLean, Hilder, Ellis and Jurgen Ryck. By far the most influential fashion magazine of the 1980s was *Follow Me*, which catered to a more urbane market moving toward a sharper, more polished look – a local version of the international trend known as 'new wave' that embraced crossovers between art, post-punk music and fashion. Grant Matthews' vibrant suburban images were typical. Along with Matthews, Monty Coles and McLean's work was featured in the first exhibition of contemporary Australian fashion photography shown in an art context, *Image Perfect: Australian Fashion Photography in the 80s*, at the Australian Centre for Photography in 1987. The curator, freelance photographer Sandy Edwards, had previously produced a critical artwork, *Narrative with Sexual Overtones* (1983), exploring the construction of female sexual identity through stereotypical images appropriated from fashion magazines (Edwards 2004: 61). Feminist ideas were strongly felt in Australia at this time within the creative and academic worlds, under the sway of Postmodern theory, and many artists sought to interrogate, rework and reconstruct images of women. For the most part, however, the more mainstream publications like *Vogue* were immune to such critiques, and simply mirrored conservative international trends towards images of athletic, healthy and business-oriented women.

Since the early to mid 1990s, a number of independent, street-style/fashion/lifestyle magazines have come on to the Australian market. Many are now established names, such as *Australian Style*, *Black and White*, *Cream*, *Oyster*, *Yen*, *Russh* and *Frankie*. The Australian market consumes more magazines per capita than any other OECD country. More magazines – each with its own house style and design formats for specialised readerships – have meant more places for publication and more varied assignments for photographers. While magazines like *Vogue Australia* tend to employ only a small number of regular photographers (Richard Bailey, Troyt Coburn and Justin Edward John Smith are some of the key names in the first decade of the twenty-first century), faster turnaround times, lower budgets and fewer advertising constraints also mean independent magazines are the chief publishing avenues for aspiring fashion photographers. As start-up magazines, designed as quick promotional tools for those involved, some are short-lived – such as Pierre Touissant's *Processed*, which had only two issues in the early 2000s. Independent magazines are also an area where fashion photographs frequently cross into an art and popular culture mix.

The well-established versions of international glossies such as *Vogue Australia*, *Australian Harper's Bazaar* (1984–) and *Australian marie claire* (1995–) are the traditional pinnacles of the magazine world, but they also tend to be the most conservative clients for fashion photography. *Vogue*, for example, tends to employ only a small number of regular photographers, and these are rarely the pages in which these photographers produce their most dynamic work. Arguably, in fact, these publications stifle more experimental and conceptual fashion photography by persistently publishing studio-based shots capturing clichéd poses and well-worn exoticisms, taking crews to locations such as India or Marrakesh.

Most fashion magazines continue to be published in Sydney, as has been the case historically. Australian fashion photographers have always been concentrated in the most populous cities, Sydney and Melbourne.

Melbourne's relative importance, however, seems to have shrunk radically since the 1950s when Myer was a major client to the Shmith and Newton–Talbot studios, which were then in full swing. Shmith and Talbot were regularly featured in *Vogue Australia* and *Flair*, but were also employed by local department stores and exclusive boutiques (van Wyk 2006: 59). Today, all of the glossies and most of the independent magazines are located in Sydney. Sydney's stronghold is so entrenched that some photographers have been told to relocate there if they hope to find work, and whole creative teams are flown around Australia for shoots, rather than resources being employed from individual states.

The small size of the Australian market has always posed a challenge. Currently, the industry in Australia is hugely competitive and fragmented; paid work consists largely of freelance contracts, principally filled by a small group of entrepreneurial individuals. Although the rewards can be high, both in creative and financial terms, fashion photography is a field that suffers generally from unregulated pay conditions. The lack of fashion magazine outlets and the general small scale of support for local creativity have always made for a difficult situation for photographers, even more so with the continued use of international photographers. Nevertheless, Australian fashion photographers have not limited themselves to working for local magazines. As well as doing assignments in Europe and the United States, Australian photographers are now regularly working in Asia, reflecting the increasing globalisation of the industry. Likewise, independent Australian magazines increasingly publish the work of international photographers. For instance, one of the most original of recent small magazines is the biannual art-fashion publication *doingbird*, edited by Max Doyle and Malcolm Watt. It features only a handful of Australian photographers, showing a preference for international photographers, models, writers and illustrators. Moreover, *doingbird* has a higher circulation internationally than locally, countering the general flow of imported magazines.

Australian fashion photographers are regarded internationally as adaptable practitioners, and many choose to work overseas because the rewards and opportunities are greater. Contemporary Australian fashion photographers who regularly work overseas include Lyn Balzer and Tony Perkins, Harold David, Liz Ham, Derek Henderson, Ingvar Kenne, Tim Richardson and Justin Edward John Smith. All exhibit their work in galleries, or they are involved with self-publishing, and many collaborate with artists and fashion designers. Some of these photographers, notably Richardson and Smith, are also experimenting with digital imaging in distinctive ways that give the body a filmic, futuristic feel awash with colour and located against fantastical backgrounds.

For many, the first step towards becoming a professional is to study a general commercial or art photography course, due to a lack of programs devoted specifically to fashion photography. In fact, the Australian Centre for Photography, a predominantly art photography, government-funded institution, runs one of the only regular courses. Historically, many start with portraiture. While documentary and fashion have traditionally been at odds with the 'real' world of the street opposed to the artificial world of the studio at photography schools, this is no longer the case, as contemporary fashion photography increasingly borrows the aesthetics of realism. Liz Ham, a well-known Sydney-based documentary photographer, has successfully transferred aspects of this style to her fashion work. On the other hand, Tim Richardson began as a graphic designer and art director, a training he believes contributes to his distinctive minimalist style.

While some see no distinction, most Australian fashion photographers tend to divide their commercial and personal work, with one often subsidising the other. These circumstances have famously been explored by photographers such as Edward Steichen, Diane Arbus, Wolfgang Tillmans and Philip-Lorca di Corcia. Art directors play a key role in mediating the relationship between photographers and magazines and the fashion houses that regularly commission some of the most experimental fashion photography. One of the best known is Melbourne-based Fabio Ongarato, who works with most of Australia's pre-eminent fashion photographers. In 2000, Ongarato curated a significant exhibition surveying contemporary Australian and New Zealand fashion photographers' works, entitled *Unpublished*, and in 2004 he was commissioned by the New York-based fashion magazine *Big* to art direct an Australian issue. However, Ongarato's most notorious contribution to Australian fashion photography occurred in 1997, in a landmark project with Melbourne fashion label Scanlan & Theodore for their tenth anniversary. As Ongarato notes:

> I wanted someone special to shoot the campaign. Working on the concept of questioning beauty and its relativity to cultural perceptions, I commissioned the artist Bill Henson to produce his own interpretation of the collection. The result was a never seen before campaign where art met fashion which created heated debate and controversy. The response was not an obvious

AUSTRALIAN FASHION UNSTITCHED

one, nor was it one we could have envisaged doing ourselves.
(Borschke 2008)

Henson's campaign featured the designers' clothes on adolescent models in a dark and moody setting more familiar from his well-known artistic practice. The images caused something of a minor scandal and raised the profile of all involved.

Predominantly, however, fashion photography in Australia continues to have a lingering obsession with the landscape – both the bush and the beach – in common with so many other forms of artistic expression in white settler Australia, from film to literature. This often ironic exploration of the Australian environment may be ascribed to an uneasy relationship with a largely uninhabitable environment now figured as the background for cutting-edge urban fashion imagery. One key exponent of this type of work is Derek Henderson, a New Zealander who spent many years working in Sydney (and who has now relocated to London). Landscape is one of the most prevalent pictorial themes in his work and features as a moody presence within the frame along with the model. In Henderson's fashion photographs clothing may be central to the shot, but it equally appears as if it just happens to be what the model put on that day before she was photographed going for a walk or leaning on a fence – such is the sense of calm and ease in his casual style.

Sex has always been the traditional mainstay of fashion photography. Desire is the fuel that drives the consumption of fashion, more than any other emotion. Perhaps strangely, then, overt sexuality is a rare feature of contemporary Australian fashion photography, and when explored it is often to reveal some strangeness with the Australian landscape. Those who do tend towards a palpable sexuality in their work include Lyn Balzer and Tony Perkins, and Justin Edward John Smith. In Balzer and Perkins' most recent photographs – inspired by French artist Marcel Duchamp's last work *Etant Donnés* (1946–66) – their model takes on a near-cartoonish appearance: she is abstractly contorted, flat on her back with legs splayed and face out of view. The quirk, however, is that she is in the Australian bush, lying down in spiky native rushes, her milky, flawless skin awkwardly coexisting with the harsh landscape. Her near-prostrate, deathly appearance in a number of the shots from this series replays an old theme: that the Australian bush is no place for the white woman. In their series for the Australian edition of

*Big* magazine, Balzer and Perkins' nubile naked model wears only a pair of thongs on her feet in the bush landscape, as if becoming native.

Balzer and Perkins' photographs destabilise the largely elegant mainstream aesthetic in fashion and present images of stark sexuality and uninhibited confidence. Theirs are highly crafted images produced in a storytelling mode. They offer a new kind of stylishness based on playfulness and an ability to fuse the body with nature in a performative way. They are in sympathy with the famous fashion campaigns for the brand American Apparel, shot by Juergen Teller. In this post-feminist approach, the female figure is naked or semi-clad but also secure, even lighthearted, about her own sexual power. Balzer and Perkins' method is largely unique to contemporary Australian photography, which is characterised by elegiac fantasies or low-key fashion narratives. Like many photographers with diverse portfolios, their gallery exhibitions and subcultural magazine work bring notoriety and credibility, while also acting as a creative outlet.

**4.4** Lyn Balzer and Tony Perkins, fashion illustration (Lee Gold Label for Qompendium), 2008

Courtesy Lyn Balzer and Tony Perkins

One of the other key Australian photographers exploring the body's limits is Justin Edward John Smith. His penchant for preternaturally pneumatic women with huge red lips, white-blonde hair and skin, and peculiar expressions plays on a deliberate doll-like quality. The concept of bodies taken over by some unseen force is powerfully explored in a series of images where the models, found in a carpark, on the beach and in a shed, are inexplicitly contorted, lying down with arms out in mysterious but suggestive ecstasy. Again, the fantasy model body is captured in an ordinary setting but one that is never 'straight', and takes an idiosyncratic look at the concept of beauty.

Globally, as the fashion mannequin increasingly competes with celebrities to be the dominant face of fashion, fashion photography has diffused into style. This turn is promulgated by websites, blogs and online newsletters that promote street fashion as today's true style barometers and sell personal style over individual brand names. In Australia, the most successful operators behind this new wave of imagery include Right Angle Publishing, a group of young Melbourne-based entrepreneurs whose weekly lifestyle e-newsletters, customised to each state on the east coast of Australia, dictate fashion by making sure they always have their cameras at the right place at the right time. These media – fed by photographers such as Hayley Hughes – are part of the deliberate confusion of fashion with lifestyle, a growing trend that sees fashion infusing all aspects of consumption. Here, fashionable but everyday young people are turned into models. These exemplars of cool are shot at the most exclusive parties, exhibition openings or on the street, and in part bring fashion photography full circle: again, the portrait is key to understanding and selling fashion. The non-professional plays out the fantasies and desires that constitute fashion photography itself. With discordantly normal people wearing the clothes that photography leads us to believe are so desirable, contemporary fashion imagery in Australia adds complexity to the ideals at its core.

## Note

1  It should also be noted that, in a decade when it was rare for women to work professionally as photographers, Janice Wakely (1935–) established the Penthouse Model Agency and Photographic Studio (1963–65) in Melbourne with co-model Helen Homewood. Wakely had begun her modelling career in 1954, working in both Sydney and Melbourne with a range of Australian photographers, having been awarded a certificate from the Mannequin Academy in Sydney in 1952. In 1956 she participated with another five

Australian models in a much-publicised fashion tour to New Zealand sponsored by the Australian Department of Trade, and in 1958 she travelled to London and was named 'Girl of the Moment'. Wakely and Homewood's enterprise functioned both as model agency and photographic studio – perhaps the first of its kind in Australia. The studio produced photographs for fashion houses, designers and retail stores, including Lisal Furs, Robert Fritzlaff, Fibremakers, Sportscraft, Como Knits, Villawool Handknits, Ada Swimwear, Avon Swimwear, Sabego Furs, Baliencia, Lillian Frank, Leopold, Edward Beale, Saga Mink, Dent's Gloves and George's of Melbourne, which were published in all the newspapers and popular fashion magazines of the time, including the *Sun-Herald* and the *Australian Women's Weekly*.

## References

*Australia's Culture Portal* (n.d.), 'Max Dupain', <http://culture.gov.au/articles/maxdupain>.

Borschke, M. (2008), 'The style of no style', *Dhub*, <www.dhub.org/articles/732>.

Crombie, I. (1989), *Athol Shmith: Photographer*, Melbourne: Schwartz Publishing.

—— (2004), 'Athol Shmith', *Photofile*, 71, p. 37.

Edwards, S. (2004), 'The eighties in retrospect', *Photofile*, 71, pp. 58–61.

McFarlane, R. (2003) in A. Sayers, *POL: Portrait of a Generation*, Canberra: National Portrait Gallery.

Maynard, M. (2001), *Out of Line: Women and Style in Australia*, Sydney: University of New South Wales Press.

—— (2006), 'What is "Australian" fashion photography? – a dilemma', in refereed proceedings of UNAUSTRALIA, The Cultural Studies Association of Australasia's Annual Conference, 6, 7, 8 December 2006, <www.unaustralia.com/proceedings.php>.

Messenger, J. (2004), 'Bruno Benini', *Photofile*, 71, p. 39.

Newton, G. (1988), *Shades of Light: Photography and Australia, 1839–1988*, Canberra: Australian National Gallery.

Newton, H. (2003), *Helmut Newton: Autobiography*, London: Gerald Duckworth.

Palmer, D. (2005), 'Tracing the origins of Australian fashion photography', *The La Trobe Journal*, 76, pp. 87–103.

Palmer, D. and Rhodes, K. (2004), 'The golden age of Australian fashion photography', *Photofile*, 71, p. 37.

Rhodes, R. (2007), 'Pye in your eye: making the pictures of wearable images', in *Katie Pye: Clothes for Modern Lovers*, exhibition catalogue, Melbourne: National Gallery of Victoria, pp. 21–6.

Sayers, A. (2003), *POL: Portrait of a Generation*, Canberra: National Portrait Gallery.

Van Wyk, S. (2004), 'Henry Talbot', *Photofile*, 71, pp. 40–41.

—— (2006), *The Paris End: Photography, Fashion and Glamour*, Melbourne: National Gallery of Victoria.

# THE ART OF FASHION

*Bonnie English*

**5.1** Katie Pye, *Junk Jacket*, 1979.

*'For "fashionability" timing is important, however, good art (in fashion) must go beyond time'* (Katie Pye)

Photo: John Lethbridge. Courtesy John Lethbridge

*Fashion as art is my creation of imagination, a freedom of expression to wrap or reveal oneself. (Linda Jackson)*

IN OCTOBER 1967 an exhibition opened in the Costume Institute, Metropolitan Museum of Art in New York entitled *The Art of Fashion*. It was a singularly important event in the fashion world, as it was one of the earliest exhibitions that acknowledged the significant interplay between fashion and art, with their shared notions of social expression, cultural heritage and current ideals. Polaire Weissman, the executive director of the gallery, commented: 'Fashion in costume documents the taste of its time in the same manner as do painting, sculpture and other works of art' (Metropolitan Museum of Art 1967: 152). Interestingly, another exhibition at the prestigious Museum of Modern Art, entitled *The Sixties: Paintings and Sculptures from the MoMA Collection*, had just finished in September of the same year; this exhibition featured work that also challenged the perceived differences between commercial and fine art. The work of the Pop artists included pieces by billboard artist James Rosenquist, comic strip artist Roy Lichtenstein and ex-shoe illustrator Andy Warhol. Considering the works on display, it seemed that the traditional definitions of painting, sculpture and printmaking had blurred and new forms, new categories and new points of reference were being established. While modern art had given way to Postmodern mixed-media installations, performance art and conceptual art, the fashion world was also whispering the words of the Dadaist, Marcel Duchamp: 'After all, what is art?'

Just as artists like Picasso[1] used *objets trouvés*, or 'found objects', to metamorphose one image into another, kids on London's Portobello Road were sifting through piles of secondhand clothing bits and pieces, attempting to use the sartorial past to enhance the present. In this fine art postwar period, the art of collage developed into the art of assemblage,[2] a means of creating works of art entirely from pre-existing – often old, worn or discarded – objects, in which the artist's contribution was to be found in making the links between them. In turn, these links created memories and meanings in both fashion and art. In Arman's *Clic-Clac Rate* (1960–66) he assembled a number of old cameras to form a relief sculpture and Robert Rauschenberg, the Neo-Dadaist, used objects such as old bed linen soiled and splattered with paint in his work entitled *Bed* (1955) to make the viewer more aware of himself and his environment. According to Rauschenberg, 'painting refers to both art and life, and the artist's job is to close the gap' (Gebhardt 1998: 199).

In much the same way, the markets became a mecca for young designers looking amongst the mayhem, with fold-up tables laden with fabrics, crumpled garments, old shoes and other fashionable bric-a-brac, to bring a new meaning to fashion enhanced with the richness of bygone days. Appealing especially to the younger designers, the search for an exotic look underlined personal expression. This was the drawcard that enticed a young Australian designer called Jenny Kee to work at the Chelsea Antique Markets under the auspices of the famous dealer Vernon Lambert, who traded in antique garments dating from the Georgian period. She described the aura of the markets as an 'Aladdin's cave crammed full of old clothes, costume jewellery, china and antiques . . . an exotic world . . . displaying a profusion of Spanish shawls, beaded dresses, Victorian lace and feather boas' (Kee 2006: 74). In a few words, Kee summarised the impact of the secondhand market on many of the young designers in the 1960s: 'Like me, they threw every ounce of the creativity into an evolving artwork called personal style', not only showing 'a passion for the clothes . . . but a dedication to art' (2006: 89). Kee's love of ethnic intricate prints and embroideries, appliqué and patchwork, and offbeat knitted jumpers would influence her design directions for years to come.

Jenny Kee returned to Australia in December 1972, the same month the Whitlam Labor government was elected. According to Kee (2006: 133), this sent a ripple of optimism to the ex-pat community in Britain and elsewhere. 'We believed Whitlam would change Australia,' she said, '[as] he had a real commitment to the arts and the creative country . . . we had a chance to do something new here.' In fact, the Whitlam government, prompted by the New Nationalism movement, encouraged the development of national – and therefore cultural – identity through the arts. Fashion historian Margaret Maynard (2001) concurs that this was part of 'an increasingly tolerant, culturally diverse, multiracial and pluralistic Australian society, which many remember as an almost legendary period of artistic encouragement' (2001: 57). Significantly, art historian Edward Lucie-Smith (1969: 145–6), underlining the correlation between nationalism and cultural pride, commented that Australian artists such as Sidney Nolan had a much greater relevance to the genesis of American Pop Art than was generally admitted. He pointed out that in American Pop Art there was 'a goodish dose of nationalism as well', which contributed to its sudden and overwhelming success. Subsequently, there was great interest shown in Nolan, who had established a new, *faux-naif* style in his 'Ned Kelly' series; this was seen as a vehicle that reflected a fairly sophisticated Australian nationalism.

Strategically, Kee opened her soon-to-be famous Flamingo Park salon on 27 August 1973 in Sydney's Strand Arcade, just two months before the official opening day of the Sydney Opera House, which attracted an international audience of 300 million television viewers. Momentarily, the eyes of the art world were on Sydney. Kee's clientele consisted of the 'arty set', members of the film industry, aspiring women professionals and a diverse cross-section of the wealthy who were searching for unique clothes to help them establish an identity. Some of the clothing, drawn from friends (Lambert) in England, consisted of 1950s Kandinsky-inspired fabrics, patchwork smocks and skirts using original 1930s and 1940s prints and Hawaiian shirts. By scouring the markets and op-shops in both Melbourne and Sydney, she added Deco ties, satin dressing gowns, interesting hats, 1950s scarves and jewellery, and Speedo navy jersey swimsuits. Emulating the visual chaos of the markets, Kee aimed to intensify the impact of colour and graphics in the interior design of her shop, laced with a feeling of the retro/romantic and kitsch in what was to become known, familiarly, as 'the Park'.

Not only did she stock her own creations – which included hand-knitted jumpers by Jan Ayres, an experienced English knitter, made from pure Australian wool and decorated with popular iconographic images from 'Oz', and the fantasy clothes of Linda Jackson that she had seen exhibited at the Bonython Galleries in Sydney – but she also sold the rather eccentric jewellery of Peter 'Ruby' Tully, made up of unusual found objects and everyday materials, many of them plastic. For Tully, 'Kitsch was King' and Australian imagery of flora and fauna was coupled with products such as miniature jars of Vegemite, skateboards, koalas, boomerangs and legendary tourist attractions such as the Sydney Harbour Bridge and Ayers Rock (Uluru).

While Tully's jewellery was fun to wear and witty in its concept, it inherently commented on the paradox of 'jewellery-as-art' rather than 'jewellery-as-status'. For this reason, he was seen as a very serious Postmodernist artist. While the work presented as a cheap, commercially mass-produced souvenir range, its underlying message was much more critically analytical in the way it questioned the nature of 'preciousness or value', both in jewellery and in nationalistic sentiment. Needless to say, his work did not really seem out of keeping with Kee's quirky Blinky Bill and gumleaf motifs. John McPhee, senior curator in Australian Art at the Australian National Gallery in Canberra, had remarked, tongue-in-cheek, that 'she was never afraid to turn the koala into a heroic figure'.[3] Arguably, Kee's versions of Australiana revealed a growing sense of patriotic pride in celebrating images that had previously been seen as childish, insipid and tacky, while Tully commented on the notion of cultural tourism and the superficial way in which tourists often viewed the 'Down-Under experience'.

Despite being in a very competitive market, Jenny Kee and Linda Jackson forged a strong and enduring friendship as kindred spirits in the Australian world of fashion. They worked together for eight years, with Linda initially supplying Flamingo Park with:

> retro-designed linen and cotton sundresses, flared shorts with bra tops in different prints, checked chiffon cocktail wear and oyster grey and pink waisted shirts and biased-cut skirts made from satin that Linda had found printed with the name Letty Lynton. (Kee 2006: 138)

Kee, who had studied design at East Sydney Technical College and Jackson, a product of the Fashion Department of the Emily McPherson College, Melbourne, had similar interests in past artists and designers alike. They spent hours poring over books and magazines featuring the work of Sonia Delaunay, the Cubist painter turned fashion textile designer of the 1920s and 1930s, Madeleine Vionnet and her exquisite bias-cut draped garments, and artist/designer Elsa Schiaparelli, with her provocative use of Surrealist-inspired imagery.

The work of the early twentieth century avant-garde abstractionists provided more inspiration for the duo, and when they visited the Pompidou

Centre in Paris in 1977 they reflected on the powerful influence of these artists on their work:

> In our Delaunay and Matisse clothes [we] saw for the fist time the paintings of these artists as well as those of Mondrian and Leger. While people looked at us, two walking artworks, we looked at the paintings that had inspired us. (Kee 2006: 189)

Perhaps more importantly, Kee and Jackson shared an innate connection to the Australian natural landscape. Kee commented on her need to 'soak up the vibrant colours of sea and sand' and to 'bring colour to Australians – have them dress in the azure, ochre, scarlet and green of their country' (2006: 134). This colour, she felt, would bring uniqueness to her clothes design. In a similar yet different way, Jackson produced paintings in cloth with a palette that referenced the bush landscape. She explained:

> The textures and colours of the bush landscape led me to experiment with many paintings and printing techniques, combining stencils and gum leaves and string in the process. The basic rules of screen printing and 'repeats' (repeating the same pattern over and over again) were abandoned so that the end result reflected all the irregularities of Nature. Metallic gold, copper and silver pigments, mixed with the brightest fluorescent colours, resulted in entirely unique fabrics with no two pieces alike. Then with these original 'paintings' on silk or cotton we would wrap and decorate ourselves with these beautiful pieces of the bush. (Jackson 1987: 85)

Both Jackson and Kee saw textiles as the greatest vehicle through which they could express their creative flair. Jackson often hand-painted silk chiffons, crêpe de chine and organzas, as they were delicate, light-weight fabrics that lent themselves to movement when draped across the body; this feature was reminiscent of Delaunay's garments (for which the poet Cendrars wrote, 'On her dress, she wore a body'). In homage, she dedicated one of her chiffon creations to the textile artist, naming it *Delaunay Chiffon* (1977). Jackson, like the amazing Vionnet, draped her original, hand-painted fabric on the mannequin first and then cut the cloth away, allowing the garment to interface with the natural contours of the body. Like both Balenciaga and Cardin, she created shaped dresses such as the *Waratah* (1984) with petal bodices and double-layered petal skirts. As an orange, pink and fuschia creation also fashioned in petal-like pieces resembled a flower itself, she chose to call it *A Rose Is a Rose Is a Rose*, much in keeping with Surrealist humour. Another garment called *Black Magic*, designed in the same year and composed of layers of black taffeta feathers, was an exceptionally powerful rendition of the native black cockatoo, reinforcing both a symbolic and a spiritual link to the land.

By 1979, individual strengths and differences were becoming polarised in the work of Kee and Jackson. Kee's love of 'patching' was a continuing passion in her work, combining colours and patterns to set up rhythmical directions of flow in her textile designs. Exoticism in her work was evident not only through ethnic pastiche, but in the loud, colourful and graphic styling that she sustained throughout her designing career.

**5.2** Jenny Kee, *Black Opal*, 1981 *'Fashion as fashion is of the moment, fashion as art is timeless.'* (Jenny Kee)
Photo: Grant Matthews.
Courtesy Jenny Kee

Inspired by a growing obsession with opals, Australia's national stone, Kee began a series of textile design drawings using watercolours and inks that captured the brilliance of the opal colours bleeding into each other and highlighted on a black background. She began tearing the paper and reassembling the pieces into visually intense collage-like compositions. She worked with Fabio Bellotti of Rainbow Fabrics in Milan to print the highly complicated designs. In retrospect, she believed that her opal fabrics were 'the most highly evolved and stylish I've done' (Kee 2006: 219). At the *Flaming Opal Flamingo Follies* parade of 1981 (Kee 2006: 217), Kee's black opal silk was a show feature along with knits called *Totem Opal*, *Abstract Opal* and *Lightning Opal*, which were 'flashing, gold-threaded interpretations of the stone'.

There were also knits with familiar poetry written into them that read 'I love a sunburnt country, a land of sweeping plains, the home of precious opal, wind, dust and scanty rains' and Margaret Preston-inspired knits that exuded a strong graphic appeal. When Jackson and Kee's work was included in a six-page spread in Italian *Vogue* by editor Anna Piaggi, their international recognition was established. Kee's Opal textile range was immortalised when Lagerfeld used her prints for sixty-five garments made in 'cotton, organza and silk on blouses, skirts and jacket linings' (Joel 1998: 249) for his first *prêt-à-porter* Chanel Spring/Summer collection in 1983.

While Jackson was renowned for her defined cut-out or stencilled prints that featured Australian floral imagery such as the Waratah, Sturt's Desert Pea and Birds of Paradise to create flat, two-dimensional abstract forms – similar to Matisse's later work – her work was to become much more subtle in the coming decade. Kee often describes this conceptual phase as reflecting a calm serenity, and applauded Jackson's very elegant and imaginative work. Undoubtedly, Jackson's exceptional layered constructions were key elements in her unconventional approach to creating fashion. Always the artist, first and foremost, her work was experimental, pushing the boundaries of textile exploration by using unorthodox methods of screen-printing and stencilling, incorporating real leaves in her creations and including metallic and fluorescent colours in her 1982 Bush Couture range.

When Jackson first visited the Utopia Indigenous community in Central Australia in 1980, and engaged with the local artists, she saw the potential for a truly unique Australian textile design industry to emerge. Having been introduced to the resist-dyeing batik technique in the late 1970s, many Northern Territory communities adopted this method and applied it to lengths of fabric used to make up fashion garments. According to Robyn

**5.3** Linda Jackson, *Black Magic, Black Cockatoo*, 1977

Photo: Linda Jackson. Courtesy Linda Jackson

Healy, 'once the calibre of these compositions was recognised, the fabric lengths were soon sold individually as artworks, and their transition into fashion was halted' (Kee 2006: 32). Despite this, the original collaboration between Jackson (and others) and the Indigenous communities inspired individuals, including the famous painter Emily Kngwarreye, and community art groups alike to forge an eminent position for themselves in Australian art history.

Arguably, from the 1960s and 1970s onwards, momentum grew with the idea that one could actually wear a work of art. The body gave the 'canvas' form and volume and the bodily movement gave the surface imagery a dynamism and liberation unrealised in Op Art or Kinetic sculpture. 'Wearable art' captured the imagination of Australia's finest. Both artists and fashion designers wished to express themselves through creative and innovative means to bridge the gap between theatre, art and life through the art of fashion. When the Art Gallery of New South Wales opened its *Project 33 – Art Clothes* exhibition in 1980–81, curated by Jane de Teliga and displaying the work of up-and-coming young artist/designers, the careers of these participants became immortalised in the journals of Australian fashion history. After the event, the curator of Textiles and Costumes, Jennifer Sanders of the Museum of Applied Arts & Sciences (now the Powerhouse Museum), bought Kee's *Opera House* cotton knit dress and coat and Jackson's *Olga Silks* to inaugurate the museum's Jenny Kee and Linda Jackson Collection.

A plethora of fashion-as-art exhibitions followed in the 1980s with the textiles of the Indigenous Tiwi Designs of Bathurst Island exhibited at the Hogarth Galleries (1983) in Sydney. The curator, Adrian Newstead (owner of the shop COO-EE and agent for the Islander group), invited urban fashion designers to create garments for their show using the Tiwi batik textiles, which reflect the green and gold colouring of the lush tropical environment of the island. Similarly, in 1985, the Art Gallery of New South Wales invited artists to create art clothes inspired by Margaret Preston's still-life of gumtree foliage, and the Australian National Gallery in Canberra held an exhibition called *Linda Jackson and Jenny Kee: Flamingo Park and Bush Couture* to celebrate the success and significance of these two renowned designers. In 1989 a Powerhouse Museum exhibition entitled *Australian Fashion: The Contemporary Art*, curated by Jane de Teliga, represented the theme of 'Australia' as interpreted by a diverse group of artist/designers. It underlined the embedded nature of cultural currency in the socio-political leanings of the 1980s.[4] When cultural links to place and region become stronger, the search for the ethnic and the essentially pure in fashion becomes a primary aim – and this seems to best epitomise this period.

Textile designer Deborah Leser worked with Linda Jackson interpreting the flashing colours of the indigenous opal gemstones and produced brilliant translations of the hues of the Australian landscape using sophisticated colouring techniques. Margot Riley (1999) explains that, by

**amalgamating her talent as a graphic artist with batik dyeing and hand painting techniques learned in Indonesia, London and Japan, Leser's unique combination of skills allowed her to design directly onto silk fabrics. (1999: 58)**

Jackson, like others, found it difficult to find unique textiles without having to import them from overseas, so local textile designers were highly sought after, as they could provide smaller amounts of fabric for one-off designs.

Others, including Glenda Morgan, also explored the rich colours and patterns of the land: the Rooftop Clothing label featured textiles with unique marbled effects and the saturated, intense hues of Rebecca Paterson's reddish-brown silk clothing captured the notion of the extreme heat and dryness of the desert. Bronwyn Bancroft, a descendant of the Bundjalung people of New South Wales, combined the Aboriginal motifs of her people and contemporary design techniques to produce some of the finest textile design work in the country. Seemingly, this strong feeling for colour became symptomatic of a great strength in Australian design and enabled the designers to produce work that was highly inventive and breathtakingly beautiful.

Also emblematic of Australian 'fashion-as-art' design in the 1980s was the designers' sense of adventure and humour. Dinosaur Designs used shimmering blue and green transparent resin baubles to construct a seductive mini-dress that spoke of the sun, sea and sex. Another key designer, Jenny Bannister, chose material from her immediate environment to reflect upon political issues that impacted upon the environment. Her *Extinct Hat* (1984), made from calfskin with stripes and spots stencilled on to it, simulated the Tasmanian tiger and was indicative of her bid to create a decidedly independent Australian fashion design. Kara Baker produced the ubiquitous Melbourne Cup hat, complete with a raffia horse's mane, to wear to the famous racing event.

When Brisbane's Kim Hodges submitted her renowned *Exquisite Lizard Dress* to the Australian Fashion Gown of the Year competition in 1980, it did not win because it was viewed by the judges as being more 'fantasy wear' than 'formal wear', but it attracted huge media coverage. The long black wool frock, featuring a soft sculpture of a lizard in silver lamé crawling up the back of the dress and peeking over the shoulder, was worn by a model wearing a green beaded skull cap. While it might be seen today as the ultimate environmental statement, undoubtedly the image of the lizard symbolised the tough, quintessential Australian archetype to the rest of the world. In an interview, Hodges revealed that the iconic dress attracted the attention of Hazel Hawke, then wife of the Prime Minister, who wished to purchase the creation to wear to diplomatic functions overseas. As it was not for sale, Australia's First Lady chose another garment titled 'Nocturnal Awakening', which did win the coveted Australian Gown of the Year in 1981 (Hodges 2008). It was a black chiffon gown and jacket, which featured an appliquéd possum and stylised branches, gum leaves and flowers in soft colours and was worn to international receptions in Jakarta, London, Paris and Washington. Not surprisingly, a fashion article in America's *Newsweek* in October 1984 stated that 'the Australians have a creativity, a spontaneity and a wildness that is way ahead of us . . . they are not afraid to do anything.'[5]

Katie Pye was a powerful contender in the 1970s and 1980s fashion stakes. A rebel at heart, art school-trained Katie opposed institutional thinking and opened a concept clothing shop called 'Duzzn't Madder' in Sydney's Balmain in 1976, where she sold eccentric 'one-offs' and secondhand clothing. Pye's unconventional clothes drew attention at her stall at the Paddington markets, but she gained instantaneous notoriety from her entries in the *Art Clothes* 1980/81 exhibition held at the Art Gallery of New South Wales. The *Young Doctors* outfit combined an eclectic mix of vinyl ventilators, an open-zippered heart motif and rather explicit medical photographs. Another entry consisted of a three-piece outfit appliquéd with both religious and sexual scenes called *Religious Cavalier*, which so horrified gallery staff that it was temporarily locked away so that the public could not view it. With controversy came notoriety and Pye's work immediately constituted a general revolt in fashion styling.

Buoyed by feminist dictates and radical women's magazines that advocated freedom, self-expression and independence, Pye indicated that the monthly alternative style publication called *Rag Times* directly influenced her design thinking. Its first editorial in October 1977 stated that the policy of the magazine was personal style, to use fashion as a means of identity, reflecting 'who you are and the way you live', and blatantly noted that Australians didn't want to be dictated to. Fashion writer Margot Riley argued that, by 'blending her anti-fashion, neo-tribal design style with the aggressive imagery and desire to shock, like "punk" fashion, she created a sophisticated mix that challenged accepted conventions of dress' (1999: 56). Like Vivienne Westwood, Pye's punk creations were visually confronting, and her hand-painted garments merged seamlessly with the look of the torn, tattered and knotted Japanese creations that dominated recession dressing in the 1980s.

Just as some of the contemporary Japanese designers' work spoke of memory and meaning – a trend especially evident in Yohji Yamamoto's garments – Katie Pye's work, entitled *Memories and Friendship* (1983) (part of her Ascension collection, exhibited in the Griffith University's *Tokyo Vogue: Japanese and Australian Fashion* exhibition held in Brisbane City Hall Gallery in 1999) revealed a very poignant and profound personal sentiment not often found in her later work. It was a deconstructivist garment pieced together with remnants of lace trim stitched to a base of recycled flour bags. In an interview (Pye 1999), she revealed that when her mother's best friend, Lucile Beet, passed away, Katie inherited a box that contained lace trim taken from worn-out underwear and lingerie that Lucile had saved over the years by wrapping it around pieces of card. In Lucile's memory, Katie reassembled the pieces to create a new garment with an old history. Working as a Postmodernist artist, she reconstructed the form through the appropriation of both material and meaning.

Her work, exhibited in the retrospective *Clothes for Modern Lovers* exhibition at the National Gallery of Victoria in 2007, polarised both her very design-based clothes that were reminiscent of the textile patterns of the Russian Constructivist designers Popova and Stepanova and Sonia Delaunay's Cubist textile designs, and her more painterly, romanticised approach steeped in Expressionism. Undoubtedly, she approaches both her structured and unstructured design work with an artist's perceptual ability to visualise the entire picture. This explains why she sees her garments as contextualised within a specific framework – that of a photograph, film, installation or performance. To an art historian, the influences are obvious: a touch of Dada, Kandinsky, Matisse and Ernst. In a forceful way, Pye challenges the observer to respond to her aesthetics. According to Australian contemporary fashion curator Danielle Whitfield, Pye wanted to make 'a clothing statement that, she declared, 'actually involved a conversation between myself and the wearer' (National Gallery of Victoria 2007: 4). In a later interview, Katie stated:

> [I am] creating an aura, cocoon or a mantle for others. Often unspoken things are more important than spoken. It is important for a designer to find a truth that resonates with the audience. Having heart and empathy for others, trying to break down the barrier, is my intent. (Pye 2009)

Arguably, within a Postmodernist visual arts context, humour is an inherent part of the artist/designer's repertoire. The names of some of Pye's garments, including *I Hate Housework* (1976) and *Hothouse Dress* (1981), allude to her feminist sentiments; *Wharfwear* (1980) references sinners, prostitutes and tarts; *The Party* (1980) is evocative in its phallic imagery; *Emoh Ruo* (1980) (backward spelling for 'Our Home') is a patchwork design that forms the map of Australia; *Fallen Angel* (1983) is made up of knots and tangles. Other titles include *Desperados* (1983) and *Mumbo Jumbo* (1984).

In an ABC radio interview, Katie Pye remarked: 'What you call fashion, I call a product. What I call fashion is art' (Pye 1983). Most recently, she commented reflectively that: '[With regard to] fashionability, timing is important but good art must go beyond time!' (Pye 2009). Throughout her designing career, Pye used her work as a means to comment on society, politics and aesthetics. Her design and textile work was experimental, constantly evolving and breaking new ground. She worked collaboratively with photographers, film-makers, musicians and theatrical technicians to create visuals that are superlative in their composition, surface rendering and drama. She was, and still is, a formidable force to be reckoned with.

Like Katie Pye, Jenny Bannister created fashion through the eyes of a Postmodernist artist. Highly experimental and unorthodox, she introduced to fashion interesting combinations of unusual materials. Leather, studs, plastics and quilted breastplates were used to create one-off garments that were part-punk, part-feminist and part-fetishist. Her first plastic dress in 1977 attracted the attention of Jenny Kee and Clarence Chai, both of whom began selling her range in their Melbourne stores. Significantly, this heralded the new trend for designers to consider limited production ranges as a viable part of the Australian fashion industry.

Daring to be different, Bannister referenced popular culture and appropriated both historical and fantasy iconography in her medieval armour, mermaids and Amazon constructions. In particular, her *Golden Beach Girl* outfit, which comments on the stereotypical 1960s bikini-clad models familiarly seen in the James Bond movies, is based on a spider web construction but made from a moulded plastic mesh of Acquaplast, which is normally used for surgical splints. This outfit is now in the collection of the National Gallery of Victoria. From the 1970s, her work featured prominently in 'art clothes' exhibitions, including the *Australian Art Clothing* exhibition for the 1986 Commonwealth Arts Festival in Edinburgh. Her anti-elitist work relies on the element of shock, and was quickly adopted into the new DIY – do-it-yourself – trend in the 1980s. *If the Art Fits, Wear it* was a most appropriate title chosen for one of her shows.

Western Australia's Rebecca Paterson and Megan Salmon created the clothing label SpppsssP in July 1996. Sharing a common philosophy, both designers studied fine art rather than fashion design, and the results reverberate in their multifaceted, innovative and cutting-edge design. The unpronounceable label name (S for Salmon and P for Paterson) is indicative of their highly charged creative explorations and experimentation. Fascinated by textiles that come out of new technologies, their ability to deconstruct, reconstruct and reinvent new 'industrial' materials and forms is undoubtedly their greatest strength. For their summer 1998–99 collection, they used layers of treated nylon over printed cottons that had been forged and moulded by heat and pressure to create a 'laminated' appearance and silk organza that had been cemented and manipulated into slabs that echoed concrete surfaces. When subjected to the same process, Tencel fabrics, developed by Courtaulds Fibres, created a 'wet link feel' that was coupled with other fabrics to achieve an unusual surface tension. In the winter collection, a range of deconstructed over-dyed knits were mixed with felt, velvets, georgette and vintage-looking fabrics. Other collections included industrial aprons, ties and wraps, clear plastic tabards worn over minimal, brightly coloured slip dresses and romantic hand-painted flowers sandwiched between layered fabrics.

According to Salmon, SpppsssP aesthetics reflected dress code possibilities triggered by global technologies. Paterson often described the label's clothing as textile-inspired fashion driven from a similar textile aesthetic to that of the Japanese fashion designers, especially Issey Miyake and Rei Kawakubo of Comme des Garçons. As well, and perhaps more importantly, the clothes were generated by a street aesthetic, counter-culture and contemporary music; they were clothes designed from a perspective of trying to understand Australian style resonating with myth, romance, decoration and space.

Having been involved in numerous textile workshops across Australia, involving batik, screen-printing and *shibori* techniques, Paterson's work in particular reflects her research in both Eastern and Western subcultural styles and is generally categorised as 'art-based' clothing. Like Jackson and Kee, Paterson participated in Aboriginal workshops exploring design possibilities on cloth while working for Desert Designs, Fremantle. The 1999 Deconstructivist/Reconstructivist Rubens series was inspired by her contact with the renowned Japanese fabric engineer Junichi Arai in textile workshops in Ahmedabad in India and the Canberra School of Art. Evolving from a workshop exercise set by Arai in 1993, Paterson applied the art of *shibori* to wool cloth, but instead of using block-out and colour she used a stripping chemical that ate away part of the fibre of the material, leaving skeletal threads to reveal the body underneath, creating a fabricated dissolve fabric. Less refined than the work of the Japanese textile artists, Paterson's experimentation resulted in a more haphazard, uninhibited and spontaneous treatment of the cloth – one she describes as 'decomposed . . . speaking simultaneously of bushfire ravaged landscapes or the pungent odour of a well charred steak on the ubiquitous Aussie barbeque' (Riley 1999: 53).

Throughout her career, Paterson has been immersed in shifting aesthetics and ideas particular to counterculture and has used styling as a methodology to deconstruct gender representation. Resonating between art and fashion, she used the contemporary medium of T-shirting to indirectly critique accepted ideologies. When she introduced her Mixed-Up Culture series as early as 2001, a number of her garments were purchased by the National Gallery of Victoria for their contemporary collection. Her 'Selfh does not support Postmodernism' T-shirt featured in the NGV's *Australian Culture Now 2004* exhibition and her 'Culture Bites' work was highlighted in the *Mixed Tape* exhibition held at the Art Gallery of Western Australia (AGWA) in December 2005 and the L'Oréal Melbourne Fashion Festival in March 2006. Her growing interest in graffiti, inspired by her son and underlined by the visual and conceptual impact that it has had on today's urban society and institutional thinking, has become a key focus in her work. She is fascinated with the concept of 'graff' as a contemporary form of calligraphy that has become a highly skilled subcultural art practice in its own right. Her work has been included in national and international exhibitions in Tokyo, London, Hong Kong and Seoul, and has been paraded in Canada and France.

Numerous other designers, including Sally Browne, Michael Glover and Wendy Arnold, David Miles and Janelle Smith of the Studibaker Hawk label (established in Sydney in 1982 and named after a powder blue '59 automobile of a similar name) conceivably fall into the 'fashion-as-art' category, each expressing their affiliations with the art world. Studibaker Hawk won several fashion awards, including the FIA's Fashion Occasions, for its outstandingly unique, brightly coloured screen-printed evening wear, which was a collaborative effort of an artist, an architect and a fashion designer respectively. While the Studibaker Hawk designers were surprised at their success, their highly original range – dubbed 'street couture' – retained a classic simplicity of line, yet a sculptural silhouette. Their work melded art, craft and fashion into a viable and exciting commercial enterprise. Glover, in particular, 'established himself as a specialist in art clothes' with his ability to achieve an emphatic tactile effect with 'his bonding of leather and suede' and to illustrate 'his uncanny talent of combining unlikely yarns in his hand-knitted garments', seen in many Australian Wool Board exhibitions (Mackay 1987: 90).

Textile art production grew from strength to strength in Australia from the 1970s onwards, as it did in most Western countries, possibly as a direct result of the renewed interest in ethnicity and indigenous practice, clearly reflected in fashion styling. While textile production developed from craft that was steeped in ancient tradition, it developed in 'New World' nations, hand-in-hand with the growth of multiculturalism. Artistic cultural practice in textiles in Australia developed, for some, as a synthesis of both European and Asian influences, clearly evident in the work of three leading artists, Liz Williamson, Patricia Black and Maggie Baxter. Undoubtedly they have made outstanding contributions to the evolution of textile design in Australia through their ability to combine the old with the new, tradition with originality and handicraft with technology in their work.

Applauded as one of Australia's leading fibre practitioners and textile designers, Sydney's Liz Williamson has spent the last thirty years experimenting with tensions created when mixing hand-made and commercially made yarns, playing with different finishing touches, exploring ideas inherent in the structure of cloth and merging computer programs and hand-woven techniques. In an interview, Williamson explains that hand-woven wraps and scarves display uneven puckered surfaces when wools with different shrinkage rates have been woven side by side, and that when nylon monofilament, in particular, is woven into the weave structure of the work it rucks and protrudes as the yarn around it shrinks, giving the wrap a folded and complex surface (quoted in Bond 2008). Her fascination with surface tensions emerged early in her practice as she travelled through Afghanistan and India and began to learn more about the cultural sensitivities associated with a textile maker's craft.

Since the 1980s, after a number of postcard-sized jacquards were given to her by a friend, she embarked on the 'Jacquard Project', which involved travelling to Canada in 1998, where she was introduced to a computerised Jacquard loom at the Montreal Centre for Contemporary Textiles. Material produced by this process, which became central to her practice, resulted in unique and unusual cloth, usually woven for limited production garments. While great subtlety in colour can be created with this type of weaving by using different construction techniques and complex weave structures, Williamson could also produce dominant, organic forms as she did in her Loop series (2008), in which necklaces worn as body ornaments were made from woven leather strips juxtaposed with fraying silk thread filaments. Her work has ranged from industrial production to artisan-inspired exhibition pieces, and since 2001 she has been involved in several development projects in Asia, working with weavers from Cambodia, Vietnam, Pakistan and India.

Williamson creates textiles that are meant to be worn on, and connected to, the body: 'The cloth is reminiscent of the surface of the skin . . . strands of memory and protections are interwoven throughout Liz Williamson's practice' (quoted in Bond 2008). Reconnecting with her own heritage, having grown up on a property in country Victoria, Williamson relates how she first learned about textiles from her mother – in particular, the art of darning, mending and repairing, and the memory and meaning associated with old and worn cloth. For Williamson: 'Darning is part of our memory, part of what people think of as their family history' and 'darns, like scars, represent a place of healing, where damage is covered over . . . revealing history and evoking memory' (Bond 2008). In her recent Darned series, she has taken inspiration directly from a handkerchief darned by her mother, which was scanned, digitally manipulated and woven on a loom using the Jacquard process. Williamson's work is represented in most major public collections in Australia.

Patricia Black is one of a number of Australian textile artists to draw inspiration from the ancient Japanese dyeing technique of *shibori*, with which she has experimented for years. Directly influenced by the Japanese

**5.4** Liz Williamson, *Loop series*, handwoven cotton and leather, 7 x 146 cm, 2008

Photo: Ian Hobbs. Courtesy Ian Hobbs

master Junichi Arai, the beauty of her textile designs is enhanced through the movement of her loose, flowing garments. Using silk and synthetic organza, she creates surface texture and tension through *arashi* and *itajime* techniques. As a colourist, her work is highly charged, full of drama and vitality, and has been acquired in collections worldwide, including in New Zealand and Japan. Her 'wearable art' pieces are produced in limited editions, and her textile designs have been commissioned for costume and set design, dance performances and art installations at the Australian National Gallery (1990), the Art Gallery of New South Wales and the Textile Museum of Venice (1997). Since the 1990s she has spent a great deal of time in Italy, where she has held workshops with Art Viva in Florence.

Like Black, Maggie Baxter also embraced a non-Western textile practice – that of India. Trained as a sculptor, she turned to textile design in 1989 and, through performance art, began to investigate the body and cloth as sculptural forms. With no formal training in textiles, she was able to rethink, experiment with and provide new perspectives on traditional forms. Immediately absorbed in Kutch culture (western India), with its vibrant colours and patterns, she had her textiles fabricated according to traditional methods and local practices of weaving, non-chemical dyeing and resist block printing. Mark-making and overlay dominate the essence of her surface designs. Line over line, stitch over line, and fabric strip over fabric strip form the dynamics of her surface renderings. According to Baxter (2006: 6):

> embroidery and/or drawn thread work . . . are reconceptualised as a graphic mark or form of drawing. Layering different weaves, print, embroidery and found objects such as buttons or bells owes as much to collage and assemblage as textile art and design.

Baxter achieves a sense of discord in her work through displacement or deconstruction of sections of cloth 'which don't quite match', deliberately avoiding a seamless registration. She argues that it is a sense of Western Australian space that informs the layout of her work, where 'actual or implied boundaries hold . . . in fields of colour and patterns.' Using the Indian *churidar* method of cutting, in which fabric twice as long as it is wide is folded to form a tube with the fabric grain on the bias, she comments that 'this drapes on the body very differently to cloth with a straight grain.' In her own way, she pays homage to the bias-cut of the couturier Madeleine Vionnet, the form and structure of Issey Miyake's clothes, the grid forms of artists such as Agnes Martin and Eva Hesse, calligraphic brush strokes and Japanese *shibori*. Clearly, the paradoxical magic of Baxter's textile work relies on her bold, striking and sophisticated design coupled with her great subtlety and sensitivity.

As argued, the aesthetic study of fashion and textiles poses questions about personal expression, individuality, exploration and experimentation and the notion that 'there is a perfect imperfection inherent in all handmade work' (ArtsWA and Australia Council 2006: 8). The art of fashion suggests a cultural paradox, an interface between Western and Eastern practice. It implies the exotic, the atypical, the exceptional. It crosses boundaries in construction, technique and design processes. Creative practice is constantly changing, mutating, refiguring and pooling new ideas. The fusion of original textile and fashion production forges a unique aesthetic. This chapter has reviewed the work of leading practitioners in the field and addressed the way each individual has contributed to the transformation of textile and fashion pieces into 'wearable art objects'. In Postmodernist terms, some work was politically or sexually charged, some was laced with humour, and some dismissed cultural boundaries and mainstream conventions. The calibre of the designers' distinctive work is undisputable and, in a commodity-driven world, their refreshing and uncompromisingly self-expressive work provides an inspirational legacy for emerging Australian designers. While all fashion is not art, when fashion does become art it evokes a powerful emotional response that resonates for generations.

## Notes

1 Picasso transformed the image of a bull by adding old bicycle handlebars for horns, playfully using a tin can for the head of a goat and creating a monkey from replica automobile parts.
2 The Metropolitan Museum of Art in New York staged *The Art of Assemblage* exhibition in 1961.
3 Comment made by curator John McPhee at the Australian National Gallery's 1985 exhibition entitled *Linda Jackson and Jenny Kee: Flamingo Park and Bush Couture*.
4 In 1984, 'Advance Australia Fair' replaced the British national anthem 'God Save the Queen'.
5 Written by Ann Sterling, a clothing importer, Los Angeles.

## References

Baxter, M. (2006), *The Unbounded Line*, exhibition catalogue, ArtsWA and The Australia Council, Perth.

Bond, C. (2008), 'Wrapped: Liz Williamson's practice', *Craft Australia*, 31 October, <www.craftaustralia.org.au/library/review>.

English, B. (ed.) (1999), *Griffith University's Tokyo Vogue: Japanese and Australian Fashion*, exhibition catalogue, Brisbane City Hall Gallery, Brisbane.

Gebhardt, V. (1998), *Painting: A Concise History*, London: Lawrence King.

Healy, R. (2005), 'Making noise: contemporary Australian fashion design', in B. Parkes (ed.), *Freestyle: New Australian Design for Living*, Melbourne: Melbourne Museum/Sydney: Australian Centre for Craft & Design, pp. 30–6.

Hodges, K. (2008), interview with Bonnie English, 23 May.

Jackson, L. (1987), *Linda Jackson: The Art of Fashion*, Sydney: Fontana.

Joel, A. (1998), *Parade: The Story of Fashion in Australia*, Sydney: HarperCollins.

Kee, J. (2006), *A Big Life*, Melbourne: Lantern.

Lucie-Smith, E. (1969), *Movements in Art since 1945*, London: Thames & Hudson.

Mackay, E. (1987), *Fashion Australia*, Sydney: Elinda Mackay Design.

Maynard, M. (2001), *Out of Line: Australian Women and Style*, Sydney: UNSW Press.

Metropolitan Museum of Art (1967), *Metropolitan Museum of Art Bulletin*, 26 (3), New York: Metropolitan Museum of Art.

National Gallery of Victoria (2007), *Katie Pye: Clothes for Modern Lovers*, exhibition catalogue.

Pye, Katie (1983), interview with ABC *Nationwide*, n.d.

—— (1999), interview with B. English, 24 March.

—— (2009), interview with B. English, 12 May.

Riley, M. (1999) 'Beyond nationality: the influence of Japan on Australian fashion and textile designers, 1975–2000', in B. English (ed.), *Griffith University's Tokyo Vogue: Japanese and Australian Fashion*, exhibition catalogue, Brisbane City Hall Gallery, Brisbane.

Wynhausen, E. (2008), 'The Face', *The Australian*, 20 December.

# INTERLACED

## TEXTILES FOR FASHION

*Liz Williamson*

**6.1** Jenny Kee wearing 'Wattle' Dress, 1995
Photo: Sue Stafford. Courtesy Powerhouse Museum, Sydney

**T**EXTILES ARE INTRICATELY interlaced with fashion, giving texture, drape, feel, detail and colour to garments. In Australia, tracing the place of textiles in the fashion industry presents a complex story of materials, individual designers, studio practices, commercial production, textiles, art, craft and design. Overwhelmingly, throughout the century, makers of textiles for fashion have shown a desire to represent Australia, its character and its spirit in cloth.

This chapter documents how textiles have been designed and made for fashion over the last six decades, focusing on designers whose practice specialised in fashion fabrics. Many of these artists and designers gained experience overseas, returning with specialist knowledge and skills. Many were highly skilled immigrants who believed that Australia presented opportunities and a new horizon after World War II. All were telling a story with designs that captured the essence of this country, defining its character through design, colour, pattern, line, texture, image and shape. These designers introduced new design practices by developing innovative approaches or using new technologies.

The chapter begins by looking at the historical place of wool in the evolution of the Australian fashion and textile industry. It then considers the organisations established to promote wool, and examines the work of the designers whose reputations were established by the end of World War II in both woven and printed textiles. Finally, it discusses designers whose style captured an Australian essence.

# Wool: the fabric of a nation

The well-known saying 'Wool: the fabric of a nation' illustrates the Australian perception of wool as a material embedded in the history of European settlement. Sheep and wool are depicted in paintings, folklore, sayings, songs and stories. From the arrival of sheep with the First Fleet in 1788 to the celebration of 200 years of wool trading in 2007, the export of fine Merino wool has been central to Australia's wealth and prosperity. While Australia's greatest role has been as a supplier of wool as a raw material to the international textile industry, local manufacturing has also been an important target for its fashion industry. Specialist organisations, established to promote and market wool and to fund research into new products, processes and markets, have played a significant role in promoting the symbiotic link between Australian fashion and wool fabrics.

Wool is a natural material with a complex biological structure and properties appropriate for many diverse applications. As a fibre, it is hard wearing, fire resistant and water repellent; it can be made into soft, warm, firm, heavy or light fabric; it can be spun into yarn for knitting or weaving; it can be felted, manipulated and given sculptural shapes, embroidered or printed. Wool's characteristics and properties make it one of the most adaptable of fabrics, perfect for fashion garments while also appropriate for utilitarian garments, military uniforms, workwear, sportswear and furnishings. According to contemporary Paris-based Australian designer Martin Grant:

> Wool is extraordinary for its sculptural qualities. Thick felted wool you can beat around, manipulate, create interesting forms. The finer weaves are amazing for their suppleness and drape. It is one of the most versatile of materials, and so intrinsic to fashion. (AWI and Powerhouse Museum 2007: 9)

By the end of World War II, the Australian wool and textile industry was in a strong position to capitalise on changing conditions with the return to peacetime activities and the enhanced consumer demand arising from postwar migration to Australia. Established companies and specialist organisations were able to meet this growing demand. In the mid 1930s, the Australian Wool Board (AWB) and the International Wool Secretariat (IWS) were specialist organisations established to improve wool production in Australia, promote awareness and use of wool products, and support research. In a unique arrangement, both the AWB and the IWS were funded by contributions from wool growers.

Yarra Falls in Melbourne was one of the first commercial spinning, knitting and weaving mills to be founded, signalling the development of a national textile industry. Established in 1917 to supply high-quality worsted and woollen yarn for knitting and weaving in Australia, the company invested heavily in modern automated equipment to become a leading supplier of quality wool fabrics with an extensive range of pure worsted wool for the fashion industry and for export. Macquarie Textiles wove woollen fabric from as early as 1869 and worsted fabrics from 1925 for use in apparel, furnishings, upholstery, blankets, bedding and knitting yarns. Located in Albury in New South Wales, Macquarie has long been a major supplier of wool fabrics for local and overseas markets. Other companies such as Moylan Woollens (1950) and Creswick Woollen Mills (1947) also played a key role in local production of woollen fabrics.

When in 1947 Christian Dior launched the New Look in Paris, metres of luxurious fabrics were needed to sculpt the softly padded feminine shapes. It was seen as a revolutionary collection after years of wartime rationing and austerity. An excellent illustration of the impact of Dior's designs is shown by this AWB advertisement from the *Australian Women's Weekly*, dated 14 February 1948:

> The look for 1948 is lady-like . . . says *Vogue* of the new fashions . . . Skirts are complete circles, or made full and feminine with pleats and gathers . . . And nearly always the fabric for these clothes is wool. More explicitly, it is men's suiting, worsted gabardine, broadcloth, plaid or handwoven tweed. Wool was chosen because it gives the desired shape and swing to skirts. It takes hip-padding and moulds easily and smoothly into close fitting bodices. In fact, ever since Christian Dior first introduced this 'belled' or 'Infanta' silhouette he and his colleagues have shown more and more wool clothes for all occasions. (AWI and Powerhouse Museum 2007: 32)

The wool industry boomed in the 1950s, due in part to the need for wool to make uniforms for the Korean War, but mainly to meet demands from international fashion markets. This called for new research and marketing because competition from synthetic and human-made fibres challenged wool's supremacy, which in turn led to greater funding for research to enhance wool's performance and functionality. Funded by the AWB, the Commonwealth Scientific and Industrial Research Organisation (CSIRO) developed processes to shrink-proof wool, while permanent pleating was developed through the revolutionary Siroset process.

The IWS, in its role of promoting wool internationally, initiated wool fashion awards in the early 1950s, with the Australian designer Hall Ludlow winning the award in 1953 for an outstanding wedding dress made entirely of wool fabric. Capitalising on this success, in the following year the IWS commissioned designers to collaborate with leading textile manufacturers to create collections presented in prestigious parades in Paris, and designers Karl Lagerfeld and Yves Saint Laurent were successful in the new talent competition (AWI 2007: 32). Subsequently, the French designer Pierre Cardin visited Australia in 1963 as a guest of the Australian Wool Board to explore wool's sculptural qualities in geometrically shaped garments using finely tailored heavyweight wools (AWI 2007: 36).

In the following decades, the Australian Wool Corporation[1] continued its strong support of the Australian fashion and textile industry in various ways, including launching Woolmark in 1964 to market pure new wool products. Italian Francesco Saroglia designed the distinctive Woolmark logo, not only to give wool an international identity but also to create consumer confidence among retailers, consumers and manufacturers and to symbolise quality standards. Campaigns such as 'Why Wool' and 'Get Real, Get Wool' advertised the advantages of wool and demonstrated the need for rural Australia to maintain and reinforce its position in the fashion industry and marketplace (Historic Houses Trust 1994: 48).

As well, international interest in wool was generated by a series of key events. Prue Acton designed somewhat controversial uniforms for the 1984 Australian Olympic Games. The athletes were described as wearing uniforms in wattle yellow wool emblazoned with koalas, emus and wombats. They carried wattle yellow wool coats, made after the style of the Driza-Bone, and waved Akubra hats. While local Australians were seemingly critical of the uniforms, they were highly acclaimed by the parade judges and Australia was named the best-dressed team in the opening ceremony (Historic Houses Trust 1994: 50). Further international acknowledgement came with the Bicentennial Wool Collection fashion parade at the Sydney Opera House on 31 January 1988. Highlighting Australian wool in contemporary fashion, nine international and six Australian designers were invited to showcase their wool collections in a highly televised and promoted event. International designers Claude Montana, Sonia Rykiel, Oscar de la Renta, Donna Karan, Kenzo Takada, Gianni Versace, Missoni, Jean Muir and Bruce Oldfield joined Australian designers Jill Fitzsimon, George Gross, Adele Palmer, Covers, Wendy Heather and Stuart Membery. Guests of honour for this high-profile event were Prince Charles and Princess Diana. Promotion was widespread, reinforcing awareness of the importance of wool to the economy and its rightful place in the fashion industry.

During the 1990s, Australia became the world's biggest wool producer and was also the main source of apparel wool entering international trade channels. However, the period also saw significant rationalisation of the total textile industry in Australia. Many companies closed or were amalgamated, including Yarra Falls, which was acquisitioned by the Australian Country Spinners in 1998. Significantly, traditional wool processing industries were challenged by China, the new manufacturing giant, replacing the once-dominant Eastern Europe. By 2003 China had become the largest processor of Australian wool.

In 2000, when the Woolmark Awards for Excellence were held, Sportwool was launched and Merino wool was recognised for its absorption qualities in active wear and its high resilience, which enabled wool to be promoted into a new market of sports uniforms. In 2006, the Wild Oats crew in the Sydney to Hobart Yacht Race attracted great attention when they wore iconic Driza-Bone style jackets made of 100 per cent Merino wool jersey, successfully promoting wool as quick drying with its natural moisture-management properties. In the corporate sphere, Australian designer Peter Morrissey created wool uniforms for Qantas staff in 2003 with an Indigenous print by Balarinji Design Studio, further underlining the cultural link with the national carrier.

The year 2007 commemorated 200 years of achievements by the Australian wool industry. In 1807 the first bale of Australian Merino wool was shipped to Britain by John and Elizabeth Macarthur intended for commercial sale, thus establishing the Australian wool trade. To celebrate this milestone, the Powerhouse Museum in Sydney held the exhibition *Fashion from Fleece: 200 Years of Australian Wool in Fashion*. Initiated and funded by Australian Wool Innovation (AWI) and curated by Jane de Teliga, it presented key fashion pieces by Chanel, Yves Saint Laurent, Giorgio Armani and Rei Kawakubo (Comme des Garçons) plus pieces by Australian designers Collette Dinnigan, Martin Grant and Jayson Brunsdon, alongside historical wool samples and garments from the Powerhouse Museum collection.

The increased demand for natural and sustainable fibres in fashion has seen more innovative Australian Merino yarns becoming available. Designers and retailers globally have worked with Australian Wool Innovation and manufacturers to develop the softest, finest and most innovative fabrics

**6.2** Kenzo romper suit in ultra fine Merino wool, Bicentennial Wool Collection, 1988

Courtesy Australian Wool Innovation Limited

**6.3** Versace pure new wool gown, Bicentennial Wool Collection, 1988

Courtesy Bicentennial Wool Collection

in high-end fashion, sportswear, leisure wear and uniforms. Recently, a featherweight jersey was developed by AWI specifically for fashion designer Akira Isogawa. This is a trans-seasonal wool fabric with qualities similar to silk in handle, drape and softness. AWI developed the fabric from a blend of Merino wool and Modal, a rayon fibre produced from beechwood. Akira used the translucent fabric for costumes for *Grand*, a Sydney Dance Company production in which he collaborated with Graeme Murphy (Cochrane 2007: 134). This is indicative of the role played by Australian Wool Innovation to develop new applications for Australian wool. AWI's important work assists designers and retailers to discover new and innovative ways to enhance the attributes of wool through researching and developing new products, and opening new markets. According to the Wool Board:

> driving the global demand for Australian Merino wool is dependent on understanding what consumers want, developing new fabrics to address consumer needs and providing marketing support to ensure sales on the shop floor. (Australian Wool Board online n.d.)

## Pioneers of Modernist textile designs

In the story of textiles in Australian fashion, several studio-based practices and design projects from the early 1940s left a legacy of originality, using colour, texture, pattern and design to represent a vision of Australia. Various craft studios and workrooms were established by Australians returning from study overseas, by recent immigrants or by textile artists attempting to visualise their heritage. Arguably, while most endeavoured to develop unique national designs for the Australian market, all in their own way were important in defining an Australian character in fashion through textile design.

Edith (Mollie) Grove and Catherine Hardress established *eclarté*,[2] a highly successful weaving studio, in 1939 'to make, for Australians, in Australia, fabrics of equal beauty and quality to those which, up to date, we have enjoyed only when expensively imported from abroad' (Frances Burke Textile Resource Centre 2000: 16). Having studied and worked in weaving and theatre in London, the pair travelled in Europe, researching fashion and textile trends. Studio production began on specially designed looms, with Hardress designing and Grove weaving tweeds for clothing. Designs were directed by an aesthetic concerned with 'texture and colour blending, and considering climate conditions in relation to weight and weaves and durability' (Frances Burke Textile Resource Centre 2000: 19). The business was launched at an exhibition opened by Prime Minister Sir Robert Menzies in 1940, with over 300 yards in their range of 'tweeds in checks, stripes and plain colours, dress fabrics for the beach, gossamer laces in wool for evening wear and furnishing materials including floor rugs, cushions and accessories' (Frances Burke Textile Resource Centre 2000: 19).

Invited by the Australian Wool Bureau[3] to demonstrate at the Melbourne Royal Agricultural Society Show, *eclarté* won great acclaim with the public and their fabrics found their way into top Australian stores, with regular displays at Myer in Melbourne (Frances Burke Textile Resource Centre 2000: 19). During the war years, when mills were producing heavier fabrics for military needs, *eclarté* was restricted by the government to producing tweeds only in commercial lengths at prices dictated by the Prices Commission. After the war, *eclarté* began to develop furnishing fabrics and enjoyed a postwar boom in housing development, working with architects and individual clients on commercial and domestic interiors.

With the move to Dandenong in 1951, the Australian Wool Bureau continued its support as *eclarté*'s hand-woven wool products were outstanding, both aesthetically and in terms of quality. *eclarté* was renowned for its extensive range of subtly coloured yarns, all chemically dyed but reflecting Grove's experimentation with shades and colours influenced by the landscape surrounding their studio. Not surprisingly, a suit woven by *eclarté* and designed by Australian fashion designer Hall Ludlow in 1960 won the gold medal in the Couture Section of the Australian Wool Bureau Fashion Awards (Frances Burke Textile Resource Centre 2000: 21) and a special award was given for the fabrics (Cochrane 1992: 179). *eclarté* collapsed in the early 1960s when the studio found it impossible to compete with mechanised factories in an increasingly industrialised environment; its designs were copied and complications arose regarding commission. Grove and Hardress proclaimed that they were 'artists, not traders' (Bogle 2002: 115).

At the time of *eclarté*'s closure, Robert Maltus' weaving studio began in Melbourne, founded by Marian Swinton with Dutch-born master tailor Adrianus Janssens as a partner. Janssens designed and produced collections of hand-woven garments that successfully combined the ancient craft of hand-weaving with haute couture fashions from 1959 to 1968. Robert Maltus enjoyed consistent wins in the prestigious Melbourne Gown of the Year competition. After Maltus closed, Swinton accepted a teaching position at Emily McPherson College (now RMIT University's Fashion Program). Janssens focused on work for private clients, and from 1974 to 1999 also lectured in the Fashion Department at RMIT. During his twenty-five years at the university, Janssens was an inspiration and mentor, especially sharing his knowledge of the craft of tailoring (Frances Burke Textile Resource Centre 2000: 12).

Alcorso printed textile designs were considered the most innovative products that reflected a truly Australian character. The company Silk and Textile Printers was established in Sydney in 1939 to produce screen-printed dress fabrics using new Italian techniques that Claudio and Orlando Alcorso had brought to Australia. At the end of World War II, Claudio Alcorso, attempting to realise his vision of an Australia that could produce its own textiles of quality and beauty, actively commissioned leading artists 'to design fabrics that reflected an Australian character for a market largely dominated by imports' (Menz 1987: 72). The first range of fabrics, exhibited in Melbourne in 1946, presented Australian motifs printed on wool and silk dress fabrics. The printed wool designs attracted international orders, were acclaimed by critics and manufacturers and were worn by hundreds of Australian women on the streets of Sydney and Melbourne. In the following year the company moved to Hobart in Tasmania, and the Modernage Fabrics range was printed using forty-six designs from thirty-three Australian artists, including Margaret Preston, Russell Drysdale, James Gleeson, William Dobell and Hal Missingham.

While many artists had never produced designs for textiles before, their designs reflected Alcorso's vision for Australian textiles with original motifs, landscapes, cityscapes, flora and fauna. The catalogue entry for *Tree Forms* by Russell Drysdale notes: 'this design was made from drawings taken from a sketch and arranged informally to complete a full screen' (Alcorso 1947: 9). It shows Drysdale's interest in the landscape of inland Australia with small groups of Aborigines wandering through a threatening, drought-stricken landscape (Menz 1987: 74). William Dobell's *Burlesque* design 37 was 'inspired by a festive woman during peace celebrations at King's Cross, Sydney' and has two variations: one for 'hangings in heavy fabrics' and the other with an 'all over pattern . . . intended for dress materials in fine fabrics' (Alcorso 1947: 28). The range extended well beyond the original forty-six designs, as they were offered in various colourways and on different fabrics. Designs were printed on wool, silk and other fabrics, as either furnishing fabrics or for fashion.

Modernage Fabrics were hailed as 'one of the boldest attempts to establish a range of exclusively Australian designs' (Bogle 2002: 212), and a review in the December 1947 issue of *South Australian Homes and Gardens* commented that:

> a few years ago it would have been considered impossible to produce locally a wide range of attractive textile designs by Australian artists. This exhibition is an important pointer to the future trend of industrial development.

Sydney Ure Smith, president of the Society of Artists, commented in his catalogue essay 'Vision and Confidence in Art for Textiles' that there was great potential in these fabrics as, in the past, 'our manufacturers had been content to copy designs from overseas, not daring to venture into new fields' (Alcorso 1947: 8). The venture generated limited commercial success because the Australian public preferred imported fabrics, but was remarkable in involving high-profile artists and using a visionary process to produce unique designs, which are now held in museum collections.

During the 1950s, several companies provided print designs to the fashion industry. In Melbourne, Prestige Limited, a manufacturer of hosiery from 1922 to 1979, established one of the first industrial design studios in Australia with European-trained textile designer Gerard Herbst as art director from 1946 to 1956. Herbst introduced printed fashion fabrics to the Prestige range, with the studio inventing several new printing techniques, including the transfer of gold leaf to fabric and a photographic screen-printing process called 'phototex'. The company's printed fabrics were showcased internationally in 1951 at the International Textile Exhibition in Lille, France. Designs were based on natural forms of the Australian environment and featured images of driftwood, lizard skin, seashells, rocks and leaves.

The studio implemented a Bauhaus-inspired program of experimental textile design to create artists' designed fashion fabrics that competed with those imported from overseas. The studio aimed to introduce a European-inspired design aesthetic to the Australian industry. While searching for a sense of identity, Herbst 'was keen to distance himself from the gumnut and koala style' and instead 'favoured more subtle designs based on moss, eucalypt, bark, leaves, logs and geological formations'. He wanted his designs 'to do justice to the Australian environment and its unique characteristics without resorting to pirating Aboriginal motifs' (Maynard 2001: 168). Prestige's main Australian competitor was Silk and Textile Printers.

The 1960s saw various forms of promotion for Australian textile design. In Sydney from 1963, the Fashion Fabric Design Awards were held annually at Blaxland Gallery, sponsored by Bruck Mills Australia Ltd, Tennyson Textile Mills and R.H. Taffs fashion house. Organised with the Contemporary Art Society, the exhibition aimed to 'allow Australian artists to express their ideas for fashion design, and to induce export demand for Australian inspired and produced textiles and garments' (Cochrane 1992: 175). Artists were commissioned to produce designs, and from the mid 1960s many of these were printed on new synthetic fabrics.

During this period, several designers and companies successfully produced and marketed their own design ranges. One of the most successful was Frances Burke in Melbourne. Burke had studied art at various institutions in Melbourne in the early 1930s and exhibited at the Melbourne Contemporary Artists Exhibition from 1936 to 1938. In 1937, Burke and Morris Holloway established Burway Prints, Australia's first registered screen-printery, becoming Frances Burke Fabrics in 1942. Burke's strongly patterned, modern fabric designs, which had a distinctly Australian spirit, often featured Australian flora, fauna and Aboriginal motifs. Burke promoted the use of innovative designs and vivid, daring colours, educating her clientele in the use of appropriate fabrics to create an ambience for the new wave of architecture. Her shop, New Design, presented a range of her popular prints, printed in repeat in fifty-two colours plus plain dyed cotton fabrics for clothing (Cyberfibres 2009a).

In Sydney, Annan Fabrics was established as a wartime enterprise in 1941 by Alexandra (Nan) Mackenzie and Anne Outlaw, and became a pioneer in screen-printing design in Australia. Having studied design, drawing and painting at the National Art School in Sydney, Mackenzie based her design philosophy on appropriate and full knowledge of all the processes involved in making the finished article (Sumner 1987: 84). Inspired by Australian flora and fauna and Aboriginal symbols, she produced large-scale designs with vibrant colours primarily suited to interior furnishing fabrics but used also for beachwear, evening wear, day dresses and sarongs. Her designs *Strelitzia*, *Banana*, *Ginger Plant* and *Bush Bunch* captured the lushness of each plant, highlighting Mackenzie's skill and expertise. After the war, inexpensive imported fabrics flooded the market and impacted on the company's viability. Relying on commissions, Annan Fabrics continued to produce hand screen-printed textiles until the mid 1950s.

Sydney-based designer Mary Shackman's designs showed great versatility, ranging from the large-scale patterns and brightly coloured prints of the 1960s to the hand-painted free-form clothing of the 1970s. They were sought after by leading Australian fashion designers. Her designs reflected the mood of the time and are said to have 'raised a few eyebrows . . . offering everything from punk, African warrior, Japanese samurai, Australian native or 50s colour or just a mass of abstract colours' (Mackay 1984: 179).

Shackman began screen-printing fabrics in 1965 after attending the National Art School. She co-founded a design studio called Printed Materials, Mary and Vicki. The studio hand-painted and printed yardage for clothing and furnishings, which sold to department stores, designers and boutiques, including George's, Farmer's, Finlandia, Carla Zampatti, John J Hilton, Simona, Merivale and Gasworks. Her design practice illustrates the shift occurring at this time towards a focus on Australian fashion designers and manufacturers using local artists and designers, rather than outsourcing from overseas or larger factories.

In 1972 Shackman began a wholesale business with her husband George Theodore, hand-painting and printing for Australian fashion labels Jenny Kee, Linda Jackson and Mark & Geoffrey. Later she established Mary Shackman Pty Ltd, creating her own resort wear ranges of T-shirts, sarongs and accessories, which sold through Sportsgirl, Country Road, David Jones, Cherry Lane and Robert Burton. In the 1980s she concentrated on painting, exhibiting at various galleries while continuing to work with fashion designers, creating hand-painted textiles for Nicola Finetta. In 1998 she began collaborating with Anthony Kendal, painting fabric designs for his Thys Collective collections in 2000, 2001 and 2002.

## Indigenous textile studios

Australian designers gradually began to receive international recognition in the European market. The use of Indigenous Australian designs, including Aboriginal motifs on women's dress and leisure wear, intensified in the 1970s and 1980s. In the 1980s major Australian fashion designers put Indigenous textiles on the map, and at the same time Indigenous labels including Designer Aboriginals, Tiwi Designs, Desert Designs and Balarinji captured the brilliance of Aboriginal stories in their design. This coincided with the Australian government's policy of developing a national identity through artistic expression.

For example, Jenny Kee believed that, by going back into history, a new contemporary fashion could be created, and that the epitome of this in Australia was the tribal art of the Aboriginal people. Her Kee *Corroboree* range, designed in 1977 with David McDiarmid, illustrated this approach. Much of the work produced in Linda Jackson's design studio Bush Couture was inspired by outback trips to central Australia in the early 1980s. Her collections were diverse, including printed, plant-dyed, knitted and woven garments with inspiration derived from time spent with Indigenous communities learning about their myths, history and art. The women of Utopia supplied her with their batik silk, incorporating many traditional motifs. One range was based on a design achieved by placing gum leaves on fabric and rolling over dyes, the leaf forming a resist and creating a pattern via the relief of the leaf (Mackay 1984: 110). Robert Burton used two of the designs, *Snake* and *Dragonfly*, for his 1983 summer collection.

**6.4** Linda Jackson in her Utopia Silks and Lydia Livingstone in Bush Couture outfit, Kata Tjuta (Olgas), 1982

Photo: Fran Moore. Courtesy National Gallery of Victoria, Melbourne

At the same time as designers were using Australian motifs, native flora and fauna to capture an Australian aesthetic, several Aboriginal labels were established, successfully marketing their designs internationally. In the previous decades, the Australian government and other agencies had to encourage Indigenous cultural production in communities, promoting self-sufficiency and employment.

Queenslander Olive Ashworth's textile designs were informed by a love of the tropical northern Australian environment, in particular the Great Barrier Reef. In 1954, her design *Aquarelle* won the Leroy Alcorso Textile Design Competition, a prize inaugurated to promote Australian textile designers and to raise the standard of local fashion design: 'This swirling pattern of delicate, marine grasses of the Barrier Reef was printed in nylon in several colourways and made into dresses of four or five styles' (McKay 1984: 8). Ashworth won again in 1955 with another swirling marine design of seagulls in flight and in the following years worked on commissions for furnishing fabrics and murals for tropical motels, hotels and restaurants.

In 1971 she established Indigenous Design of Australia, a textile company that specialised in furnishing and dress fabrics (Cyberfibres 2009b). Her fabrics, labelled 'distinctively Queensland', were produced for local resorts and were:

> [a] kaleidoscope of tropical and animal life . . . she is captivated by waves and currents of the reef, and in her Barrier Reef designs seeks to depict, above all, the tidal rhythm and flow of the sea . . . it is from Australia's own flora and fauna, marine life and Aboriginal legend and art that we must produce our tourist fabrics. (McKay 1984: 18)

In the late 1960s, Ernabella artists were introduced to the wax-resist technique of batik. This proved popular, quick to produce, easily transportable and appropriate for translating traditional body painting designs. In the hot conditions of the desert, batik proved an ideal process to capture stories, and from 1971 became a signature art form for Ernabella. Batik spread to other communities, with the Utopia women being introduced to the technique in late 1977. Their earliest creations were translated on to T-shirts and wrap-around skirts. Both groups visited the Batik Research Institute in Jogjakarta, Indonesia. Emily Kngwarreye worked with fabric before turning to painting on canvas in 1989. As a ceremonial elder, Kngwarreye was among the Utopia women who took on leadership of the batik project. They preferred brushes to *tjanting* (the traditional tool used to apply wax), so their batiks took on a painterly quality, a style far removed from the traditional Indonesian craft. Techniques were adapted to local conditions, with the artists folding the fabric loosely in their laps to apply the wax or anchoring the corners on a flat surface with sand-filled tins: 'The result, unlike the rhythmically formal Indonesian style, is free-flowing, asymmetrical and abstract' (Cosic 2009). Each Utopia artist developed her designs from traditional ceremonial ground and body paintings and personal totems.

The Tiwi Design Aboriginal Corporation was established in 1969 on Bathurst Island, near Darwin, to 'preserve, promote and enrich Tiwi culture' (Parkes 2006: 250). The Tiwi Design group currently represents about 100 artists working in traditional and contemporary media. Their textiles include hand-screen-printed textiles for fashions, with many of the original 1970s designs still being produced, demonstrating an 'enduring quality' and the timelessness of Indigenous designs. In 1983 curator Anthony (Ace) Bourke exhibited Tiwi Designs at the Hogarth Galleries in Sydney. Major Australian fashion designers Jenny Kee, Linda Jackson, Katie Pye and Robert Burton chose fabric for the Tiwi people to print for fashion garments, creating a fashion application for the textile designs (Cochrane 1992: 329).

Also highly successful was the Jumbana Company, launched in 1983 under directors Ros and John Moriarty. The company is now based in Sydney, with its major label Balarinji; it specialises in cross-cultural collaborations – that is, Aboriginal and non-Aboriginal. Balarinji caters for the middle leisure wear and tourist market while the company targets high-profile companies that are marketing themselves as uniquely Australian. Rainbow Dreaming T-shirts, Sand 'n Shore bathing costumes and Barramundi swimwear that 'make peace with fish spirits' all continue the tradition of Aboriginal motifs appearing on women's leisurewear (Maynard 2001: 176).

Bronwyn Bancroft ran Designer Aboriginals in Rozelle, Sydney from 1985 to 1990, one of the first retail outlets for quality, one-off, hand-printed and painted clothing and jewellery designed by Aboriginal artists. In 1987, Bancroft and four other Koori designers were invited to present their hand-painted and printed clothing at the prestigious department store Au Printemps in Paris. In 1996, Bancroft expressed concern that clothing was no longer a suitable medium for Aboriginal artists, as it received little recognition. Aboriginal designers, she felt, needed to make art.

Desert Designs originated in Western Australia in the 1980s using designs created by Jimmy Pike, with a goal of marketing products into the commercial world of contemporary fashion while maintaining the essence of

Pike's creativity as well as Aboriginal cultural integrity. Desert Designs opened several stores in Australia, with all fabric designs having an Indigenous name, information on the artist and the design, as well as its symbolic meaning, attached to all products. In 1986 Desert Designs established licensing agreements with accessory and textile manufacturers Oroton and Sheridan, giving access to national and international markets with ranges of both children's clothing and women's fashion. At the same time, the *Jimmy Pike: Desert Designs* exhibition travelled to Japan and, after a second tour in 1989, the designs were licensed for ranges of skiwear and beachwear.

## 1990s fashion designers focus on textile design

The 1990s saw several innovative studio-based practices established, including those of Rae Ganim, Glenda Morgan and Rebecca Paterson. Rae Ganim created clothes that were naïve in their pattern and construction, using simple garment styles to highlight her fabrics. Ganim completed an art design course, majoring in printed and woven textiles, before joining Prue Acton in the mid 1970s and later setting up her own business. Her self-professed 'childlike approach' is demonstrated in large blocks of colour and humorous prints – for example, bacon-and-egg and fish-and-chip outfits from the 1980s. At this time, Ganim commented that: 'Anything goes in Australian fashion right now. The whole idea of looking to overseas collections for our direction has gone, the designers and the market are much more confident' (Mackay 1984: 98).

Glenda Morgan set up Reptilia Studio in Sydney in 1983, specialising in hand-printed and painted furnishing and fashion textiles, characterised by random repeat patterns. Her designs possessed a uniquely Australian quality inspired by the landscape and a 'painterly style' in which 'the paint is usually layered in a thick, rich impasto that speaks for a variety of brush techniques' (Singleton 1988: 68). Reptilia fabrics were widely exhibited throughout Australia and are represented in numerous collections. Morgan revealed that:

> I wouldn't call what I do art, since it's not an intellectual process as such, but more of an emotional one. I like this spontaneity of approach because it keeps the fabric fresh . . . Once I've got my feelings down in paint on the fabric I may question the visual effectiveness of it all, and perhaps make adjustments. (Singleton 1988: 69)

Rebecca Paterson is a Perth-based textile designer, clothing designer and manufacturer. With a background in the visual arts, she 'views clothing, textiles and the body from a different perspective, outside the trend driven mainstream fashion industry' (Powerhouse Museum online n.d.). Her label, SpppsssP, was launched in 1996 in Western Australia with Megan Salmon. Both trained as painters and met in 1990 while working at Desert Designs. Paterson worked for a time with leading Japanese textile innovator Junichi Arai, and their summer 1998 collection included pieces patterned with *shibori*, the Japanese resist dye technique. SpppsssP has been described as 'Australian culture slamming into Japanese textile processes' (Boland 1998).

Paterson launched Breathless in 2000, with 'dramatic textiles and bold forms continuing her focus on process, concept and the designing and making of clothes that blur the boundaries between art and fashion' (Powerhouse Museum online n.d.). With concepts derived from politics, feminism and spirituality, her passion for experimenting with new technologies drives her work. Deconstructionists and Japanese designers – particularly Rei Kawakubo of Comme des Garçons – are the major inspiration for the label: 'We do anything with our fabrics. Let's see what happens when we put the fabric on the floor and have a party' (Anderson 1997).

## Asian influences

Over recent years, various Asian countries have played a key role in the design, making and production of textiles for the individualised work of Australia's contemporary fashion designers. Many Australian designers are expressing their individual aesthetic through the use of original and hand-crafted textiles. Leading designers are sourcing fabrics from Asian countries, and are collaborating with their traditional artisans to create unique one-off textiles.

Easton Pearson's inspiration for garments comes directly from the textile. Fabrics sourced and commissioned are hand-embroidered, crocheted, knitted, woven, beaded and embellished from artisans and craftspeople in India and Vietnam (Parkes 2006: 112). Lydia Pearson and Pamela Easton make frequent trips to these countries with a passion and respect for their cultures and the welfare of their people. Collaboration with an Indian women's cooperative has enabled embroidery and traditional techniques to be incorporated into their garments. Easton Pearson stated:

> It's so much more exciting to work with fabric you have designed,
> I guess there is some sort of spirituality about the process. It has
> a bit more heart. We will often include a little story about where
> the fabric comes from. It makes the garment more special. (Coffey
> 1998: 137)

Most of the embroidery is from Mumbai in India, with the garments being constructed mainly in Brisbane. The paper patterns are sent to the embroidery workshops with the fabric and, once completed by the artisans, the garments are cut and assembled in Australia. A small percentage of production occurs in Hong Kong, which is justified by the fact that the skill base is still lacking in Australia. The label now sells in Europe, Japan, Russia, the United States, Asia and the Middle East.

Caravana was launched in 2004 by Cathy Braid and Kirsten Ainsworth at Sydney's Fashion Week and quickly became known as 'a label with a conscience' (Cochrane 2007: 122). Caravana designs are produced by Pakistani artisans using their traditional embroidery skills. In 2003, Braid and Ainsworth lived in the Chitral Valley, Northwest Pakistan and established work centres in which women could be trained. Designs take inspiration from the local environment and, through each woman's individual interpretation, each garment is made with a personal imprint of both designer and maker.

Akira Isogawa, one of Australia's most original designers, grew up in Kyoto, Japan, a city founded on the ancient silk trade. It is apt that a designer who is passionate about textiles comes from a city that exists essentially because of fabric. His work fuses Japanese traditions with Western influences. In 2001–02 his solo exhibition at Object Gallery, Sydney demonstrated his commitment to textiles and emphasised his belief in the process of collaboration. Within the industry, he has searched for skilled artisans, craftspeople, specialists in embroidery and print, and textile producers in places such as Bali, Hong Kong, India and Vietnam, with the aim of developing 'experimental textiles' (Parkes 2006: 156):

> I'm part of an industry – part of a society – I don't aspire to lead
> or to have a particular impact. But what I'm really interested in is
> collaborating – to be able to work with other creators. So I'm not
> ambitious to lead the industry, but to work within. That is what
> I do. I'm very privileged to be able to work with other creators.
> (NGV online n.d.)

To make his embroidered silk organza *Wedding Bird Layered Dress*, Isogawa worked with Chinese embroiderers to dramatically loosen and scale up their work to create an exaggerated laced effect. He has also collaborated with Signature Prints, drawing inspiration from the archive of Florence Broadhurst. Akira's designs are driven by the texture of fabrics and the endless possibilities of cloth, as he works by physically draping the cloth over the figure to create his garments. Every collection is conceptually driven; however, Isogawa has stated that: 'If you cannot wear it then I'm defeating the purpose – and that is a mistake. This is the trick – to find the balance between what is wearable and what is art' (NGV online n.d.). In his 1998 Spring/Summer collection entitled Botanica, he bravely used calico, it being the only fabric available to him during a trip to Indonesia scouting for embroidery. He 'adopted it as an ironic foil for his most lavish workmanship' (Coffey 1998: 38). Clearly, in his inimitable humble way, Isogawa was challenging existing practice and, through paradox, posing alternatives to contemporary methodologies.

Georgia Chapman and her co-founder Meredith Rowe launched Vixen in 1993. Vixen produces beautifully feminine hand-crafted textiles 'driven

**6.5** Akira Isogawa, three red outfits from his solo exhibition at Object Gallery 2001–02

Photo: Brett Boardman. Courtesy Object Gallery, Sydney

by the surface decoration rather than the product'. They began designing scarves and sarongs because they were uninterrupted lengths of fabric that required little in the way of manufacturing (Parkes 2006: 262). Chapman's textile designs are a collaboration of specialists' and designers' work, with the textile and the garment being created in tandem, each evolving as ideas and processes influence the other. Her eclectically mixed patterns and colours have become her signature. For over a decade, Chapman has been devoted to labour-intensive, manual techniques: 'Everybody loves decoration. I think that's why people react so strongly to what we are doing. Its almost a backlash against all the plain clothes that are around' (Coffey 1998: 168). Vixen began showcasing its textile designs by supplying high-end fashion labels, such as Scanlan & Theodore, Collette Dinnigan and Country Road.

## Technological advances

Major technological advances in textile research and development, as well as global changes, have impacted upon the textile and fashion industry, resulting in reorganised production methods and manufacturing practices and the introduction of new digital technologies. These new directions have addressed the rapidly changing needs of the marketplace. Fashion is constantly developing, demanding new and innovative materials from the textile industry. Digital printing is one of the major changes impacting on the fashion industry.

Longina Phillips is one of Australia's largest textile design company operators of ink jet technology, using reactive, acid and disperse dyes – similar to desktop printing – and thus eliminating the need for messy and labour-intensive screen-printing. The ink jet equipment is ideal for small or exclusive orders, essentially for designers to have sample ranges produced because it can print directly from a computer image. She says:

> A designer can come in here with an idea, we can create the design, print the fabric and then have it back to them. The Australian fashion industry is very sophisticated, demanding new concepts all the time. (AWI online n.d.)

## Conclusion

In the postwar period, the place of textile design within the Australian fashion industry has continually evolved, with fashion designers, textile designers and manufacturers presenting designs that reflected the colour, character and nature of the land, its people and its location. Australian wool, the nation's fabric and its associated industry, is intricately involved in providing exquisite fabrics, new developments and innovative finishes. Above all, textile and fashion designers have interlaced ideas of the Australian spirit and Australia's place in the world into each inspiring design range.

## Acknowledgement

With thanks to Kate Daniel, research assistant and the Powerhouse Museum Research Library.

## Notes

1  See chapter 1 endnote 1.
2  *eclarté*, always written in lower case, is a word formed from *clarté*, French for 'enlightenment'; prefaced by the letter 'e', this word represents excellence and the high ideals the business sought to achieve.
3  See chapter 1 endnote 1.

## References

Alcorso, C. (1947), *A New Approach to Textile Designing by a Group of Australian Artists*, Sydney: Ure Smith.

Anderson, M. (1997), 'cum quat may', *Oyster Magazine*, summer.

Australian Wool Board (n.d.), <www.wool.com.au>

Australian Wool Innovation Limited (AWI) (2007), *Australian Merino Wool: Celebrating 200 Years*, Sydney: AWI.

—— (n.d.), AWI Publications, <digital.wool.com.au/default.aspx?iid=5289&startpage=page0000024>.

—— and Powerhouse Museum (PHM) (2007), Fashion from fleece, exhibition curated and catalogue, essay by J. de Teliga, Sydney: Powerhouse Museum.

Bogle, M. (2002), *Designing Australia: Readings in the History of Design*, Sydney: Pluto Press.

Boland, Y. (1998), 'The future of fashion', *Oyster Magazine*, summer.

Cochrane, G. (1992), *The Crafts Movement in Australia: A History*, Sydney: UNSW Press.

—— (2007), *Smartworks: Design and the Hand Made*, Sydney: Powerhouse Museum.

Coffey, D. (ed.) 1998, *Catwalk: The Designer Collections*, Sydney: ACP Creative Books.

Cosic, M. (2009), 'Fabric of the desert revealed in new creative form', *The Australian*, 5 January.

Cyberfibres (2009a), *Online Register of Australian Fashion and Textile Design*, <www.cyberfibres.rmit.edu.au/francesburke>.

—— (2009b), *Online Register of Australian Fashion and Textile Design*, <www.cyberfibres.rmit.edu.au/biogs/TRC0003b.htm>

de Teliga, J. (1989), *Contemporary Australian Fashion: The Contemporary Art*, Sydney: Powerhouse Museum and Bernard Lesser Publications.

Demasi, L. (2003), 'Market forces', *Sydney Morning Herald*, 26 February.

English, B. (1999), *Griffith University's Tokyo Vogue: Japanese/Australian Fashion*, Brisbane: Griffith University, Queensland College of Art.

Frances Burke Textile Resource Centre (2000), *Studio Weaving in Australia: Robert Maltus and eclarté*, Melbourne: RMIT.

Gale, C. and Kaur, J. (2004), *Fashion and Textiles: An Overview*, Oxford: Berg.

Healy, R. (2006), 'Making noise: contemporary Australian fashion design', in B. Parkes (ed.), *Freestyle: New Australian Design for Living*, Sydney: Object: Australian Centre for Craft and Design/Melbourne: Melbourne Museum, pp. 30–7.

Historic Houses Trust (1994), *Wool in the Australian Imagination*, Sydney: Historic Houses Trust.

Joel, A. (1998), *Parade: The Story of Fashion in Australia*, Sydney: Harper Collins.

Mackay, E. (1984), *The Great Aussie Fashion: Australian Designers 1984–1985*, Sydney: Kevin Weldon.

—— (1987), *Fashion Australia*, Sydney: Stuart Lodge.

Maynard, M. (2001), *Out of Line: Australian Women and Style*, Sydney: UNSW Press.

McKay, J. (1984), 'Barrier Reef fabrics of Olive Ashworth', *Australian Business Collection Annual*, pp. 18–19.

Menz, C. (1987), '1946: Modernage fabrics', *Craft Australia*, 4 (Summer), pp. 72–7.

National Gallery of Victoria (n.d), <www.ngv.vic.gov.au/akira/resources/rb_akira.pdf>

Parkes, B. (ed.) 2006, *Freestyle: New Australian Design for Living*, Sydney: Object: Australian Centre for Craft and Design/Melbourne: Melbourne Museum.

Powerhouse Museum (n.d.), <www.powerhousemuseum.com/hsc/paperbark/influence.htm>.

Singleton, Kate (1988), 'Reptilia Designs', *Craft Arts*, February–April, pp. 60–2.

Sumner, C. (1987), 'Annan Fabrics', *Craft Australia*, 1 (Autumn), pp. 83–5.

# THE SPECTACLE OF FASHION

## MUSEUM COLLECTION, DISPLAY AND EXHIBITION

*Craig Douglas*

**7.1** *Martin Grant Paris* installation, National Gallery of Victoria, Melbourne (9 December 2005 – 7 May 2006)
Photo: Helen Oliver-Skuse. Courtesy National Gallery of Victoria, Melbourne

*Fashion is designed to be worn on living bodies. In the contemporary museum one of the biggest challenges for the curator of fashion is to somehow recreate some of the life that was originally intended for those garments. (Roger Leong, 2008)*

**A**T THE BEGINNING of the twenty-first century, it is clear that large-scale social, political and cultural changes are in progress. Cultural theoreticians have labelled this period, amongst other terms, as 'Post 9/11'. Even closer to our immediate times, the term 'global recession' – as both a name and a condition – is emerging as an economic and, by association, cultural force that will shape the years ahead. No matter what label is applied, the period from the 1990s through to the present has seen paradigmatic change that continues to affect social structures, relationships and value systems. Hooper-Greenhill, writing in 2004, stated:

> Museums, expository spaces charged with garnering, caring for and exhibiting those objects that symbolise some of our deepest feelings and hopes, are one of the most vulnerable of institutions at this time of radical change. (Hooper-Greenhill 2004: 557)

## Museums: products of the Enlightenment

Museums originated in the Age of Enlightenment. They are an expression of reason and rational thought. They sculpted their position through grand narratives and what Lyotard calls 'meta-narratives' (1992: 138), which were understood outside the site (the museum) from which they were spoken. The museum, in developing a reliable picture of the world, has always employed observation, shaped through the processes of classification and presentation to knowledge constructs.

The pre-twentieth-century history of the museum can be divided into two main stages. The first, in broad terms, spans the late seventeenth and eighteenth centuries – the Age of Enlightenment, also known as the Age of Reason. The second occurred in the nineteenth century, when the production and dissemination of knowledge were the focus of the Modernist museum. This type of museum was intended to be encyclopedic, drawing together a complete collection to act as a universal archive. The nineteenth-century history of the museum is one of consolidation and extension of the emergent principles of classification, which were often used as a strategy to distance this type of public institution from the contemporary popular museums. However, the most defining feature of the nineteenth-century public museum was that it provided access to public citizenry (Altick 1978). This *ideal* twenty-first-century museum adopts a more democratic stance towards its visitors. This democratisation has allowed fashion into the art museum as opposed to just the ubiquitous textiles and dress displays synonymous with museums of earlier eras.

**7.2** Jean Antoine Watteau, *Gersaint's Sign*, 1720
Source: Schloss Charlottenburg, Berlin

# Fashion commercialism and the museum

In 1720, the French painter Jean Antoine Watteau returned to Paris and stayed with his friend E.F. Gersaint, an art dealer. For him, he completed *Enseigne de Gersaint* (Gersaint's Sign), a painting of the interior of Gersaint's shop intended for use as a signboard (see Figure 7.2). In the painting, Watteau depicts two women visiting a commercial art gallery dressed in *robes volantes*.

The woman in the foreground of the painting is seen from the back, a view that emphasises the graceful lines of her dress as she peers at an uncrated painting in front of her:

> The dresses worn by the women in *Gersaint's Sign* are made of simple striped and plain silks . . . this simplicity reflects the importance of the *robe volante*'s influence on fashion . . . a new style of dress with double box pleats at the centre back that flowed loosely from the neck to the floor. (Parmal 2006: 27)

The woman's gown depicted in Watteau's painting developed from the *robe de chambre* (or, in England, the nightgown), a loosely fitted over-garment that took its inspiration from the Japanese kimono. This evolutionary process, evident during the reign of Louis XIV, sees the nightgown take on increasing informality as it moved from the boudoir to the outdoors (Parmal 2006). French dressmakers of the period often referred to the boxed-pleat style of the *robe volante* as 'Watteau's pleats'.

The Watteau painting provides evidence that the fine arts and fashion have a long and inextricably linked history. *Gersaint's Sign* conflates fashion, dress, taste, collecting and commercial enterprise into the broader sensibilities of the Enlightenment. Fashion and painting as commodity and style are at play in this picture. It is interesting to note that the idea of the *museum* (literally translated as 'house of the muses', with a lineage dating back to classical Greece) emerged during this period, when the Louvre became the first public art museum in Paris in 1789–90.

As the Age of Reason gave way to the might of industrialisation, and the city and town emerged as features of a new and growing middle class immersed in trade, the museum had different roles to play. During the nineteenth century it embraced its role as a Cabinet of Curiosities, displaying the wealth of nations and individuals as collectors. However, an equally significant role for the museum, and in particular the art museum at this time, was as a site of civilising rituals. During this century, the serious museum audience grew enormously. At the end of the century, 'the idea of art galleries as sites of wondrous and transforming experience became commonplace among those with any pretensions for *culture* in both Europe and America' (Duncan 1995: 16). The same can be said about the colonies of New South Wales and Victoria, and their respective public art gallery spaces.

If, as Duncan suggests, art museums are sites of ritual, it is the visitor who enacts the ritual. Many museum professionals have also considered the notion of the art museum as a performance field. Philip Rhys Adams, once the director of the Cincinnati Art Museum, 'compared art museums to theatre sets' (Duncan 1995: 12). Maybe that is why the contemporary art museum can, with some imagination and commitment, engage with fashion exhibitions and events. Here I'm thinking of the extravagant fashion shows that have replaced the weekly parades held by the French fashion houses until the early 1980s. In 2006, Chanel chose to show its Spring/Summer collection in the Grand Palais in Paris. But as contemporary art museums curate or host exhibitions on fashion and associated events, it is important to acknowledge the museum's *liminality* – a state of withdrawal from the day-to-day world, where time and space in the sense of the normal business of life are suspended. The corporeal experience of being with displayed objects, and the particular space that is the museum, can also be intellectualised. It has been said that:

> no country has modernised its economy or polity without concomitant changes in costume or without media to diffuse information and feedback about those changes and their significance. Modernity everywhere was just as much a corporeal experience as an intellectual one. As Gilles Lipovetsky (1991) demonstrates, the rise of a fashion culture is closely linked to deeper changes in society. (Hartley 2009: 170)

## The contemporary museum

Today, there are many simplistic assumptions about the nature of fashion and the role and functions of the public art museum. While both engage in the commerce of the sign, their signification has similarities and differences. In both fields of contemporary cultural practice, audiences have come to appreciate the finished product, be it the fashioned garment or the exhibition. Readers of fashion magazines, those who visit the ubiquitous fashion parades and catwalk spectacles, and those who visit fashion exhibitions in a public gallery or museum are all unaware of the complex stories, developments and negotiations that lie behind these events.

The idea of the muse is a daunting proposition for both the fashion designer and the museum fashion curator. Both creators are tethered to the related themes of influence, historical connections and the genealogies of their respective creative and institutional endeavours. However, while they may be read as separate zones of inquiry – fashion and the museum – fashion as exhibition in the museum allows for fertile conversations to occur, aesthetically and intellectually. Here, the essentialism of the fashion system[1] can also be revealed and considered. Both the fashion industry and the art museum rely on the centrality of display. Both engage with their respective modes of production, distribution and consumption.

Between 1997 and 2002, at her own gallery (Judith Clark Costume) based at London's Notting Hill, the now London School of Fashion academic and curator Judith Clark 'consistently questioned the value of established disciplinary boundaries between the categories of art, history and fashion and offered visually stunning display solutions' (Breward 2004: 12). In 2004, the Fashion Museum (ModeMuseum) in Antwerp commissioned Clark to produce the exhibition *Malign Muses: When Fashion Turns Back*. 'The exhibition itself stands as a record of the development of a concept. It is very much an exhibition about the process of research rather than a simple outcome' (Breward 2004: 14). It pays homage to Anna Piaggi's famous double pages for *Italian Vogue*'s juxtapositions of contemporary as well as historical fashion references. This exhibition incorporated a compelling narrative and a curatorial understanding that fashions emerge out of a continuum of relationships (Breward 2004: 14).

Today, different concepts of art history can exist in the art museum. The processes of self-analysis and critique established in the 1960s, and explored by cultural theorists such as Lyotard (1986), Clifford (1988) and Jameson (1990), heralded the emergence of Postmodern cultural and demographic changes. Museums began to view their collections and temporary exhibitions as vehicles by which the viewer and the curator could enter into dialogues. The audience and its needs became fundamental to the new museum.

The museum-building boom of the 1980s and 1990s saw the introduction of yet another curatorial shift – to a more qualitative understanding of display. Exhibitions moved from static to more dynamic models. New meanings were gleaned from art collections and artworks, with interpretation replacing absolute truths. It could be argued that Clark's 2004 curatorship of *Malign Muses: When Fashion Turns Back* is an excellent example of interpreting fashion. Her curatorship sees a more radical compression of past and present. As Clark states:

> Historical references in dress have never been about evolution continuity. There are others ways of plotting this. In dress, surfaces float free of their histories . . . Curating is like creating a new grammar, new patterns of time and reference . . . Unlike language, but more like the multiple meanings of a pack of tarot cards, objects can be read back to front and side to side. (Breward 2004: 12)

While curatorship within the art museum is in continuous revisionist mode, over the last twenty years two modes of presentation have become dominant: the *ahistorical* installation and the *monographic* display (Greenberg et al. 1996).

The *ahistorical* approach eschews chronology and evolution, taking works of art out of their cultural and historical contexts. Again, Clark's *Malign Muses* embraces this form of curatorial inquiry. It has been suggested cynically that this form of curating is elitist by stealth, dealing in obfuscation instead of information. (Szeemann, Fuchs and Hoet in the 1970s and 1980s were ardent exponents of this form of curatorship.) On the contrary, *ahistorical* curatorship as exemplified by *Malign Muses* was:

> an exhibition project to build ideas in space, sometimes through details of historical dress glimpsed at a distance, sometimes as a massive constructivist set with moving parts that bring past and present fashion together in new, ever-changing constellations. Together, these add up to an exhibition that is a monument to ideas. (Evans 2004: 42)

The idea of the contemporary public museum continues to play a central and important role in the way Western culture is defined and understood. The concept of the museum has been labelled a *rational myth* – an institution constructed around and driven by a persistent, powerful applied and shared set of beliefs. In general, this museum (and the same could be said about fashion) reflects developments in modernist, post-industrial and postmodern society. A number of theoreticians have commented on a crisis in the contemporary museum. The reality is that, since the eighteenth century when the first public museums appeared in Europe, politics and social change have made this institution one that, if it were to survive and be relevant, would forever be in change or crisis mode.

After World War II the art museum, in international terms, became eclipsed by the performing arts. Postwar reconstruction and economic recovery led to the emergence of a mass tourism market into the 1970s and 1980s. The interdisciplinary Pompidou Centre in Paris opened in the 1970s with its library, and the gallery coexisted with the other elements. This arts centre allowed for information and entertainment to become connected to a new understanding of culture:

> This concept expanded the reach of the art museum towards a whole new audience that had so far taken no interest and dismissed the institution as stuffy and irrelevant to modern life . . . The Pompidou exhibitions [emphasised] a pan-European dialogue and an interdisciplinary cross-fertilisation. (Schubert 2000: 59)

## New museology

Over the last twenty years, the concept of the new museology (Vergo 1989) has shaped the way museums have reconsidered the visitor's experience. Interpretation and visitor-focused engagement has replaced the object as central to a museum visit. In a number of museums, it has become common to readily assess the effectiveness of their exhibitions and displays through visitor evaluation (Pearce 1995). In Australia, the Powerhouse Museum in Sydney was one of the first public museums in this country to develop a dedicated visitor evaluation department.

In the late 1980s, curatorship in the museum realigned itself on the basis of the broad ideals of the new museology – that is, from the object-centred authority of the museum to collections and exhibitions that become more visitor focused. At this time, Australian fashion was also searching for a new design language. It could be argued that certain public art galleries and museums were complicit, along with organisations such as the Fashion Council of Australia, in providing new voices and forums in which local Australian fashion could be considered. Annette Van den Bosch (2005) correctly observes that the boom in the capitalist Western art market from the mid 1960s through to the late 1970s had direct and lasting implications on and for Australian public art museums.

The acquisition of Jackson Pollock's *Blue Poles* by the 1972 Whitlam Labor government for the national art collection was a defiant symbol of the establishment of Australia as a modernist democracy in its own right. The National Gallery of Australia's foundation director, James Mollison, understood that a new era in Australian political history could symbolically be referenced by the acquisition of a Modernist work into the National Collection. *Blue Poles* fulfilled a number of symbolic functions. It provided the fledgling national collection with an international currency. While there was no National Gallery building at this time, *Blue Poles* symbolised untold possibilities in terms of alliances and exhibition potential for both the collection and the National Gallery.

At this time, the centre–periphery circumstance of Australia to the world was also being played out in the local fashion industry. Local dress culture was 'burdened with clichés regarding conservative nationalistic referencing and worth' (Healy 2007: 30). Locally produced was seen as inferior. However, the independent creative spirit that gave Pollock licence to paint *Blue Poles* was also resonant in particular Australian fashion designers' creations. Their work would contribute to a unique, emerging post 1960s Australian fashion industry.

Robyn Healy (2007), in her essay *Making Noise: Contemporary Australian Fashion Design*, identifies the independent designer as responsible for shaping difference. 'It's Time' – the Labor Party campaign slogan and the subsequent election promise of the 1972 Whitlam government – spoke of the potential of the arts to build a very different Australia at that time. Synergies and interdependent relationships shaped early 1970s visual (including design and craft) practices. The National Gallery of Australia (a Whitlam government initiative), established in 1973, reported in its first annual report (for 1976–77) that 'The Australian National Gallery will acquire objects in the decorative arts. It will be particularly interested in those objects of artists/ craftsmen and designers' (Bell 2002: 249). The Gallery's annual report went on to identify, under the broader category of decorative arts, fashion and the theatre arts as two distinct areas of interest. The Gallery would collect 'costume that represents notable, influential and characteristic fashion design of a particular period' (Bell 2002: 249).

## A Postmodern Australia and beyond

As post-Whitlam Australia was moving economically and artistically into a new era, so too were certain independent fashion designers. The same Anna Piaggi, who had influenced Judith Clark's curatorial framework that subsequently informed *Malign Muses: When Fashion Turns Back* in 2004, announced in *Italian Vogue* in December 1977:

> A fashion arrives from another hemisphere. Over a six-page spread the influential stylist enthuses about the latest Flamingo Park designs, the work of Linda Jackson (b. 1950) and Jenny Kee (b. 1947). She writes that theirs is 'one of the inventive free collections we've seen in recent years'. Animated colour, gigantic pattern and idiosyncratic motifs, combined with the beginnings of unstructured dress forms, make a liberating style. It appears so different from all others. (Healy 2007: 31)

Flamingo Park (1973–82) fashion became known as Australiana – or the first true Australian style. As Robyn Healy aptly states: '[It] became an icon of independence in line with the political agenda of the federal Whitlam Government' (2007: 31). This highly individual fashion design duo was influenced by such luminaries as Sonia Delaunay and her textiles, Sergei Diaghilev's Ballets Russes, couturier Madeleine Vionnet, costume from Japan and China, and of course the Australian landscape as championed by Margaret Preston and Indigenous art practitioners. Linda Jackson had been interested in Indigenous art practices since the 1970s, but travelled to the Northern Territory in 1980 for the first time. She worked with various communities, successfully collaborating with Utopia to incorporate batik fabric into fashionable garments (Healy 2007). Kee and Jackson either created their own textiles or commissioned artists to work with them. Kee's spectacular *Black Opal* design was contracted by Karl Lagerfeld and incorporated into his inaugural 1983 Chanel ready-to-wear collection (Healy 2007: 31–2).

While the National Gallery of Australia (hereafter referred to in this chapter as the National Gallery) was only established in 1973 and Kee and Jackson's fashion design had synergistic connections to the spirit of the times, it must be noted that other Australian public art galleries and museums had a history of collecting fashion, costume and textiles that dated back to the late nineteenth century. 'The first textiles were acquired in 1895 by the National Gallery of Victoria' (Somerville and Leong 2008). While the Powerhouse Museum in Sydney was established in 1988, its first acquisition was a dozen 'doilies' (actually dress trims) embellished with iridescent beetle wings and two cashmere smoking caps from India donated by Professor Liversidge, a founding trustee in 1883 (Jones 2009). The Powerhouse Museum has as its antecedent the Technological, Industrial and Sanitary Museum, established in 1880.

Both the Powerhouse Museum and the National Gallery of Victoria, established as they were in the nineteenth century, emerged in the colonies as civilising influences. The Powerhouse Museum has its origins in the Sydney International Exhibition of 1879, while the National Gallery of Victoria, established in 1861 and significantly enhanced by the Felton Bequest of 1904, became at that time one of the richest art museums in the world. Through stealth and opportunism, this public gallery and its collections have grown to embrace the encyclopedic ideals of the universal art museum.

In 2003, with the opening of the refurbished galleries on St Kilda Road, the National Gallery of Victoria established NGV International on the site. To celebrate the occasion, a series of publications exploring different aspects of this museum's diverse international collections were produced:

> The first group of textiles was acquired by the NGV in 1895, and consisted of a small group of Indian block-printed textiles. However, it was not until 1948 that the first major group of fashion-related clothing came into the collection, with the presentation by the Misses Butler of a collection of nineteenth century garments. (Vaughan 2003: 6)

Like the National Gallery of Australia, which established a decorative arts acquisition policy outlined in the gallery's first annual report (1976–77), the National Gallery of Victoria had also established a Decorative Arts Department – only earlier. In 1980, John McPhee was appointed the National Gallery's first Curator of Decorative Arts: 'With his appointment the collection of ceramics, glass, textiles, metalwork and furniture were brought together with the express purpose of showcasing Australian achievements' (Bell 2003: 249). In 1981 the National Gallery of Victoria's costume and textiles collection became a separate collecting area. In 1995 it was renamed 'Fashion and Textiles' to reflect the changing nature of the collection. Throughout the early twentieth century, the National Gallery of Victoria's Fashion and Textiles collection grew through significant acquisitions and gifts.

For example, the Gibson-Carmichael collection of embroidery was gifted in 1911, the Dr G.E. Morrison collection of Chinese costume and textiles was presented in 1920, and a collection of fans was gifted in 1927. With the addition of the Una Teague collection of Eastern European costumes and textiles presented in 1942, the National Gallery of Victoria's fashion and textile collection became truly international in scope. Significant benefaction has supported the gallery's collection, with the 1904 Felton Bequest being one of the richest in the world at that time. In 1974 and again in 1978, the Schofield gift of nineteenth- and twentieth-century costumes and accessories further strengthened this collection.

In 1973, a group of costumes from the productions of the Ballets Russes established the National Gallery's collection of decorative arts within the gallery's International Art Department. From 1980 to 1986, Diana Woollard was the curatorial assistant responsible for Australian and international arts within the International Art Department. Robyn Healy, who had also been responsible for the fashion collection from 1979 to 1989, took over Woollard's role in 1986. Both John McPhee and particularly Robyn Healy must be acknowledged for their stewardship, insightful curatorship and well-considered fashion and textile acquisitions, displayed and collected throughout the 1970s and 1980s.

From 1983, Robyn Healy at the National Gallery curated a number of exhibitions that drew from and acknowledged the gallery's growing and important fashion collection. Exhibitions such as *Mariano Fortuny* (10 October 1983 to 18 March 1984), *The Twenties* (13 October 1984 to 31 March 1985), *Plastic, Rubber and Leather: Alternative Dress and Decoration* (22 March to 2 November 1986), *Diaghilev's Designers: The Second Generation* (15 November 1986 to 14 June 1987) and *New Fashion for the 80s* (16 May to 2 August 1987) are examples of insightful exhibition curatorship, informed and supported by savvy acquisitions.

In 1985, some twelve years after Jenny Kee opened the store Flamingo Park and three years after Linda Jackson opened her own shop, Bush Couture, John McPhee (then) Senior Curator in Australian Art and Robyn Healy curated *Linda Jackson and Jenny Kee: Flamingo Park and Bush Couture*. Writing in the exhibition catalogue, McPhee stated that 'both Linda Jackson and Jenny Kee consciously reject current fashion trends and seek their inspiration in the art of the past' (McPhee 1985: 2). While this was true, the exhibition also acknowledged both Kee's and Jackson's spirited collaborations with designers such as Peter Tully, Rolley Clarke and David McDiarmid. The Australian landscape and certain cultural/art practices by Indigenous communities, such as those on the Tiwi Islands and at Utopia, shaped these designers' practices. Two *molorrk* necklaces (c. 1984) and another necklace made of bark and ochre (c. 1984), both from the gallery's collection, appeared in the exhibition under the names of the little-known Aboriginal artists. A reproduction of Mike Molloy's Cibachrome photograph dated 1984 and entitled *Universal Oz Tribe* 1984 fashion illustration for Flamingo Park appears in the catalogue (see Figure 7.3).

**7.3** *Universal Oz Tribe*, 1984, fashion illustration for Flamingo Park
Photo: Mike Molloy. Courtesy Jenny Kee

In the same year, Elina Mackay authored a full-colour publication titled *The Great Aussie Fashion: Australian Fashion Designers 1984–85*; the same Molloy photograph is prominently displayed in this book. This publication was part designer profiles, part trade journal. Writing in the foreword, Mackay notes:

> Australian designers have come to terms with their unique environment. Our lifestyle creates a specialised demand for fashion that complements and reflects the easy, relaxed, often sporty activities of Australian people . . . The real richness in Australian fashion lies in the multi-cultural background of our people . . . there are no boundaries . . . (1984: 1)

The exhibition titled *Plastic, Rubber and Leather: Alternative Dress and Decoration*, which was curated by McPhee and Healy for the National Gallery in 1986, championed in part 'art-clothes' – a term coined by Jane de Teliga who, as Assistant Curator of Prints and Drawings, curated an exhibition at the Art Gallery of New South Wales in December 1980 titled *Project 33 – Art Clothes*:

> This exhibition was a seminal display, positioning local contemporary fashion in line with avant-garde art movements. And [it was] staged in context of a contemporary art project housed in a state gallery that did not represent fashion in its permanent collection. (Healy 2007: 32)

*Project 33 – Art Clothes* embraced designers such as Peter Tully and Katie Pye with their sensationalist design flair. Wearable art objects from this exhibition were purchased by the National Gallery of Australia and the Powerhouse Museum. In 1996, the Powerhouse Museum, under the curatorial directorship of Judith O'Callaghan and Robert Swieca, and supported by Glynis Jones, curated *Absolutely Mardi Gras: Costume and Design of the Sydney Gay & Lesbian Mardi Gras*. This exhibition explored the phenomenon of Mardi Gras and celebrated the work of designers such as Peter Tully. This designer was 'inspired by the way tribes created an identity through their ceremonial or party costumes, [and] Tully was determined to create a cultural identity for his own gay tribe . . .' (Jones et al. 1996: 64). Writing in the exhibition catalogue, Glynis Jones stated:

> when people think of Sydney Gay & Lesbian Mardi Gras, they usually think of costumes for these embody all the reasons for the parade itself: celebration, identity, community, creativity, fantasy, subversion and politics. (Jones 1996: 35)

The last three decades of the twentieth century saw the National Gallery of Australia, the National Gallery of Victoria and the Powerhouse Museum curate a broad range of fashion exhibitions. Collectively, these exhibitions enabled thousands of museum visitors to see dress not only as a form of personal expression, fantasy and creativity, but also as a vehicle that individually or collectively spoke about the particularity of being Australian.

In Melbourne, the Fashion Design Council of Australia (FDC) also championed creative individuality. The Council was established there in 1984 as a peak body representing the interests of individual fashion designers. It encouraged young designers to be provocative and experimental, separating themselves from the conventions of mainstream fashion. While the fashion curator used the exhibition and museum to objectify dress, the FDC exposed fashion through photography, film, performances, catwalks, a retail shop, nightclubs and business seminars. For example, it supported dance performances such as *No Fire Escape from Fashion*, staged by the provocative artists Leigh Bowery and Michael Clarke & Co, and extraordinary parades starting with *Fashion 84 Heroic Fashion*. These events and others extended the rather safe parameters of fashion displayed in the museum. As Robyn Healy contends, 'perhaps the real legacy of the FDC is in the ambitious infrastructure it pioneered . . . Essentially [it] targeted the future . . .' (2007: 34).

The FDC stimulated and supported local highly creative and innovative fashion designers, especially those based in Melbourne. In 1989, curator Jane de Teliga took Australian fashion overseas in the exhibition *Australian Fashion: The Contemporary Art*. The Powerhouse Museum developed this exhibition in partnership with London's Victoria and Albert Museum. Terence Measham the (then) director of the Museum of Applied Arts and Sciences (which administered the Powerhouse Museum) stated in a foreword to the exhibition catalogue:

> [T]he Powerhouse Museum was very pleased to accept the invitation of the Visual Arts/Craft Board of the Australia Council to be the organising museum for *Australian Fashion: The Contemporary Art*, our first major overseas exhibition . . . The London showing of this exhibition offers the first opportunity for innovative Australian fashion, textiles and jewellery designers to exhibit overseas. The collection reflects our multicultural heritage, the unique Australian environment and our distinctive dry humour and a sophisticated awareness of international trends. (Powerhouse Museum 1989: n.p.)

*Australian Fashion: The Contemporary Art* was, as de Teliga wrote in the catalogue, 'an extraordinary collection of things to wear by more than 50 Australian designers' (Powerhouse Museum 1989: 5).

## Curating fashion and the twenty-first century

The 1990s saw further growth in the fashion and textiles collections of the National Gallery, the National Gallery of Victoria and the Powerhouse Museum. This growth, plus a certain positioning by these public galleries to articulate difference, afforded all museums opportunities to explore the strengths of their collections. *Dressed to Kill: 100 Years of Fashion*, curated by Roger Leong for the National Gallery in 1994, is one such example. *Dressed to Kill* was the first major exhibition that focused on the entire history of high fashion drawn principally from an Australian public collection. From the gallery's press release dated 30 November 1993, Leong is quoted as saying:

> We have tried to capture and express the excitement, the drama, and the humour with which the very best fashion is associated, in order to communicate the designer's aesthetic and intellectual idea . . . the new concepts and visions of dress which the designers have brought to fashion are the major focus of our interpretation . . . [this] exhibition is a multi-media display.

At the beginning of this decade, the diversity of Australia's unique Aboriginal and Torres Strait Islander cultures was showcased at the Powerhouse Museum from April 2000. James Wilson-Miller and Steve Miller, both Indigenous men, curated *Bayagul: Speaking Up – Contemporary Indigenous Communications*. A music curator, Michael Lea, and decorative arts curator, Lindie Ward, completed the team. A new dedicated Koori Gallery located the exhibition. In the exhibition catalogue, a section titled 'Fashion and design: colours of the land' explained:

> Traditional clothing shows ingenuity for making do with available natural materials . . . Contemporary Indigenous fashion shows a similar ingenuity but the materials are more likely to be silks, cotton and wool. The emphasis is on the textiles and the vibrant Aboriginal colours and images created from dyes, batik, screen-printing and even direct application of paint. (2000: 21)

In the emerging twenty-first century, exhibitions have become the medium through which most art becomes known. In the political economy of art and the museum, exhibitions are the primary sites of exchange where signification is constructed, maintained and occasionally deconstructed:

> Part spectacle, part socio-historical event, part structuring device, exhibitions – especially exhibitions of contemporary art – establish and administer the cultural meaning of art. (Greenberg et al. 1996: n.p.)

Realising a set of ideas by incorporating objects, images, text and multimedia in a particular physical structure, the temporary exhibition has become the core business of today's museum. What to curate is, more than ever before, a question that has currency. The answers lie in a myriad of criteria the museum uses to measure relevance and success, with the most obvious of these being attendance and the least understood or examined being the curatorial premise. While museums have been called 'safe places for unsafe ideas', the last nine years in Australia have arguably witnessed some remarkable curatorship of exhibitions about fashion, textiles, dress, creativity and inspiration. In this essay, I have singled out two exhibitions which I believe speak with conviction about the ongoing yet ever-changing role of the contemporary public art museum and fashion design.

As previously stated, the temporary exhibition has currency only if the curatorship has contention. A sound rationale gives an exhibition its legitimacy. *Martin Grant Paris*, curated by Katie Somerville, opened at the National Gallery of Victoria in December 2005 (see Figure 7.1). This exhibition depended on a trustworthy working relationship between the fashion designer Martin Grant, the curator and the gallery. As Somerville stated in a recent interview about the show, 'this exhibition was more akin to a contemporary art installation' (Somerville 2008). The Martin Grant exhibition, like Judith Clark's *Malign Muses*, was about ideas, inspiration and associative connections – the conceptual processes with which a fashion designer like Grant constantly engages in order to translate ideas into fashioned garments.

Somerville's somewhat *ahistorical* curatorship is further understood when we consider how this exhibition was constructed, both physically and metaphorically. While this exhibition employed a chronology embracing 'works spanning the years from the early 1990s, designed after [Grant] established his label in Paris, through to the [then] recent collections for spring-summer 2006' (Somerville 2005: n.p.), it was intersected with the introduction of 'garments, drawings, paintings, photographs and installations created by Grant and some of his other artistic collaborators'. Included in this exhibition were additional objects, which offered 'an insight into this fashion designer's influences, and the recurring themes and sculptural forms that characterise his approach to design' (Somerville 2005: n p).

Like Judith Clark in her 2004 *Malign Muses* show, Grant regularly employs the history of fashion as a reference tool. This designer also has a fascination with the silhouette. In Grant's National Gallery of Victoria exhibition, the silhouette – translated by the theatrical lighting integral to the exhibition – acts as a shadow or a trace. The shadow can be read as a trace or echo, perhaps homage to past fashion designers. In her introduction to Walter Benjamin's *One Way Street and Other Writings*, Susan Sontag (quoted in Evans 2004: 43) argues that 'Benjamin, in his writing on the city, spatialises time'. Somerville, in collaboration with Grant, has attempted to spatialise time within the physicality of the exhibition.

Most curators begin with a topic, develop a list of objects that evidence the theme of the exhibition, and then work with an exhibition designer to make it happen. In contrast, Somerville and Grant developed spatial solutions in the exhibition that allowed objects to speak for this fashion designer's abiding interest in fashion history, his collaborations with other artists and designers, his innate understanding of the city that is Paris, and the abiding resonance of the crinoline as both an anchor point for ideas and time, and a theatrical entry point into the exhibition. The crinoline references a past event in Grant's engagement with the sculptural. In 1994, Grant created *Habiller Déshabiller*, a site-specific sculptural installation in the famous gardens of *Château de Courances*, south of Paris (Somerville 2005: n.p.). The filmic and totemic references to the crinoline in the exhibition take the museum visitor back in time to another era. The crinoline is also cross-referenced to the ball gown painted by Grant when he was in kindergarten. The designer's childhood painting was also displayed in this exhibition.

The *Martin Grant Paris* exhibition drew heavily on Grant's private collection, whether it was a framed mirror (displayed in the exhibition) once *in situ* in one of the shops in Melbourne's famous Block Arcade, or the hand-stitched detailing of his *Stitch Coat 2004*. This garment was inspired by the collaborative nature of Grant's and Rosslynd Piggott's friendship. This work and others in the exhibition provided a conscious meditation on their mutual interests. Maybe the exhibition *Martin Grant Paris* could be understood as a group of memory rooms, with each room understood through the objects on show. Or possibly the exhibition could be interpreted as a memory theatre. Frances Yates (quoted in Evans 2004: 45) explains that 'memory systems impressed on imaginary or real architectures [were] first used by the ancient Greeks.'

*Martin Grant Paris* represents a new form of curatorship. The curatorial rationale allows the museum visitor to partially chart the conceptual and creative processes of the fashion designer. Grant's way of thinking and doing has been exposed. Peter Vergo's *New Museology* (1989) (where the museum experience became more visitor focused) has been enhanced by Somerville's new form of curatorship. *Martin Grant Paris* became a laboratory of ideas, exposed for all museum visitors to see. Some garments from the *Martin Grant Paris* exhibition were acquired by the National Gallery of Victoria for its permanent collection.

Another equally innovative exhibition, *Sourcing the Muse* (12 April to 21 July 2002), was curated by Glynis Jones, Assistant Curator, Decorative Arts and Design at the Powerhouse Museum. Jones employed the museum's collection as a *wunderkammer*, or cabinet of curiosities:

> The origins of [this exhibition] lie in the Powerhouse Museum's rich dress and textile collections and the emergence over the last decade of a new generation of Australian fashion designers whose original and distinct signature styles [have drawn] accolades both locally and internationally. (Jones 2002)

Like the National Gallery of Victoria's *Martin Grant Paris* exhibition, the curatorial premise for *Sourcing the Muse* (see Figure 7.4) was built about revealing the fashion designer's creative processes. Eleven fashion designers – Akira Isogawa, Lydia Pearson, Pamela Easton, Gwendolynne Burkin, Michelle Jank, Nicola Finetti, Peter Boyd and Denise Sprynskyj, Rosemary Armstrong, Georgia Chapman and Maureen Sohn – working as eight Australian fashion labels were invited by the Powerhouse Museum to consider the 'textile and dress collection and [choose] one or more items to use as a source of inspiration for a new work they would create' (Jones 2002). It is worth noting that the Powerhouse Museum collection now includes more than '30,000 items of men's, women's and children's clothing and accessories from all over the world, as well as fashion plates, drawings, photographs, textiles, swatch books, designer archives and fashion magazines' (Jones 2009). With such a rich and diverse collection, *Sourcing the Muse* was a well-considered strategy by the curator to give this museum's collection a currency and relevance for contemporary fashion designers. Each designer or team of designers was encouraged to investigate the museum's collection 'as a source of inspiration and information' (Jones 2002). While museum collections always remain

**7.4** *Sourcing the Muse*
exhibition installation, 2002

*wunderkammers*, their curiosity value lies not only in the diversity and sheer number of objects they house, but also in the resonance of each object to its original circumstance, location and culture.

Glynis Jones rightly acknowledges the significance of museum fashion, dress and textile collections when she quotes the late Richard Martin (former curator at the Costume Institute, Metropolitan Museum of Art, New York). Martin once stated that 'one is aware that ours is no mere echelon of objects but a museum's extraordinary capacity to offer history for potential contribution to a creative future' (Jones 2002). A designer's inspiration comes from many sources simultaneously. In the case of the *Sourcing the Muse* exhibition project, museum object(s) selected by the fashion designers allowed each person or team to engage in or with the materiality of the chosen objects. For example, Akira Isogawa selected a silk taffeta brilliant blue aniline dyed day dress with bustle c. 1870 for his inspiration, whereas Easton Pearson considered a little Balkan tunic and a fan skirt from the collection. The tunic fitted with a silhouette on which they had been working. They were interested in the inside construction of old garments. Each designer or team created specific garments to be shown as part of the exhibition, inspired by their curious selections. Jones, as curator, had some preconceived ideas of the objects the designers would find of interest. What she found was that they were attracted to 'construction, dress components, decorative techniques and embellishments and, even in one case, the deterioration of historic textiles' (Jones 2002). Designers chose garments from a broad range of cultures, from 'Egypt to Zaire and China and Europe and with dates ranging from the mid-nineteenth century to the 1990s' (Jones 2002).

However, while *Sourcing the Muse* focused on the breadth and depth of the Powerhouse Museum's extensive collection, this exhibition articulated – albeit within a museum framework – the idea of collaboration. To provide the museum visitor with a better understanding of design processes, a designer's *creative process box* – containing designs, drawings, production photographs and a mannequin displaying the designer's new outfit – formed part of the exhibition (Jones 2002). In addition, the designers were asked by the museum to employ their own stylists, makeup artists and photographers to achieve *an image* of the garment they specifically created from their engagement with the museum. The chosen object from the collection was then placed alongside the newly designed garment in the exhibition. While fashioned garments are synonymous (in the main) with living bodies, the fashion image (photograph) incorporated into the exhibition provided an opportunity for the various aspects of the fashion industry to be highlighted.

While the display of dress and textiles in museums follows strict guidelines, the individuality of the fashion designer was championed in this exhibition. Curiosity and wonderment are integral to the museum visitor experience. And while:

> we are now experiencing a kind of historical *ricorso* to curiosity, whose effects are often perceptible just where we might least expect them . . . curiosity has the valuable role of signalling to us that the object[s] on display is invariably a nexus of interrelated meanings. (Bann 2003: 119)

Somehow, *Sourcing the Muse* was as much about exposure as it was about curiosity. The expository spaces of museums such as the Powerhouse allow for grand narratives to be staged. These 'meta-narratives' were employed in this exhibition to underline the multiple stories and creative processes of fashion designing alive in contemporary Australia. *Sourcing the Muse* allowed aspects and players relevant to the contemporary Australia fashion industry to form credible engagements with the museum. At the time of the exhibition, there were many closures and failures with offshore manufacturing and increasing imports, which suggested impending doom for the local fashion industry. Yet the industry was 'growing thorough internationalisation, innovative design and marketing' (Jones 2002). The eight design labels invited to participate in *Sourcing the Muse* are ahead of the field in innovation and limited high production values. These fashion designers have shown – and continue to show – the way through their individuality, creating about them an aura of uniqueness.

Unquestionably, there is a place for fashion in the museum. While the museum provides a liminal space in which to contemplate objects and collections, it is fashion's intimate association with people's lives, according to curator Glynis Jones (2008), that provides a wonderful base from which to explore the technological, social, economic and political forces that shape the world.

## Note

1  Roland Barthes (1915–1980) was a French literary theorist, philosopher, critic and semiotician. Barthes' work extended over many fields and he influenced the development of schools of theory including structuralism, semiotics, existentialism, social theory, Marxism and post-structuralism. In 1983 his original 1967 publication, *The Fashion System*, was translated into English and published by University of California Press.

## References

Altick, R.D. (1978), *The Shows of London*, Cambridge, MA: Harvard University Press.

Bann, S. (2003), 'The return to curiosity: shifting paradigms in contemporary museum display', in A. McClellan (ed.), *Art and its Publics: Museum Studies at the Millennium*, London: Blackwell, pp. 117–32.

Bell, R. (2002), *Material Culture: Aspects of Contemporary Australian Craft and Design*, Canberra: National Gallery of Australia.

—— (2003), *Building the Collection: National Gallery of Australia*, Canberra: National Gallery of Australia.

Breward, C. (2004), 'Spectres: when fashion turns back', in J. Clark (ed.), *Spectres: When Fashion Turns Back*, London: V&A Publications, pp. 10–15.

Duncan, C. (1995), *Civilizing Rituals: Inside Public Art Museums*, London: Routledge.

Evans, C. (2004), 'A monument to ideas', in J. Clark (ed.), *Spectres: When Fashion Turns Back*, London: V&A Publications, pp. 42–8.

Greenberg, R., Ferguson, B.W. and Nairn, S. (1996), *Thinking about Exhibitions*, London: Routledge.

Hartley, J. (2009), *The Uses of Digital Literacy*, Brisbane: University of Queensland Press.

Healy, R. (2007), 'Making noise: contemporary Australian fashion design', in B. Parkes (ed.), *Freestyle: New Australian Design for Living*, Sydney: Object: Australian Centre for Craft and Design/Melbourne: Melbourne Museum, pp. 30–6.

Hooper-Greenhill, E. (2004), 'Changing values in the art museum – rethinking communication and learning', in B. Messias Carbonell (ed.), *Museum Studies: An Anthology of Contexts*, London: Blackwell.

Jones, G. (1996), 'Outrageous costume and confections', in G. Jones, J. O'Callaghan and R. Swieca, *Absolutely Mardi Gras: Costume and Design of the Sydney Gay & Lesbian Mardi Gras*, exhibition catalogue, Sydney: Powerhouse Museum.

—— (2002), *Sourcing the Muse*, exhibition website, Sydney, Powerhouse Museum, <www.powerhousemuseum.com/sourcingthemuse>.

—— (2009), interview by C. Douglas, Powerhouse Museum, Sydney, 11 February.

Jones, G., O'Callaghan, J. and Swieca, R. (1996), *Absolutely Mardi Gras: Costume and Design of the Sydney Gay & Lesbian Mardi Gras*, exhibition catalogue, Sydney: Powerhouse Museum.

Leong, R. (1994), *Dressed to Kill: 100 Years of Fashion*, exhibition catalogue, Canberra: National Gallery of Australia.

—— (2008), interview by C. Douglas, National Gallery of Victoria, Melbourne, 31 December.

Lyotard, J.-F. (1992), 'Answering the question: what is postmodernism?' in C. Jenks (ed.), *The Post-Modern Reader*, London: Academy Editions.

Mackay, E. (1984), *The Great Aussie Fashion: Australian Fashion Designers 1984–85*, Sydney: Kevin Weldon Associates.

McPhee, J. (1985), *Linda Jackson and Jenny Kee: Flamingo Park and Bush Couture*, exhibition catalogue, Canberra: Australian National Gallery.

Messias Carbonell, B. (ed.) (2004), *Museum Studies: An Anthology of Contexts*, London: Blackwell.

Parmal, P.A. (2006), 'La mode: Paris and the development of the French fashion industry', in *Fashion Show Paris Style*, Hamburg, Germany: Ginko Press Verlag GMBH in association with MFA Publications.

Pearce, S. (ed.) (1995), *Art in Museums*, New Research in Museum Studies 5, London: Athlone Press.

Powerhouse Museum (1989), *Australian Fashion: The Contemporary Art*, exhibition catalogue, Sydney: Powerhouse Museum.

Schubert, K. (2000), *The Curator's Egg: The Evolution of the Museum Concept from the French Revolution to the Present Day*, London: One-Off Press.

Somerville, K. (2005), *Martin Grant Paris*, exhibition catalogue, Melbourne: National Gallery of Victoria.

—— (2008), interview by C. Douglas, National Gallery of Victoria, Melbourne, 31 December.

Somerville, K. and Leong, R. (2008), interview by C. Douglas, National Gallery of Victoria, Melbourne, 31 December.

Van den Bosch, A. (2005), *The Australian Art World: Aesthetics in a Global Market*, Sydney: Allen & Unwin.

Vaughan, G. (2003), Introduction, in R. Healy (ed.), *Fashion and Textiles in the International Collection of the National Gallery of Victoria*, Melbourne: National Gallery of Victoria.

Vergo, P. (1989), *The New Museology*, London: Reaktion Books.

Wilson-Miller, J. and Miller, S. (2000), *Bayagul: Speaking Up – Contemporary Indigenous Communications*, exhibition catalogue, Sydney: Powerhouse Museum.

# AGAINST THE GRAIN

## AUSTRALIA AND THE SWIMSUIT

*Christine Schmidt*

**8.1** Hotel Bondi Swim, bikini with 'LOCAL' embroidery, 2008
Photo: Derek Henderson. Courtesy Hotel Bondi Swim Pty Ltd

*The fabric threads fall into place when drawn with the grain and fray and ravel when drawn against the grain. (Ruby Lorner Campbell, 1971)*

**F**ROM ITS BEGINNINGS as a penal colony at the periphery of the West, Australia evolved into a nation with a unique identity: 'a nation of swimmers with an enthusiasm for sport and the beach' (Cordell, *The Original Mermaid*, 2004). Australians embraced the temperate climate and pursued outdoor activities such as swimming and bathing from the early 1800s. Australian Midge Farrelly, a surfer who won the first world surfing championship held at Manly Beach, Sydney in 1964, describes the colony in a documentary titled *Nothing to Hide*, which tracks the swimsuit's journey in Australia:

> We may have been the descendants of white outcasts from England . . . they threw us in a wonderful place . . . in Australia. They consigned us to heaven and they stayed in hell. (Rymer 1996)

In this heavenly location, major cities and towns grew close to the coastline and beaches were accessible to all. Australian society was neither classless nor a cultural desert; however, with a number of the population starting life in Australia as convicts or their jailers in an isolated and often inhospitable landscape, the fashion mode was different. The clothes worn and the type of production that evolved in Australia provide an opportunity to explore how geography, lifestyle and a nation stitched to social outcasts contributed to the evolution of the swimsuit – a garment synonymous with the 'Australian lifestyle' and beach culture.

The swimsuit is a modern invention that has evolved over the last 150 years, and was not initially classified as a fashion garment. It was much more likely to be worn in temperate geographic regions with accessible beaches; therefore, it was open to influences from Australia and other countries not traditionally associated with fashion. The swimsuit goes 'against the grain' of 'old world fashion', and it was swimmers and those on the fringe, rather than the aristocracy, who were marked as its early adopters.

Early swimsuits for men and competitive female swimmers were produced by underwear manufacturers, and were primarily functional garments that did not require the tailoring and manufacturing skills needed for more complex items of clothing. Fashion curators and scholars Richard Martin and Harold Koda have suggested that in America the swimsuit was driven by consumer demand for a product to suit the lifestyle of a 'health-worshipping nation' (Martin and Koda 1990: 75). Similarly, Australian swimwear manufacturers proved capable of producing inventive, well-constructed swimsuits epitomised by iconic swimwear brands such as Speedo. The Sydney-based company introduced an innovative design in 1929 called the Racer-Back swimsuit (trademark name) – a design that reduced the back width and centralised the straps to ensure they did not slide off the shoulder, which was essential for the serious swimmer and beachgoers negotiating the surf.

## Explosive fashion

A key benchmark in the evolution of the swimsuit was the invention of the bikini by Frenchman Louis Réard in 1946. The design – essentially two triangles of cloth each for the top and bottom – provided minimal concealment and sold in miniature boxes 'emphasizing not only how small the costume was but how scandalous it might seem' (Alac 2002: 39). The bikini was not immediately adopted by any nation, and the one-piece swimsuit continued to be the dominant design. Most swimsuit historians consistently reference the 1960s as the decade in which the bikini gained social acceptance as a result of the Youthquake revolution that equated nudity with liberalism (Alac 2002; Batterberry and Batterberry 1977; Glynn 1978; Lencek and Bosker 1989; Rymer 1996). Lencek and Bosker (1989) report that, in the 1940s and 1950s, 'Americans were horrified by the spectacle of so much bared flesh', rejecting this skimpy costume as naughty and French and un-American (1989: 90–3).

By contrast, a number of Australian beachside locales, particularly Queensland's Surfers Paradise, eagerly embraced the bikini. Swimsuit designer Paula Stafford was designing and selling bikinis from as early as 1946, although beach inspectors battled the trend, demanding that women cover up or be sent off the beaches. Wearers were not deterred, however, and bikini sales were brisk. Stafford is remembered as one of the first and best bikini designer/manufacturers in Australia, continuing to expand her business and promote the bikini in Sydney and Melbourne and later successfully exporting it to the United Kingdom and Asia. Not only were her reversible bikini and backless bikini 'world firsts' in 1953, but the bikini parade at the Sydney Town Hall in 1956 was a 'world first' for Australia as well. Unlike the Americans, who patriotically avoided the French innovation, Europeans wholeheartedly embraced the bikini but displayed greater sophistication in the way it was worn, particularly at resorts on the French Riviera. The French version was briefer and was as much about promenading as engaging in beach culture.

In the 1950s, American swimsuits were considered 'the world's classic suit, exported everywhere and imitated around the globe' (Lencek and Bosker 1989: 104). Joel (1998) and Wells (1982) report that the Australian market was dominated by the big American swimsuit manufacturers, Jantzen, Cole of California and Rose Marie Reid. These companies had a huge impact on the style of swimsuits available in major fashion centres and, more importantly, both Jantzen and Cole of California had factories in Australia. A 1952 review of the Jantzen ranges in *The Draper of Australasia* suggested that Jantzen designers and stylists looked at key trends on the Continent and in the United States, concluding that 'the Australian beach girl has her own decided preferences. She looks to practical glamour or fashions that are swimmable.' The report continued by defining the Australian swimwear market as one with specific requirements – swimsuits with endurance to take on long, hot summers and wearers who actively participated in water activities (*The Draper of Australasia* 1952).

Fred Cole, president and founder of Cole of California, visited Australia in 1953 to inspect the operations of the local subsidiary, California Productions Limited, which had factories in Sydney and Bathurst in New South Wales. He commented that the standard of the Australian operation 'equalled, if not exceeded, that of the main factory in the USA', observing that Australian girls 'look healthier and use less make-up than the American girls' and that the beaches surpassed any in the world (*The Draper of Australasia* 1953). The market relied upon an imitation of the Australian approach to beach culture, which responded to the specific needs of wearers who required a practical, durable, yet fashionable swimsuit.

## Muscling in on the action

It seemed only natural that Australian designers would feel best equipped to supply the local market as well as to export the antipodean attire to the rest of the world. In 1952, David Waters, working in a knitting factory by day and cutting out garments for his mother's stall at Melbourne's Victoria Markets at night, decided to experiment with a small swimwear line that he trialled at the markets. By 1959 his Watersun label was exporting to Singapore and Hong Kong and he was creating innovative swimsuits that targeted young, fashion-conscious wearers.

Meanwhile, in Queensland, Paula Stafford began her business by cutting out her two-piece and bikini designs on a flattened canvas secured in the sand at the windbreak hire business she ran with her husband. Continuing to experiment, she made up pattern pieces cut from tea towels and tablecloths on her kitchen table. In 1952 a model wearing a Stafford swimsuit was ordered off the beach by a male beach inspector who deemed it too brief. Stafford regrouped and, showing entrepreneurial skills, arranged for newspaper reporters, the mayor and a priest to witness five girls on the beach the next day in similarly daring swimsuits. As a result, the Gold Coast became the bikini capital of Australia and a Stafford bikini 'became a status symbol', indicating that 'you had "travelled"' (Wells 1982: 113).

Arguably, the labels Watersun and Paula Stafford represent a distinctly Australian approach to swimsuit design. These visionary designers saw a gap in the market and created designs that would compete with more established international swimwear brands locally, and be exported successfully to clients in the United Kingdom, the United States and Asia. The designs lacked the structure, sophistication and finish of a Jantzen swimsuit, yet compensated with youthful styles, prints and innovative cuts.

While Jantzen swimsuit designs included fashion features, the bulk of the range was directed towards functional swimwear for the mass market. By comparison, Cole of California's primary objective was to create swimsuits 'to look beautiful in'. Fred Cole had started his career as an actor with Universal Studios and continued his connection with Hollywood by designing for a number of film stars, including MGM's golden girl Esther

**8.2** Watersun, strappy maillot, 1966

Photo: John Waddy. Courtesy *Vogue Australia*, The Condé Nast Publications

Williams (Lencek and Bosker 1989: 51). Williams in a swimsuit was an opulent and glittering vision, and her aquatic prowess did not diminish her glamour. It was an active glamour that was first espoused by Australian long-distance swimmer, diver, vaudeville performer and silent movie actress Annette Kellerman (1886–1975). Interestingly, Williams played the part of Kellerman in *Million Dollar Mermaid* (1952), a movie loosely based on Kellerman's life story.

From her early days in Australia, when she performed in underwater displays at the Melbourne Aquarium, Kellerman developed a mermaid persona through water ballet sequences. After a season at the London

Hippodrome in the early 1900s, she travelled to the United States to perform at the White City Amusement Park in Chicago, and then at the Wonderland Amusement Park at Revere Beach in Boston. She was allegedly arrested for indecency in 1907 while preparing to swim along the coastline in 'her Australian man's bathers' (Gibson and Firth 2005). Vaudeville, and later the series of silent movies in which Kellerman starred – including the first movie to cost a million dollars to produce, *Daughter of the Gods* (1916) – were vehicles for popularising the modern swimsuit and an aesthetic for the twentieth century, which expressed a natural unaffected beauty that predicated an athleticism suited to bodily spectacle.

Using Kellerman as a prototype, Hollywood directors used splashy, colourful aquacades to showcase Williams' athletic body in glamorous swimsuits. More than any other movie star in the 1940s and 1950s, Williams contributed to fashioning the swimsuit with a sporty theatricality, and designers such as Hollywood's Margit Fellegi collaborated with Cole of California to create commercial versions in figure-hugging jersey with panelling, back zippers and padding to enhance the bust for eager wearers around the globe.

## Stretching the swimsuit's potential

The 1950s were the decade when 'swimwear expressed geography . . . and confirmed that travel was an intrinsic part of the post-war adventure with the sea and swimming' (Martin and Koda 1990: 105). International fashion photographers such as Norman Parkinson and Louise Dahl Wolfe travelled to exotic locations, situating the swimsuit in its perfect habitat – the tropical paradise. According to Muffie Sproat, in a feature about iconic *Vogue* photographers who chose Australian beaches to showcase their work, it was not so much the location that inspired them but the concept of 'a society with real freedom and enviable quality of life'. The result was a fusion of fashion and laidback lifestyle that decidedly 'did not equal a lack of sophistication' (Sproat 2007).

In 1959 *Vogue Australia* was launched and the first fashion shoot was swimwear photographed by Helmut Newton titled 'Early Beach Appearances' – a reference to the first beach experience of the season. The main image has the model immersed to the knees in an expanse of water with delicate ripples circling her lithe frame. There is a sense of space and no specific geographic location. Symbolically, the model surrounded by water suggests

Australia's island status and isolation from cosmopolitan hubs. The images in this issue capture an essence of Australia characterised by expansive stretches of beaches and water and space, but without the typical tropical backdrop of palm trees. Instead, Newton deliberately captures the model in unique and relaxed poses, without obvious jewellery, sarongs or umbrellas.

Again, in 1964, Newton's photographs for American *Vogue* depict Australia as a global landscape through its exotic beach locations and references to those local beach icons, the surf lifesavers. Reinforcing the Australian setting, in another image Newton introduces humour and wit by focusing on a model stretched out on the sand with blue seas and rippling waves in the background, holding a leashed kangaroo. The image describes an Australia where the swimsuit is at home and not taken too seriously. If we analyse it further, there is an incongruity in the caption 'The Special Look of American Sports Clothes' when the subject is the swimsuit and the location is an Australian beach!

During the 1960s, Speedo's primary objective was to develop and manufacture serious performance swimwear, as opposed to high fashion or beach swimwear. From 1959, 'the brand started to grow globally' as a result of Speedo's profile at the 1956 Melbourne Olympic Games where Speedo sponsored the Australian team, who blitzed the competition wearing sleek, silk/cotton racer styles and winning eight gold medals (Newbery 2007: 62). At the 1960 Rome Olympic Games, the Australian team wore swimsuits made from a revolutionary textile nylon Tricot (a combination of bri-nylon and terylene/polyester), exclusively warp knitted by Prestige Fabrics in Melbourne. A lightweight, strong fabric, it not only absorbed minimal water but also had the added advantage of taking dyes and prints. For the 1964 Tokyo Olympics, swimming athletes from twenty-one countries wore Speedo swimsuits. A universal connection between the brand name and performance swimwear was consolidated when seventeen out of the eighteen competitors won gold medals.

The Australian team, wearing swimsuits with vertical gold and green stripes – a first in international swimming, where teams had always worn block colours – had the local advantage of testing and training in Speedos prior to competitions. Speedo improved the performance for male swimmers by designing a skirtless trunk that produced less drag, creating a body-revealing style that filtered quickly through to the fashion market. In the first decade of the new millennium 'Speedo' is now included in most dictionaries to define any pair of short, close-fitting men's trunks and it is the classic foundation block for men's swimwear. While, stylistically, Speedo swimsuits were functional, the association with sport – particularly at an Olympic level – added another dimension to swimsuit design, and fashion stylists for *Vogue Australia* adopted this approach by the mid 1960s. Layouts favoured the one-piece that had the sporty simplicity of Speedo with accompanying text describing one swimsuit as 'strappy strategy – athletic back', and a model wearing the Melbourne label Maglia striding out in a streamlined black swimsuit featuring a bold side racing stripe, suggesting a sporty, active aesthetic.

The emphasis on youthful athleticism was reinforced when the British designer Mary Quant introduced the miniskirt, which focused on the natural body, challenging a fashion aesthetic that favoured the elegant woman with a rigidly structured silhouette engineered with complex undergarments. The result was similar to the impact of the 1920s swimsuit in that women were freed and enslaved simultaneously by the stark exposure of their bodies. The swimsuit had set the scene at the beach; now the mini was taking it to the streets.

One style of bathing suit introduced in 1964 by 'anti-establishment' Austro-American designer Rudi Gernreich stretched the conventional boundaries as to how much flesh could be exposed in public with his 1964 topless monokini design. Gernreich believed that, once fashion was inspired from the streets, clothes were no longer just clothes but a form of communication that could challenge gender stereotypes and engender equality. Due to the sensationalistic nature of the design, the monokini received extensive press coverage and was perceived as one of the last frontiers in the battle to bare all. Although Gernreich thought he was freeing women from the bonds of fashion, the monokini was ridiculed by the media and provided more witty entertainment than women's liberation, and all at women's expense! The more conventional 'Scandal Suit' was introduced by Cole of California in the same year, daringly using see-through net to reveal tantalising glimpses of the body while technically still covering it. The styling was copied by other American West Coast manufacturers and fashion designers intent on infusing the swimsuit with a glamorous edge.

Textiles played an important role in the development of the swimsuit, with the same essentials for both performance and fashion swimwear. Since the early 1900s, when swimsuits were produced in woollen knits, the goal has been to attain stretch and control with minimal drag or sag when wet. The first innovation developed in the second decade of the twentieth century by Jantzen was an elastic rib knit similar to those produced on jumper and cardigan cuffs, with noticeable lengthwise ribs that had more elasticity and durability than plain knits. Although this was a marked improvement, the woolly swimsuits were heavy and ugly once immersed in water, and required lengthy periods to dry.

The 1930s was the decade that saw technological advances in textiles for the swimsuit with the introduction of Lastex, a yarn with an extruded rubber core encased with rayon, silk or cotton threads. Initially manufactured and patented by the Adamson Brothers Company, a subsidiary of the US Rubber Co., it was a rubber yarn that, unlike its predecessors, had considerably more stretch and control and gave designers the flexibility to create more figure-hugging and daring swimsuits. Australians did not hesitate to embrace Lastex, with distributors for Dunlop Perdriau Rubber Co. importing the 'miracle yarn' from 1934 (*The Draper of Autralasia* 1934). However, Lastex also proved to have limitations. Regular contact with salt water and swimsuits that were not dried out thoroughly after use caused perishing of the rubber component and garment sag.

DuPont would make the most important breakthrough with nylon, a synthetic polyamide, commercialised in 1939, followed by the introduction of Lycra in the late 1950s. An elastane fibre that is always blended with other fibres, Lycra is a strong, lightweight fabric that contours and shapes to the body like a second skin – although the issue of how to stabilise fabrics with Lycra content was not resolved until the 1970s.

## Fine-tuning: gym and swim

Australian swimwear labels such as Watersun, Paula Stafford and Maglia had built the foundation blocks in the 1950s and 1960s, designing fashionable swimsuits primarily for the local market. In the early 1970s they were joined by newcomers Brian Rochford, Sunseeker, Seafolly and Berlei Seabodies. A diverse range of styles were available in prints and plains for both the one-piece and the bikini. The lean and leggy body aesthetic of this decade was complemented by swimsuits stripped of internal structuring, which reduced opportunities to create an illusion of a proportioned body. The new natural look led to more intensive exercise and dieting regimes than seen in previous decades: 'Suddenly, discipline and artistry were no longer bad words when it came to preparing the body for public display' (Lencek and Bosker 1989: 131). The women who embraced this new athleticism regularly participated in sports like swimming and gymnastics, with the swimmers clothed in swimsuits that provided the same freedom of movement men had enjoyed since the 1930s.

Brian Rochford catered for the youth market with the swimwear label Splash Out, deconstructing the bikini top, removing the underwire and experimenting with different cuts, styles and prints in lightweight Lycra fabrics. While Speedo had worked with DuPont to create technologically advanced, performance-enhancing swimsuits for competition, Rochford went further, closely collaborating with DuPont and Heathcote Textiles in Melbourne to create new fabrics that showcased the body for fashion. As a result, Australian designers had a competitive edge, creating snugly fitting, sleek swimsuits that did not sag when wet and dried quickly.

According to Rochford, swimwear during this period was a form of fashion where there was nothing to copy, countering a criticism that has long been directed at Australian designers. Rochford argues that Australian swimsuit designers produced some of the best swimsuits in the world due to an affinity with the beach combined with high levels of participation in outdoor activities, both for sport and for leisure pursuits (personal correspondence, 5 March 2007). Rochford's vision was to thread form and function to create youthful, edgy swimsuits, which were fashion garments with an ability to withstand high usage.

This modernist approach to swimsuit design was adopted by a number of enduring Australian brands that also commenced business in this decade. Warren and Vicky McKinney started Sunseeker, a Western Australian-based company, in 1970 after returning from a sailing holiday in the Caribbean. The swimsuit designs were driven by the idea of a beach lifestyle and having fun. Starting with crocheted bikinis and moving on to the production of distinctively clean, sharp designs manufactured in imported textiles, Sunseeker became the dominant brand nationally over the next twenty years.

Seafolly, currently one of Australia's largest swimwear companies with a major export market, was launched in 1975. Again, designs focused on the beach lifestyle, practical separates and bold prints. Seafolly, Sunseeker and Splash Out (later Brian Rochford) were building on a tradition created by early Australian swimsuit companies in the 1930s that reflected the sporty beach lifestyle of many coastal-dwelling Australians – brands such as Black Lance and This'le Fit, which produced swimsuits attributed with qualities such as Speed Cut, Surf Cut and Surf Suits.

One of Australia's fashion-forward swimsuit designers in the 1970s was Robin Garland, a former international fashion model, who created minimalist

swimsuit designs for well-proportioned bodies. Joel describes her designs as 'racy', and although some David Jones buyers had reservations due to the minuscule size of the swimsuits, they sold like 'hot cakes' (Joel 1998: 207). Garland's swimsuits were manufactured in both Australia and Europe from textiles produced and printed in Italy. Garland's bikinis were 'appealingly brief . . . fluid, feminine and sexy' (*Vogue Australia* 1976) and bikini designs from the 1974 collection provided 'Bondi' with tantalising product placement boldly printed on the bikini bottom, ensuring everyone knew that the place to be seen at or associated with was an Australian beach.

Yet Australian designers were not designing the briefest bikinis. The skimpiest styles, including the Tanga, first appeared on the beaches of Rio de Janeiro around 1974. In the same year Rudi Gernreich created a similar design, dubbing it the 'thong'. The Tanga famously appeared, worn by Christie Brinkley captured in a suggestive pose crouched in the foaming ocean waves. The image appropriately appeared in a 'paper that portrayed the world as a "man's dream", *Sports Illustrated*' (Alac 2002: 162). Launched in 1964, this was a magazine dedicated to providing readers with images of celebrity fashion models and movie stars posing in daring swimsuits, often set in exotic locales. The models appeared robustly healthy, veering towards the Amazonian, rather than the waif-like fashion ideal of the 1960s associated with models such as Twiggy.

Whereas baring the navel and torso had been revolutionary in previous decades, the focus had shifted to the thighs and buttocks. The fitness craze of the 1970s led to sporty styling, and in the May 1978 issue of American *Vogue* the Speedo swim cap was touted as 'the snuggest, sleekest' and a 'real find . . . Racers wear them.' The elite sporting accessory and product of an iconic Australian brand had been adopted and adapted as a fashion item. Not all swimsuits were pared down to racing minimalism, however. Rochford embellished his designs with innovative details including frills, real jewel trims and zigzag binds, while Robin Garland, Seafolly and Sunseeker focused on striking prints. Australian swimsuit designers created a distinctly Australian combination of sporty, functional fashion swimwear branded by lifestyle, the beach and the pool.

The swimsuit moved to centre stage in the 1980s as a garment that could expose and emphasise a body's musculature with the one-piece, a shared design template with leotard styles for working out. *Vogue Australia*

**8.3** Robin Garland, dart-shaped, front-tied bikinis, 1973
Courtesy *Vogue Australia*, The Condé Nast Publications

**8.4** Seafolly catalogue, 1989–90

Photo: Grant Mathison. Courtesy Seafolly

told readers: 'The key to success is a good body, narrow as an arrow, curved where a girl should be curved.' With a tall, broad-shouldered, muscular frame, Elle Macpherson was a model who exemplified this new body aesthetic. Slim-hipped and leggy, she had the look to enhance any swimsuit design. According to Valerie Steele, the 1980s models were a breed who would in time be referred to as 'Glamazons' (Steele and Fashion Institute of Technology 1997: 135) – women with a steely inner strength expressed through bodies that had been rigorously exercised into shape. In 1989, *Time* magazine nicknamed Macpherson 'The Body', a title cemented by the fact that she was the supermodel most closely associated with the swimsuit. A regular cover girl for *Sports Illustrated*, Macpherson was an ambassador for

Australia, while visually connecting the swimsuit and fashion through a glamorous athleticism.

Eighty years earlier, Kellerman had established her credentials when a Harvard professor, Dr Dudley Sargent, measured her as one of over 10 000 participants involved in the first research project about physical fitness in women. Sargent was seeking a woman who radiated health and physical beauty with similar measurements to the Venus de Milo, and in 1908 he declared that Kellerman most closely resembled this mythical beauty and named her the 'Perfect Woman'.

Kellerman and Macpherson represent a physical ideal: healthy outdoor beauties, both national and global identities, with the swimsuit as the garment most closely linked to their public image. Their bodies were their entrée to building diverse careers. For Kellerman that included vaudeville, silent movies, a book titled *Physical Beauty: How to Keep It* and a swimwear label with the New York knitting mill, Ashby. For Macpherson, it was global business ventures including an 'Intimates' lingerie range manufactured by New Zealand company Bendon, 'The Body' workout videos and calendars and, in 2007, a range of beauty products named 'Elle Macpherson The Body'. The common threads entwined in their career paths centre on an ethos that, through strenuous exercise, women can attain a desirable body worthy of display in a swimsuit. What Kellerman initiated was 'brought home' by Macpherson, and the swimsuit established a fashion niche, promoted through Australian bodies and outdoor beauties who were deemed to be the ideal.

Fashion editorials continued to emphasise the sporty, energetic angle of the Australian swimsuit. In 1986, the basic Speedo maillot was converted to a fashion swimsuit in the pages of *Vogue Australia* with the accompanying caption, 'Swimsuit patterned for the all-Australian girl'. The model is caught in mid-air, engaged in an athletic jump under an exotic backdrop of palm trees. Other swimsuits in the September issue reinforced the value of functionality, with captions like 'the muscle-back' and 'the understatement', further suggesting that 'Australia takes the lead in swimwear design'. In 1989, the trend continued with a fashion spread called 'Swim' – 'If you could only have one outfit this summer, what would it be? Swimwear! You wouldn't be an Aussie without a cossie' (*Vogue Australia*, September 1989).

In the 1980s, Australian fashion designers made their mark in a global market with designs adorned with Australiana motifs. Olivia Newton-John launched the Koala Blue boutiques in the United States, showcasing designs that were unashamedly Australian, and fashion designer Jenny Kee, one of her regular suppliers, created knits with distinctly Australia motifs including kookaburras, koalas and Waratah flowers. In 1989, Kee collaborated with Speedo to create a swimwear range that was a spectacularly colourful representation of Kee's signature style and, according to Craik (2006: 20) demonstrated 'a new level of Australian confidence and pride'. However, the use of Australiana and Aboriginality was not a regular event and Hawaiian flowers and African motifs were a more likely choice of print for swimwear designers. It was the swimsuit itself that communicated a sense of national identity and style.

## Fashion casts its net

In 1991 Grace Coddington, fashion editor at American *Vogue*, told readers: 'Designers have stretched the concept of the bathing suit so far that it now includes pieces as sophisticated as evening dresses.' A spread entitled 'Beyond the Beach' captured voluptuous models attributed with 'star-level presence' gazing off into urban landscapes. The vision for the swimsuit harked back to the glamour of the golden years of Hollywood and included designs by Norma Kamali and Karl Lagerfeld for Chanel. The Chanel swimsuit, reminiscent of a 1920s-style boyleg swimsuit, featured the brand's signature buttons and jacket pockets, and it was suggested that Lagerfeld had crossed 'another boundary – with a great "little black dress" that's really a swimsuit' (American *Vogue*, May 1991). This was designed as a fashion garment influenced by existing styles associated with the brand and as an exclusive luxury item that might never actually be worn in the water. In 1992, *Vogue Australia* teamed a Brian Rochford streamlined black maillot with a Chanel belt. Accessorising an Australian designer swimsuit with Chanel not only further fused the swimsuit with high fashion, but also linked the local product to international celebrity. As well, its functional performance qualities were glamorised by inclusion in the 'fashion bible', *Vogue*.

Although the swimsuit was now included in designer collections, fitness and sport regularly influenced its styling in fashion magazines. In an American *Vogue* (April 1991) fitness feature, special reference was made to 'the overexercised generation' and the importance of fitness if women wanted to continue wearing fashionable clothes. The article tracks the fashionable swimsuit's evolution from weighty wool to high-tech second skin and its cross-breeding with sportswear, underwear and exercise wear that had resulted in the interchangeable fashion of the 1990s, predicting that 'it may be that the sports enthusiast will emerge as fashion's true avant-garde.' *Vogue Australia* continued to celebrate the Australian summer and its sporting heroes, in particular the iron men and surf lifesavers who had shaped 'a lasting national identity' and defined 'the way we look at fitness' (*Vogue Australia*, November 1993). Images depict an energetic slice of beach life with models wearing swimsuits designed by Speedo and Brian Rochford.

In 1991 the Pentland Group, a British company, purchased a controlling interest in Speedo licences in America and Europe and officially took over Speedo Australia, renaming it Speedo International. A core design focus was the continuing development and refinement of a swimsuit for competitive swimmers by reducing drag and improving race times. In 1992, research and development culminated in the S2000 one-piece cat-suit, followed by the Aquablade in 1996 and the Fastskin in 2000.

On 12 February 2008, Speedo launched an Olympic performance-enhancing swimsuit called the LZR R®, which contributed to the breaking of a number of world records. The LZR Racer is so tight it has been likened to a corset with panels that stabilise the abdominal core to minimise fatigue during a race and give the swimmer a better body position in the water. The suit's introduction has been plagued by controversy, with a number of commentators and the Fédération Internationale de Natation questioning the value of the records achieved, and inferring that it is a form of 'tech doping' and as such renders the swimmers who wear it cheats. An alternative perspective recognises the aspirational desire of designers and sporting participants to attain elusive and challenging goals. It is the inevitability of an evolutionary design path determined by a restless desire to forge new frontiers – to be makers and markers in fashion and sport. As a result, Speedo collaborated with the American space agency NASA and the Australian Institute of Sport to create the LZR Racer and has discovered that the key to fashion swimwear lies in collaborating with high-profile designers. Since 2006, Rei Kawakubo of Comme des Garçons has produced swimsuit collections for Speedo that retain the classic maillot silhouette while incorporating distinctive graphics that reflect Kawakubo's design aesthetic.

The 1990s was the decade in which swimsuit design caught up with fashion, reflecting trends in colours, patterns and prints with styling not restricted to any one cut. Bikinis, one-pieces, thongs and boylegs were all

**8.5** Zimmermann bikinis, 2007

Photo: Simon Lekias. Courtesy Zimmermann

fashionable, inspired by anything from Hollywood glamour to 1960s hipsters and halters.

While established swimwear labels Brian Rochford, Seafolly and Jets continued to extend their market share in the 1990s, newcomer Zimmermann's approach to swimsuit design was more edgy and fashion oriented. The company's philosophy was affordable, fast fashion, with Nicky Zimmermann noting that: 'We don't create garments for you to have for ten years' (Coffey 1996) – a sensible approach for swimsuits, considering their short lifespans. Anthea Loucas reported in the *Sydney Morning Herald* that Zimmermann's designs were 'sassy and stylish', featuring 'graphic prints and risqué cut-away designs . . . illustrating that a swimsuit could be more than a pair of Speedos'. Zimmermann commented: 'We just never understood why swimsuits and fashion had to be exclusive' (Loucas 2003). Through inclusion in Australian Fashion Week since its inception in 1996, the Miami Swim Fair and IMG's first Australian Swim Week on the Gold Coast in 2009, Zimmermann has built an international reputation as a fashion-forward swimwear company producing designs with distinctive cut-out designs and bold and dramatic prints – a quality product that has used its Australianness and connections to Sydney and Bondi Beach to carve a niche in a competitive global market.

Over the last decade, a new generation of Australian swimwear designers continues to benefit from an Australia clothed in the imagery of the beach and pool. Tigerlily, launched in 2000 by Jodhi Meares, a successful model and entrepreneur, is a brand associated with glamour. Tigerlily's early collections included exotic and expensive designs such as a A$500 000 pearl-encrusted bikini. Swimsuits have a playful edge, with design details often strategically placed on bikini bottoms. Anna & Boy was started in 2005 by two *Vogue* fashion editors, Anna Hewitt and Lill Boyd, who believe their inside knowledge of the industry enabled them to identify a gap for their individual stylistic approach (Huntington 2006); and Hotel Bondi Swim was created by Fern Lavack and Damion Fuller, with a focus on unique prints that reflect the local 'colour' of iconic Bondi Beach. These swimwear labels and a number of others that have sprung up over the last few years all draw on either nostalgic childhood memories of beach holidays or notions of local beach life to reinforce connections with a uniquely Australian lifestyle. As stated in the Hotel Bondi Swim company profile:

> In Bondi summer means surfing, wet dogs, guitars, swimming off the boat ramp and endless hours of snorkelling. In Bondi bikinis are a way of life . . . Every print, every bikini that is created by 'Hotel Bondi Swim' is made especially to express the personality of this colourful and beautifully Australian backyard. (Hotel Bondi Swim 2008)

Over the last sixty years, Australian swimwear designers have developed a strong market position connected to geography and lifestyle, creating a point of difference from overseas competitors. These designers have consistently worked towards producing swimsuits that fuse performance and styling, manifesting in fashion swimwear for the beach or pool that is durable and will last through the long summers. With an international image as a beach culture and a nation of swimmers stretching back to the illustrious Annette Kellerman, Australian swimwear producers have made their mark in global fashion.

Brazil, also remote from the fashion hubs of Europe and the United States, has developed a swimwear profile representative of a lifestyle that is also tropical, exotic and always on holiday. A sunny, relaxed approach to swimwear has been characterised by daringly brief Tangas teamed with skimpy bikini tops. However, this minimalist approach to swimwear may have contributed to a national problem. Newbery (2007) reports there is evidence that Brazilian women have body image issues, with Brazil rated second only to the United States for plastic surgery procedures. According to a study by Unilever, in 2006 over 800 000 breast enhancements were performed, and allegedly 'before the Carnival, it is common to hear on the news that the country has run out of silicone' (Newbery 2007: 71). By contrast, in Australia women of all shapes and sizes gathered on Bondi Beach for the world's biggest swimsuit shoot that culminated in 1010 bikini-clad women setting a Guinness World Record in 2007. *Cosmopolitan* magazine editor Sarah Wilson, who coordinated the event, commented: 'we love a challenge, we're not afraid to show our bodies, we love the beach and we don't take ourselves too seriously' (Safe 2007). This suggests that, in Australia, swimsuit design has attained a balance between form and function.

## The finished garment

> Place continues to convey meaning and such meanings – however clichéd, stereotyped, fanciful and unsubstantiated – continue to motivate us; influencing our consumer choices. (Polhemus 2005: 85)

Fashion commentator Norma Martyn described the Australian look as 'fashioned by geography' (Martyn 1976: 11) and influenced by sea, sand and sun. Reflecting on an Australian fashion landscape, when Kimberley Busteed, Miss Universe Australia 2007, appeared wearing a swimsuit and a lifesaving cap for the national costume segment of the pageant, Martyn said to the world that Australia had undoubtedly taken the crown for its swimwear – and it would seem that, in Australia, less is definitely more.

## References

Alac, P. (2002), *The Bikini: A Cultural History*, New York: Parkstone Press.

Batterberry, M. and Batterberry, A. (1977), *Mirror, Mirror: A Social History of Fashion*, New York: Holt Rinehart and Winston.

Campbell, R. L. (1971), 'Development of self-instructional material for learning beginning sewing skills', MSc, Home Economics Education, Oregon State University, Corvallis.

Coffey, D. (1996), 'Fashion news', *Vogue Australia*, August, n.p.

Cordell, M. (director) (2004), *The Original Mermaid*, television documentary, Sydney, NSW: SBS.

Craik, J. (2006), 'The Australian-ness of Australian fashion and dress', paper presented to Fashion and Dress in UNAUSTRALIA Workshop, UNAUSTRALIA: The Cultural Studies Association of Australasia annual conference, Canberra.

*The Draper of Australasia* (1934) 'The miracle yarn', pp. 20–1.

—— (1952) 'Jantzen review of summer fashions', pp. 26–8.

—— 'Cole of California visits Australia' (1953), pp. 30–1, 42.

Gibson, E. and Firth, B. (2005), *The Original Million Dollar Mermaid*, Sydney: Allen & Unwin.

Glynn, P. (1978), *In Fashion: Dress in the Twentieth Century*, London: George Allen & Unwin.

Hotel Bondi Swim (2009), media release, 20 March, www.hotelbondiswim.com.

Huntington, P. (2006), 'Once were critics: Fashion Week's golden tickets', *Sydney Morning Herald*, 22 April, <www.smh.com.au/news/fashion/once-were-critics-fashion-weeks-golden-tickets/2006/04/21/1145344277851.html>.

Joel, A. (1998), *Parade: The Story of Fashion in Australia*, Sydney: HarperCollins.

Lencek, L. and Bosker, G. (1989), *Making Waves: Swimsuits and the Undressing of America*, San Francisco: Chronicle Books.

Loucas, A. (2003), 'Sisters on the springboard, with designs on a ripple effect', *Sydney Morning Herald*, 5 May, p. 3.

Martin, R. and Koda, H. (1990), *Splash! A History of Swimwear*, New York: Rizzoli.

Martyn, N. (1976), *The Look: Australian Women in their Fashion*, Melbourne: Cassell Australia.

Newbery, M. (2007), *Global Market Review of Swimwear and Beachwear: Forecasts to 2013*, Bromsgrove: Aroq Limited.

Polhemus, T. (2005), 'What to wear in the global village?', in J. Brand & J. Teunissen, *Global Fashion Local Tradition*, Arnhem: Uitgeverij Terra Lannoo BV.

Rymer, J. (1996), *Nothing to Hide*, video recording, Malvern, Vic.: Learning Essentials (distributor).

Safe, G. (2007), '1010 bikini babes on Bondi Beach', *The Australian*, 27 September.

Sproat, M. (2007), 'Bathing beauties', *Vogue Australia*, December 2007, pp. 85–9.

Steele, V. and Fashion Institute of Technology (New York), Museum (1997), *Fifty Years of Fashion: New Look to Now*, New Haven: Yale University Press.

*Vogue Australia* (1976), 'Australian design Spring '76', August, p. 55.

Wells, L. (1982), *Sunny Memories: Australians at the Seaside*, Melbourne: Greenhouse Publications Pty Ltd.

# BEYOND THE BOUNDARIES

## AUSTRALIAN FASHION FROM THE 1960S TO THE 1980S

*Roger Leong and Katie Somerville*

**9.1** *Prue Acton in London,* 1967
Courtesy Newspix

**F**ROM THE 1960S to the 1980s, Australian fashion looked beyond the boundaries of tradition and place to find a distinctive voice. At the start of this period, Australian women continued to closely follow the dictates of the leading international centres of high fashion. Subsequently, the most revered Australian fashion icons were the society dressmakers of Sydney and Melbourne with their skilful translations of Parisian haute couture. This deference, however, was already beginning to be eroded from the late 1950s along with changes in the way fashion was being sold and reported upon. Stores began to feature Australian fashion more prominently and magazines such as *Flair* and *Vogue* were being published in Australia expressly for the local market from 1956 and 1959 respectively. A growing number of industry awards propelled Australian talent further into the public realm. These developments provided the means by which home-grown fashion was increasingly endorsed.

During the early 1960s, Australian fashion moved beyond the exclusive milieu of the salon to the more democratic world of the boutique. In the process, Australian ready-to-wear designers emerged as a new creative force. These designers embodied the rebellious spirit of a new generation of younger consumers by responding to their desire to distinguish themselves from their parents.

In the 1970s, a number of expatriates came home armed with a fresh take on Australian culture. They forged a unique approach that explicitly put the energy of contemporary Australia in the foreground. The relaxed

Australian lifestyle was also inspiring designers to redefine the possibilities of casual wear, particularly through the extensive use of denim. At the other end of the spectrum, designers were responding to the broader market, especially the increasing numbers of professional women who required innovative variations on tailored classics.

By the 1980s, the profile of mainstream Australian designers had reached a new level with increased national and international exposure. At the same time, an alternative culture of independent fashion was emerging, particularly in Melbourne. Closely aligned with the club and music scenes, these young designers recalibrated the structure of the local market by reviving a more artisanal approach to making clothing and relating to their clients.

At the prestige end of the Australian market, the creed at the beginning of the 1960s maintained that the best fashion came from overseas, emanating above all from the Parisian haute couture. Central to this conviction was the practice of importing models: original couture garments that were reproduced and reinterpreted for local clients. A number of local dressmakers, especially in Melbourne and Sydney, had built their exclusive made-to-measure businesses on this basis. With the patronage of the country's most prominent society women, these Australian couturiers stood as ambassadors of European elegance.

The clientele that supported Australia's most exclusive custom-made scene comprised mainly the wives of prominent businessmen, professionals and pastoralists. In the early 1960s, these women continued to patronise charities, cultural institutions and racing events, and they remained loyal to the establishments that dressed them for the many glamorous and often formal occasions over which they presided. In Sydney, the dressmakers Germaine Rocher and Beril Jents and milliner Henriette Lamotte retained their prestige, as did Le Louvre, La Petite, Magg, Hall Ludlow and milliner Thomas Harrison in Melbourne.

The demand for exclusive, custom-made clothes and hats was, however, shrinking in tandem with the growing informality of the Australian way of life during the 1960s. Some dressmaking establishments, such as Le Louvre, responded accordingly and began importing deluxe ready-to-wear clothes, which became the key to their ultimate survival against the growing tide of closures among the exclusive dressmaking scene during the late 1960s and early 1970s. At the same time, the practice of reproducing models from Parisian couturiers was being more widely

**9.2** Lucas, cover of *Fashion Book,* 1961, Autumn range

Courtesy National Gallery of Victoria, Melbourne

offered by ready-to-wear companies such as Lucas of Ballarat and the department stores. In 1959 the manufacturer Lucas negotiated a tie-up with Pierre Cardin, which lasted from 1960 to 1963, enabling Lucas to reproduce Cardin's designs. Both George's and David Jones ran their model salons, where French couture copies made Parisian chic more accessible, as late as the early 1970s.

Within a few short years, attitudes had changed considerably. Haute couture was losing its grip on fashion-conscious women around the world. The spirit of youth, informality and egalitarianism was gaining momentum and a new generation of Australian designers emerged. All of this was taking place against a background of entrenched conservatism. The ensuing friction erupted into a nationwide scandal when the famous English model Jean Shrimpton appeared at Melbourne's Derby Day races in 1965 wearing a minidress. The fact that Shrimpton was not wearing the obligatory hat, gloves and stockings for a race meeting further shocked the sensibilities of conventional Australia. This moment was a turning point – the death knell for the outdated notion of respectable elegance had been sounded.

From this point on, Australia's new breed of fashion designers broke the mould of traditional practice and worked in tune with the latest youth trends. The new generation modelled their businesses on the example of younger British ready-to-wear designers such as Mary Quant. Moving away from the existing working methods and established client base, a handful of designers, including Prue Acton and Norma Tullo, championed a new vitality in their approach to the creation, promotion and retailing of accessible fashion for a burgeoning youth market. The key to their success and influence during this decade was their capacity to be responsive to the dynamic whims of an expanding market. They excelled at the production of affordable, ready-to-wear clothes and accessories produced in quick succession. This approach met the heightened desires of the women who saw fashion as a potent means to express and distinguish themselves from all that had gone before. Acton had a very clear sense of who wore her clothes, and was able to reflect her customers' impulses via her rapid-response designs. The spectacular rise and rise of hemlines was a perfect example of this:

> All the kids who I was supplying, all the eighteen- to twenty-year-olds said: 'That's what I wanna look like.' And overnight we were cutting the skirts. We were cutting two inches off, and the next week, another two and another two. (Acton 2003)

The shift towards an overt democratisation of fashion translated to immense commercial success for Tullo and Acton, both in Australia and overseas. With a growing list of outlets and licensees, they were both able to develop large-scale production and distribution of their designs around the world from the mid 1960s onwards. While still in her twenties, Acton had built up a multimillion-dollar business selling across four continents. As well as this assured commercial success, it is also worth noting the significant relationship that Tullo developed with the Australian wool industry, which had the added benefit of raising Tullo's profile both at home and abroad.

During this time, designers such as Acton also came to personify a new approach to the power of the designer's own style and personality, which played a key role in promoting and selling fashion to younger women looking for garments that reflected their own tastes and aspirations rather that those of their mothers.

The most successful designers of this era made the most of the rapidly growing youth market within a local and ultimately international context. This extended to the way that their ideas were presented and styled, and radically influenced the nature of the spaces in which their fashion was sold. New-generation boutiques sprang up, offering a more relaxed, playful and immersive atmosphere in keeping with the precedents set by London's Carnaby Street and the Haight-Ashbury district of San Francisco. The House of Merivale boutique opened in Sydney in 1960. Decked out like a Victorian bazaar, it anticipated the trend for boutiques as a mix of commerce and pop culture. The brainchild of John and Merivale Hemmes, the shop originally stocked clothes by young, local and overseas designers. After a few years Merivale, the designing half of the duo, was creating her own ranges for women. Later, in 1967 under the Mr John label, she designed 'daring, colourful, sophisticated and suave' clothes and accessories aimed at young men (Whitfield 2005: 17). Catering for both sexes, and eventually selling their funky wares under the one roof, the House of Merivale and Mr John was a flamboyant beacon for unisex fashion.

The informality that pervaded youth fashion in Britain and North America spread rapidly and dovetailed perfectly with the relaxed Australian lifestyle. Local designers and retailers were at the forefront in anticipating the international emergence of designer casual wear by harnessing and extending the creative possibilities of undervalued materials such as denim and canvas. Opening The Stag Shoppe in 1965, alongside factories and warehouses in Melbourne's Flinders Lane, Joseph Saba began selling fashionable menswear separates and imported denims well ahead of the mainstream denim mania that took hold later in the decade. Before long, his sales of Levi's in Melbourne made his business one of the American company's top ten accounts in Australia (Rosenthal 2005). In order to cater to the multiple and fast-changing desires of the local market, Saba launched his own iconic range of denims under the label Staggers. Recollecting the experience, Saba said: 'That was an extraordinary era; a great awakening among young people in everything from their music to the way they dressed' (Cawthorne 2005: 50).

In a similar vein, Adele and Rob Palmer started their label JAG in 1972 with an initial venture into the sale of imported denim garments from the United States, replaced a short time later with Australian designed and made clothes. Unlike most of their Australian contemporaries, the Palmers were focused on international markets from the inception of the company. Early success saw the business relocated to its largest market, the United States, in 1975, ensuring its status as the first Australian sportswear company to achieve such a significant foray into American retailing and manufacturing. JAG created a distinct aesthetic by extending the ways in which denim was used, taking it beyond jeans and jackets into a full range of garments from skirts and unstructured pants to shirts and dresses. Critical to their design signature was the use of softer, more fluid denim fabrics in a broader palette, as well as the innovative use of exterior brand labelling that was combined with decorative embellishments.

Just as the casual sportswear market had developed rapidly during the 1970s, a number of Australian designers established successful businesses catering for the expanding workforce of executive and corporate women. Sydney designers such as Trent Nathan, who established his label in 1960, and Carla Zampatti, who founded her company five years later, worked from the basis of a focused design philosophy that filled the gap between the casual, youth-oriented styles and the exclusive – and usually more mature – end of the Australian market. Zampatti and Nathan produced flexible and affordable collections of coordinates that functioned on a number of different levels, such as the office, after hours and travel. As Zampatti explained:

> Because I'm a businesswoman, I've always understood the need for clothes that are stylish, flattering and versatile – the kind that can go effortlessly from office to evening engagements. (Cawthorne 2005: 57)

Both designers tapped into the zeitgeist of the late 1970s, when men and women embraced the tailored suit as the sartorial symbol of corporate ambition. In tune with her Milanese contemporaries, Zampatti drew on her Italian heritage and experience as a working mother to create 'impeccably tailored clothes that oozed European chic, mixed and matched with ease' (Cawthorne 2005: 57). Trent Nathan focused on what he referred to as the 'core basics', such as the turtleneck, navy jacket and pants, as the foundation of a succession of well-coordinated separates (Nathan 2007). His flair for simple unadorned silhouettes, particularly the classic suit, paralleled the ethos of Calvin Klein in New York and Yves Saint Laurent in Paris.

**9.3** *Dress with Sunglasses Designed by Carla Zampatti for Polaroid,* 1974

Photo: Zampatti Bicentennial Wool Collection. Courtesy Carla Zampatti

By the middle of the 1970s, many of the Australian designers who had started their businesses a decade or so earlier were now household names and running substantial businesses catering for a broad market. Their success in the mainstream of Australian fashion created a vacuum that was progressively occupied by a new generation of talent drawn from outside the traditional fashion industry. A number of Australian expatriates and art school graduates provided the local fashion scene with revitalised perspectives on Australian culture and the place of clothing within it. These artist-designers, such as Jenny Kee, Linda Jackson and Katie Pye, brought a combination of irreverence and passion to their work – an attitude that was new to Australian fashion.

After a number of years of extensive overseas travel throughout Asia and Europe, Jackson returned to Australia. Kee had also come back from several years ensconced in the dynamic whirl of swinging London. Their meeting in 1973 was the start of a creative partnership centred in the iconic Sydney boutique Flamingo Park, where they set a new paradigm for the design, retailing, parading, styling and photographing of Australian fashion. Kee and Jackson championed an explicitly home-grown approach to fashion design, which took into account the imagery, brilliant colour palette and climate particular to Australia. Inventive, adventurous and vocal in their commitment to the development of an independent Australian fashion identity, they sought direct inspiration in their immediate environment. Their work referenced symbols of Australian popular culture such as Blinky Bill, the Sydney Opera House and, increasingly, the natural wonders of the Australian environment.

The extraordinary impact of Kee and Jackson's pioneering use of local symbols validated the use of Australian motifs on clothing, which eventually flowed through to the mainstream and tourist markets. One of the first to celebrate the sunny character of Australian urban life was the painter Ken Done, who created a series of vibrant images of Sydney Harbour during the 1980s and had them printed on T-shirts. Their immense popularity made Done a household name and inspired many other permutations of contemporary Australiana. Leading up to the Australian Bicentennial celebrations in 1988, numerous leisure clothing labels, including Kangarucci and retailers such as Olivia Newton-John's Koala Blue in Los Angeles, capitalised on the patriotic fervour.

In 1977, Katie Pye opened Duzzn't Madder, her own concept clothing shop in Sydney. A product of her art school training, Pye considered clothing a wearable canvas. Through the making, cutting, manipulation and embellishing of cloth, she engaged in a form of fashion as a personal performance, one frequently laden with social commentary. This spirit of creative defiance was manifest in the influential *Project 33 – Art Clothes* exhibition of 1980, curated by Jane de Teliga at the Art Gallery of New South Wales. The exhibition included works by Katie Pye alongside clothing and accessories by Linda Jackson, Jenny Kee, David McDiarmid, Kate Durham, Peter Tully and Jenny Bannister.

Melbourne's Jenny Bannister was another key figure when it came to bridging the gap between art and fashion in the late 1970s and early 1980s. A passionate advocate for the development of an independent Australian

**9.4** Jenny Bannister and Ken Gensrich, *Medieval Stud Dress and Belt*, 1980

Photo: National Gallery of Victoria, Melbourne. Courtesy Jenny Bannister and Ken Gensrich

fashion design identity, Bannister was highly critical of the tendency to copy overseas trends. Designing from a personal perspective, she created clothes for people who wanted to make an artistic statement. Theme parties, music gigs and social events were the catalyst for her inspired creations. Her work during this period incorporated eclectic materials, styles and construction techniques, of which paint-splattered or slashed plastic dresses and studded leather outfits were some of the most recognised examples.

The unconventional clothes by designers such as Bannister were found in offbeat boutiques like Chai, Clothes and Accessories in Melbourne's Crossley Lane and Vanilla in Chapel Street, as well as Black Vanity in Sydney's Oxford Street. From the 1970s through to the 1980s, the network of alternative fashion practice gathered pace as artists, designers and craftspeople, and the boutiques and galleries that supported them, grew in number around the country. While labels such as Studibaker Hawk, established in Sydney in 1982 by Janelle Smith, David Miles and Wendy Arnold, successfully took their arty blend of painterly screen-printed fabrics and extravagant sculptural silhouettes to a broader market, the majority of the smaller, independent labels continued to develop their practice outside the mainstream. In Perth, the clothing and textile artist Rebecca Paterson started her punk-inspired Nu Rotics label and shop in 1980 before relocating to Sydney in 1983. Throughout the 1980s a new breed of artist-knitters flourished, including Maureen Fitzgerald and Michael Glover in Melbourne and Peter Bainbridge and Rose Borg of Vain Extremities in Sydney.

The 1980s stand out as a defining era when the sheer number of independent Australian fashion designers reached a critical mass. Particularly evident in Melbourne, and closely aligned with the energetic club and music scenes, these young designers embraced the anarchic spirit of the post-punk and New Wave subcultures. Many of them worked at the intersection of art, design and music, creating clothes for both sexes and engaging in a range of alternative forums to show and sell their work.

## The Fashion Design Council

A year after its first successful parade, the Fashion Design Council (FDC) was established in Melbourne in 1984 by Robert Buckingham, Kate Durham and Robert Pearce to harness the collective energies of the new designers and their creative associates. With the assistance of the Victorian Ministry for the Arts and the Australia Council, the FDC was a non-profit organisation focused on representing, assisting and promoting emerging fashion designers. It was renowned for its theatrical fashion parades, held annually in Melbourne and Sydney, and its exhibitions of fashion photographs, textiles and accessories, as well as its retail outlet in Collins Street from 1989 to 1992. The cumulative effect of these various forums built an audience for the young designers' work and, in general, raised the bar for design practice within the independent sector of the industry.

Designers such as Martin Grant, Kara Baker, Christopher Graf, Inars Lacis, Brigid Lehmann and others established themselves during this period, designing for a small but influential client base. Their work was distinguished by strong silhouettes and innovative pattern-making. They worked with a new-found respect for traditional construction techniques and a quality harking back to the bespoke practices of earlier decades. Other FDC members, such as Sara Thorn and Bruce Slorach, tapped more directly into the burgeoning street and club scene by designing and making their own fabrics to create unique offerings for this new market.

The 1980s also witnessed a renaissance in the production of hand-printed textiles in Australia. In addition to Thorn and Slorach, the Printintin studio (Douglas McManus, Matthew Flinn and Andrea McNamara) and the artist and club promoter Gavin Brown experimented with bold and vibrant imagery that became an important element of alternative fashion. Their free-form designs comprised complex visual narratives that found expression in combinations of clashing patterns and fabrics, incorporating visual puns and transgressive imagery. Many of these screen-printed fabrics became the inspiration for outfits that were then worn to nightclubs, parties and the flamboyant Fashion Design Council parades.

By the end of the decade, the momentum of the art-fashion movement had reached a high point. The success of designers such as Kee, Jackson, Pye and Bannister created the opportunity for a range of hybrid practices to thrive. This was happening alongside, and sometimes in relation to, the achievements of independent-minded designers working throughout the country during the fertile and supportive era of the Fashion Design Council.

Many of these disparate but loosely connected energies were brought together, literally under one roof, in *Australian Fashion: The Contemporary Art*, a major exhibition incorporating craft and design practices as diverse as clothing, textiles, millinery, shoemaking and jewellery. Work was featured from over fifty designers and craftspeople, including Jenny Kee, Linda Jackson, Morrissey Edmiston, Kara Baker, Peter Tully, Mandy Murphy, Tamasine Dale, Utopia Batik, Tiwi Designs, Bima Wear, Bronwyn Bancroft, Liz Williamson, Deborah Leser, Gavin Brown and Fiona Scanlan. The exhibition was launched at the Victoria and Albert Museum in London in 1989 before moving to the Powerhouse Museum in Sydney later that year.

The work of mainstream Australian designers was also celebrated with an extravagant parade organised by the Australian Wool Corporation when

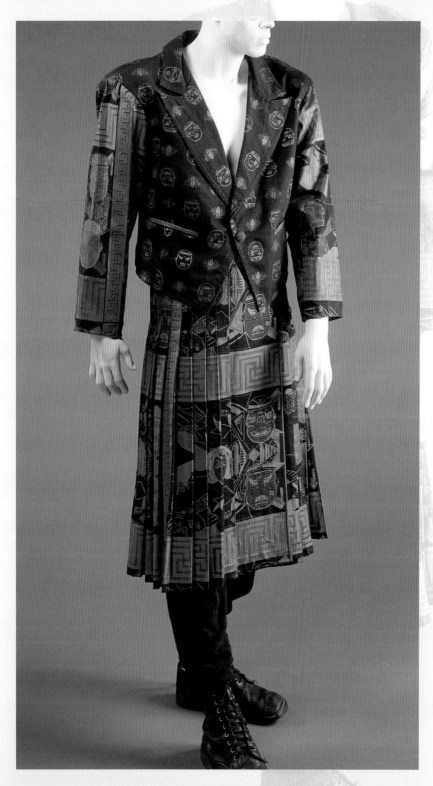

**9.5** Sara Thorn and Bruce
Slorach, ABYSS, *Jacket and
Kilt*, 1985, screen-printed
cotton

Photo: National Gallery of Victoria,
Melbourne. Courtesy Sara Thorn

it presented the Bicentennial Wool Collection at the Sydney Opera House in January 1988. Televised across the country and internationally, the event juxtaposed the work of six Australian fashion houses: Covers, George Gross and Harry Who, Wendy Heather, Stuart Membery, Jill Fitzsimon and Adele Palmer alongside nine international designers including Claude Montana, Jean Muir and Gianni Versace in a celebration of design excellence.

In the decades from the 1960s through to the 1980s, Australian fashion moved beyond the limits of a predominantly European tradition to discover new paradigms of creative inspiration, design practice and professional recognition. During the 1960s, the exemplar of imported Parisian haute couture, the exclusive dressmaker and the private client was losing its appeal. Ready-to-wear fashion became the norm, and younger customers rejected outdated notions of elegance in favour of a more informal attitude to fashion. The younger clients shopped in up-to-the-minute boutiques, seeking out the latest fashions from local designers who themselves embodied the spirit of youthful optimism.

## Summary

This new market was the first to foster a widespread belief in Australian fashion as a viable alternative to international design. By the 1970s and early 1980s, many Australian designers were achieving the recognition and celebrity status that had once been the preserve of their international counterparts. As mainstream success ensued for many local fashion houses, a quite different group of artist-designers surfaced, working between the boundaries of art, craft and fashion. Their irreverent attitude to fashion and their fresh take on Australian culture invigorated debates about national identity and the role of art and fashion in society. As the 1980s progressed, a new generation of independent designers emerged, inspired by the anarchic spirit of punk and New Wave culture. Coalescing in Melbourne under the banner of the state government-sponsored Fashion Design Council, this groundswell of local talent saw the rise of provocative, visionary and experimental methods of production and retail. This formative period of burgeoning creativity, spanning over three decades, was vital to the development of a uniquely Australian fashion culture.

# References

Acton, P. (2003), interview by G. Negus, *George Negus Tonight*, ABC TV, 13 October.

Cawthorne, Z. (2005), *Australia in Fashion: Six Great Designers*, Melbourne: Australian Postal Corporation.

de Teliga, J. (1981), *Project 33 – Art Clothes*, exhibition catalogue, Sydney: Art Gallery of New South Wales.

—— (1989), *Australian Fashion: The Contemporary Art*, exhibition catalogue, Sydney: Museum of Applied Arts and Sciences in association with the Australia Council.

Joel, A. (1998), *Parade: The Story of Fashion in Australia*, Sydney: Harper Collins.

Leong, R. (1997), 'Sydney's most fashionable Europeans', in R. Butler (ed.), *The Europeans: Emigré Artists in Australia*, Canberra: National Gallery of Australia, pp. 209–10.

—— (2010), 'Making and retailing exclusive dress in Australia', in M. Maynard (ed.), *Volume 7: Australia, New Zealand and the Pacific Islands* of J.B. Eicher (ed.), *Berg Encyclopaedia of World Dress and Fashion*, London: Berg.

Maynard, M. (2001), *Out of Line: Australian Women and Style*, Sydney: UNSW Press.

Nathan, T. (2007), interview by M. Trevorrow, *The Conversation Hour*, ABC Radio Queensland, 2 May.

Rosenthal, L.S. (2005), *Schmattes: Stories of Fabulous Frocks, Funky Fashion and Flinders Lane*, Melbourne: Lesley Sharon Rosenthal.

Whitfield, D. (2005), *Flair: From Salon to Boutique – Australian Fashion Labels Through the 1960s*, exhibition catalogue, Melbourne: National Gallery of Victoria.

# AUSTRALIA, PARIS THEN NEW YORK

## NAVIGATING THE WORLD'S FASHION CAPITALS

*Danielle Whitfield*

**10.1** Akira Isogawa, catwalk image of outfit, Spring/Summer 08/09
National Gallery of Victoria, Melbourne. Courtesy Akira Isogawa

**I**N MAY 1999, Sydney-based fashion journalist Marion Hume was invited to give her verdict on the fourth Australian Fashion Week for the national newspaper. The case in question was whether or not local designers had lived up to all the hype. Was the Australian fashion industry truly capable of competing on cultural and creative terms with other outstanding designers worldwide? In truth, the answer was really both yes and no. Yet, as fashion historian Margaret Maynard (2000) has noted, Hume's (1999) rapturous pronouncement that:

> it took designer Akira Isogawa just seventeen minutes to prove the answer to be an enthusiastic yes . . . with only a few oblong lengths of Australian cotton, some printing done in Sydney, some machine embroidery zigzagged on in Melbourne and some ideas that were all his own marked a supposed turn in the fortunes of the Australian fashion industry.

Hume's assertion inspired confidence in an event that had begun as 'an idea based on a group of designers the world's never heard of' (Singer 1998). It also validated the capacity of Australian Fashion Week to provide opportunities for antipodean designers who until then had lacked profile in domestic and international markets, in stores and on runways.

As regional identities within a global fashion system, Australian designers now stand before an international audience. Many are recognised for their distinctive and original approaches; Collette Dinnigan became the first Australian to be invited by the Paris Chambre Syndicale de la Couture (CSHC) to present a full-scale, ready-to-wear parade in 1998.[1] Akira, Easton

Pearson and Martin Grant (working in Paris since 1992) all regularly show their work on and off schedule at Paris Fashion Week. And in 2004, Sass & Bide made their on-schedule debut at New York Fashion Week, paving the way for Toni Maticevski, Josh Goot and Kit Willow to follow.

Collectively, these designers are the beneficiaries of a reconfigured local fashion industry. Individually, each of them has played an important role in navigating the global fashion system to staunchly redress perceptions and knowledge of contemporary Australian design.

## The 1990s: Australians in Paris

By the early 1990s, Australian fashion faced a grim future. In broad terms the economy was in recession, while the legacy of reduced tariffs in the 1980s had brought cheaper foreign imports and caused widespread job loss and decreased levels of textile, clothing and footwear manufacture. Emerging designers had limited avenues for exposure and faced ever-diminishing access to resources. Incredibly then, in 1996 – cited by industry journal *Ragtrader* (16–29 May 1996) as one of the worst retail years on record – the very first Australian Fashion Week was launched.

High-profile, part corporate and part government financed, the event was founded by Simon Lock and Australian Fashion Innovators Pty Ltd. Its aim was to insert the Australian spring/summer collections into the international Fashion Week calendar. Despite apprehension about import costs and the obvious seasonal imbalance between Australia and the Northern Hemisphere, Lock hoped that Australian Fashion Week would engender widespread opportunities for both emerging and established designers as they presented to the fashion media, buyers and possible new markets.

As academic Christopher Breward (2006) has noted, fashion today has become an important contributor to the creative economies of major global cities, assigning prestige and establishing new patterns of production, design and consumption. Likewise, David Gilbert (2006) has observed that fashion plays an active role in 'spatialising the world', sorting cities into a hierarchy of places of greater or lesser importance – think Paris, New York, London or Tokyo. Considered in this context, Australian Fashion Week not only represented a potentially critical platform from which to promote the merits of Australian fashion before an international audience, but was in itself a necessary mechanism for participation in a globally recognised, metropolitan fashion culture.

Although poorly attended by international buyers and criticised by journalists for looking 'more like an intimate replay of the fashion weeks of New York or Milan', the inaugural Australian Fashion Week did highlight the talents of a handful of emerging designers (Tulloch 1996). Zimmermann, Collette Dinnigan and Akira were all singled out for exhibiting a fresh, individual stamp. Chiefly, however, the event served to stimulate public discussion about Australian design integrity. The consensus was that, if Australian fashion was to come of age, then it needed to differentiate itself from the copy-cat tendencies that were perceived to be endemic to the market.

## Morrissey Edmiston

Dubbed 'king and queen of urban chic' by the press, Sydney-based designers Peter Morrissey and Leona Edmiston consolidated the international reputation of their label at the 1996 Australian Fashion Week. Established in 1983, the label was one of the first to successfully pioneer the idea of the celebrity fashion designer in Australia through savvy marketing activities and self-conscious promotion and to be stocked by prestigious department stores overseas.

Initially retailing from a shop in Sydney's Strand Arcade, Morrissey Edmiston quickly gained a reputation for its 'tight, tough and drop-dead cool' aesthetic (Joel 1998). Inspired by aspects of contemporary street culture, music, film and pop icons, the designers' ironic visual sampling lent an international outlook to the ranges. Morrissey and Edmiston had courted a clientele of rock stars, hairdressers and party-goers throughout the 1980s, which helped to raise the profile of the label both at home and abroad. Fans of their clothing included influential style-setters such as Kylie Minogue, Elle Macpherson, Jon Bon Jovi and INXS. That Kylie and rock-star boyfriend Michael Hutchence chose to wear Morrissey Edmiston to the film launch of *The Delinquents* in 1989 was an indication of the label's association with a sexually charged glamour.

Celebrity endorsements generated enormous editorial coverage and saw Morrissey Edmiston become a highly desirable label abroad (Upton Baker 1993). Named by American *Harper's Bazaar* as one of twenty hot new designers in the world, in 1995 its range was launched with an extravagant party at the legendary Fifth Avenue store Henri Bendel. As American designers like Calvin Klein had done in the 1970s, Morrissey Edmiston self-consciously promoted its brand through witty marketing and advertising campaigns. Each season the duo art-directed and produced collectable catalogues or 'mailers' that they posted to clients as a means of disseminating the label's design mantra of 'slick, sexy and modern'.

Before its acrimonious closure in 1997, Morrissey Edmiston had set new precedents for commercial labels seeking to challenge the traditional constraints of the Australian fashion industry.

## Collette Dinnigan

Arguably the most influential Australian designer to emerge during the 1990s was South African born, New Zealand trained and Sydney-based Collette Dinnigan.[2] Setting new benchmarks, Dinnigan achieved enormous international success in an environment where Australian designers had previously lacked visibility and credibility.

Launching her self-titled luxury lingerie label in 1990, Dinnigan's designs were characterised by intricate workmanship, antique fabrics and a kind of seductive femininity that drew from historical styles. While popular with a small private clientele, her underwear received little interest from local retailers. Undaunted, she took a small range to New York which was picked up by Barneys and then by Harvey Nichols in London. This international patronage encouraged Dinnigan to open her own store in Paddington, Sydney in 1991 and to extend her ranges into evening pants, dresses and pyjamas.

By 1994, symbolic and commercial imperatives prompted Dinnigan to target Paris as the means to situate her work within an international context. As undisputed fashion capital, Paris not only represented the epitome of glamour and prestige, but was also the measure by which individual designers were judged. Since the nineteenth century Paris' specialist institutions, couture structure, licensing systems, elite designers and fashion houses and twice-yearly seasonal parades before buyers and the press have given the city an authority to dictate styles beyond its own limits (Gilbert 2006).

In 1995, displaying equal degrees of ambition, business acumen and a good dose of naivety, Dinnigan took a small range to Paris, staging an off-schedule show during the Paris spring/summer *prêt-à-porter* collections. Presenting a collection of her signature lingerie-inspired dresses in vintage fabrics and lace at Angelina's – an old-world coffee shop on the Rue Rivoli – Dinnigan exhibited her sophisticated, modern take on femininity.

Articulating her philosophy in 2008, she stated:

> the product is not necessarily about a new shape each season, it's much more about the details . . . the intricacy of the work, the quality of the workmanship. Every piece, beaded or lace is hand-cut one by one, a lot of it is couture and it's made in Australia. (Demasi 2002)

Pivotally, however, it was the response to her follow-up collection that captured the attention of media and buyers. Not since Jenny Kee and Linda Jackson's assault in the 1980s had international journalists and buyers shown as much interest in Australian design. Given a double-page spread plus the cover of American fashion bible *Women's Wear Daily*, Dinnigan's clothing was described as the 'embodiment of dreams that are hip, sexy and sometimes brash'. American *Vogue* listed one of her lace-edged slips as one of its ten most wanted items in April. After only two seasons in Paris, Dinnigan was invited by the prestigious CSHC to participate in the official schedule at the main venue, Carrousel du Louvre, in 1998. This was a major achievement: Dinnigan still remains the only Australian-*based* designer to date to have been invited to show on-schedule.

Dinnigan's sexy-yet-glamorous clothing, with its rich, hand-worked detailing and old-world associations, found an appreciative audience among the glitterati of Hollywood. Early on she had courted and dressed a number of high-profile Australian celebrities for red-carpet events. Among others were Sarah O'Hare, who wore a Dinnigan wedding dress for her marriage to Lachlan Murdoch, and Kylie Minogue, who donned a Dinnigan gown for the premiere of *Moulin Rouge* – although neither generated as much publicity as Halle Berry, who appeared in a brief, semi-transparent, silver-beaded Collette Dinnigan gown at the LA premiere of the Bond movie *Die Another Day* in 2002.

Such credentials, coupled with industry acclaim, generated sales and solidified Dinnigan's reputation as Australia's most successful designer. Within five years, she had opened a store in London's Chelsea Green and designed an exclusive line, Wild Hearts, for the English firm Marks & Spencer. Equally as important, however, was the fact that Dinnigan's validation by the Paris fashion elite meant she was regarded as an innovator rather than as an imitator. This was crucial in helping to change outdated perceptions about the merits of Australian design and in drawing attention to other antipodean designers working at the luxury end of the fashion market.

## Akira Isogawa

Feted by the press, Akira Isogawa was another key designer whose unique signature helped to redefine the terms of Australian fashion. Elevated to visibility at the 1996 and 1997 Australian Fashion Weeks, Isogawa was one of several designers whose distinctive aesthetic '*mélange* of cultural elements' was seen as capable of catapulting Australian fashion into the international arena. Reflecting a shift in estimations, overseas editors celebrated the 'exotic' imprint of designers such as Akira and Easton Pearson as 'a fresh alternative to less creative times' (Singer 1998). Local journalist Jane de Teliga (1996) declared: 'Australia's image is being revamped, free of the archetypical icons of ockerism and outback . . . Australian designers are thinking globally' (Maynard 2001, n.p.).

Born in Kyoto, Japan in 1964, Isogawa immigrated to Australia in 1986 and soon afterwards enrolled in fashion design at the Sydney Institute of Technology. After graduation, he began retailing under the label Akira through small boutiques in central Sydney. Isogawa's designs were a synthesis of Eastern and Western aesthetics: loosely structured, layered and inventive. His postmodern reworking of antique kimono fabrics, brocade, embroideries, delicate silks and velvets rejected conventional Western tailoring methods to preference aspects of his Japanese material cultural heritage.

By 1996, Isogawa had opened his own boutique in the upmarket suburb of Woollahra, staged his first collection, Not Made in Japan (1994), in an outdoor laneway, and presented a collection of Kimono-inspired dresses at Australian Fashion Week. However, it was his 1997 Sartori collection presented at Australian Fashion Week in May that established his credentials at an international level. Viewed by highly influential international commentators such as Anna Piaggi (*Italian Vogue*) and Hilary Alexander (*Daily Telegraph*), the entire collection was purchased by Browns, London and in June *Australian Vogue* placed supermodel Naomi Campbell on the cover in a red sleeveless Akira silk print shift.

Two years later, Isogawa's distinctive sartorial vision had earned him an Australian Designer of the Year Award and saw him presenting twice-yearly, off-schedule parades in Paris during the seasonal *prêt-à-porter* collections to widespread acclaim. In part, Isogawa's ability to transcend national boundaries with his designs was pivotal to his favourable reception. As with Dinnigan, craftsmanship rather than commercialism was fundamental to his syntax, being the 'implement with which to realise [his] vision' (Isogawa online n.d.). This ethos was manifested in Isogawa's material vocabulary of imported hand-embroidered fabrics from India and the privileging of artisanal textile techniques in his designs, such as hand-beading, *shibori* and origami in combination with digital and screen printing.

Unlike his contemporaries, Isogawa has also extended into other artistic disciplines. Inside Australia particularly, he has moved beyond the convention of the catwalk to exhibitions, furniture design and an ongoing collaboration with the Sydney Dance Company. However, Isogawa is quick to emphasise that what he does is not art: 'If you cannot wear it then I'm defeating the purpose – and that is a mistake' (Somerville 2005a).

In 2005 he collaborated on an exhibition with the National Gallery of Victoria, which examined the artistic journey behind the production of his spring/summer collection, presented during Paris Fashion Week in October 2004. *Akira Isogawa: Printemps-Eté* investigated the collaborative, creative process by which Isogawa transformed his two main sources of inspiration – a series of collaged paper dolls and origami techniques – into wearable garments. In doing so, the exhibition also illustrated the technical aspects of his practice, viewed by Isogawa as 'like engineering, you've got to be able to mathematically work everything out . . . how it fits, how it moves' (Isogawa online n.d.).

Articulating a complex and multi-layered process, the exhibition comprised enlarged versions of the paper dolls, small-scale origami works in newsprint, calico toiles, ten finished garments and accessories. This all showed how Isogawa's unique visual and conceptual language has engendered novel approaches to medium, materials and technique (see Figure 10.1). By consistently stepping outside of traditional fashion discourse, Isogawa has also more broadly helped to demonstrate to the world the growing maturity and sophistication of the Australian fashion industry.

## Easton Pearson

Also gaining attention during this period for an 'ethnically eclectic' imprint was Brisbane-based label Easton Pearson, established in 1989 by designers Pamela Easton and Lydia Pearson. Preferring to define its practice as 'more about a sensibility than fashion' (Davenport 2003), Easton Pearson's distinctive aesthetic has depended less on trend-based design than on its continuing experimentation with textiles and technique.

Established locally and retailing in upmarket boutiques such as Belinda in Sydney, Easton Pearson debuted at Australian Fashion Week in 1998. The label's collection showcased an 'exoticism' derived from a diverse mix of Indigenous textile traditions, rich fabrics and Western silhouettes which held great appeal for international buyers. Following the parade, Easton Pearson was picked up by the prestigious department store Browns in London and Joyce in Hong Kong, which gave the designers the confidence to consider joining other antipodean designers already showing in Paris. The following year, they embarked on their first trip with no appointments, simply taking a suitcase of clothes and setting up in a hotel room during Fashion Week. By 2004, Easton Pearson boasted more than seventy international clients in twenty-five countries, with Italy and the United States its biggest markets (Alderson 2003).

With backgrounds in fashion and art, Easton and Pearson privileged attention to detail and visual play in their garments, citing inspiration from a shared love of 'vintage clothing and textiles, opera, antiquities and old cinema'. Early in their career, romantic ranges emphasised surface decoration, finish and delicate handiwork, which resonated with the bohemian trends found on international catwalks. Later, this look evolved into boldly executed collections incorporating vivid prints, customised fabrics, unusual palettes and intricate detail. For example, the label's 2002 spring/summer collection was based on vintage African books published in the 1930s and 1940s, and contrasted simple cotton and silk blouses decorated with embroidery and beading with voluminous patchwork skirts executed in block-printed fabrics based on traditional Indian and African patterns.

Central to Easton Pearson's design philosophy is a dedication to producing unique fabrics. Each collection begins with the textile and to this end – like their peers working at the luxury end of the market – the duo has built a relationship with skilled Indian artisans who produce exclusive fabrics for the label. An ongoing collaboration with a workshop in Bombay (and more recently with a cooperative in Gujarat) now employs ninety people who work exclusively for the Easton Pearson label, weaving or embellishing the fabrics each season. Often lengthy, the process can take up to eighteen months from conception through to manufacture (Davenport 2003).

Travelling to India about four times a year, Easton and Pearson work in partnership to design and construct each collection at their Brisbane studio. Working from paper pattern to toile and often through a series of fittings, they give intimate attention to all aspects of making. The process is time-consuming, with garments sometimes taking up to three months to construct, then another four months for the bulk production. For Easton

Pearson, however, it is the difference between the specificity of the hand-worked over the banality of the mass-produced.

Lecturing in 2000, Margaret Maynard suggested that this 'style pluralism' was evidence of important changes in the nature of consumption and the way Australian designers were positioning themselves to accommodate the global marketplace. Certainly by the late 1990s, the perceived originality of Australian design was being attributed to both geographic isolation and a multicultural outlook that differed from our traditional cultural devotion to leisurewear. Interviewed in 1998, Simon Lock had attested that 'diversity and the lack of an Australian look [are] a key strength of the industry' (Singer 1998). *Vogue* editor-in-chief Marion Hume affirmed that 'when you live this far away you live with blinkers on' and Australian designers 'have no interest in what the rest of the world is doing' (Steinhauer 1998). Regardless of whether or not isolation produced innovation, it certainly had consequences for designers aiming to work within a competitive, international fashion system.

## Martin Grant

At the same time that luxury labels such as Collette Dinnigan were first presenting collections to an international audience in Paris, Melbourne-born Martin Grant opened his own atelier on Rue des Rosiers in the Marais district. Associated with the Fashion Design Council (1983–93)[3] throughout the 1980s, Grant's profile quickly surpassed the independent fashion scene. His simple, structured garments, which cleverly reworked classic forms, appeared in nearly every Australian fashion magazine from *Vogue* to *Stiletto*, and he had received national acclaim by winning two Young Designer of the Year awards.[4] Relocating first to London and then Paris, Grant established his ready-to-wear label in 1992 and soon acquired a dedicated following of private clients that included style denizens Cate Blanchett and Lee Radziwill.

Grant's aesthetic was a fusion of femininity, modernity and exacting tailoring. His elegant collections typically comprised staples such as shirt-dresses, coats and cocktail wear in subdued palettes. Defined by precise silhouettes and little embellishment, Grant's garments revealed couture hallmarks in subtle detailing and immaculate finish. Some of his signature techniques included welted and topstitched seams. For Grant, the most important thing was 'concentration on the structure of the clothing . . . the whole process of pattern-making . . . it's very much about shape and form and the female figure' (Somerville 2005a).

Quietly holding casual off-schedule soirees for his clients each season during Paris Fashion Week, Grant landed on the fashion map in March 1999 when Naomi Campbell made a cameo appearance in his autumn/winter parade at the request of influential American *Vogue* editor-at-large André Leon Tally. The episode proved to be a key turning point. The following day, Barneys placed an order for the entire collection, and four years later Grant was signed to design for the 'Barneys New York' private label. By October 2006, he had been invited to present his first on-schedule *prêt-à-porter* parade during Paris Fashion Week.

Grant's aesthetic vocabulary often drew upon his former background in sculpture, visible in the clever manipulation of materials and his use of historical references. However, his passion for the history of fashion itself also provided an ongoing source of inspiration. Many of his clothes reference the work of mid-twentieth century couturiers such as Dior and Givenchy, evoking a sense of refined glamour that journalists have interpreted as encapsulating 'the dream of French chic'. Yet his fascination has also been reflected in recent works such as the *Corneille Dress* (2006/07 autumn/winter), which reinterpreted the little black dress through the décolletage of sixteenth-century dress styles and the *Napoleon II Coat* (2000/01), which ingeniously reworked a nineteenth-century garment form.

Like Akira Isogawa, Grant has also brought a wider conceptual framework to his creative practice and was the subject of a solo exhibition at the National Gallery of Victoria in 2005–06 (see Figure 10.2). Through collaborative exhibitions such as *Material Evidence: 100 Headless Woman* (1998 Telstra Adelaide Arts Festival) and *Habiller Déshabiller* (a site-specific installation at the Château de Courances held in 1994 where Grant dressed the garden sculptures in giant made-to-measure crinolines), he has explored ways of extending fashion into other disciplines.

Proximity to Paris has given Grant both a level of success and a knowledge of cut and fabric that he could not have acquired had he stayed in Melbourne (*The Age* 2004). For Grant, Paris provides a symbolic as well as a geographic context for his practice. As academic Agnes Rocamora (2006) has argued, the continuous representation of Paris in fashion discourse as a place where style and creativity are in the atmosphere, or even anthropomorphised as a sentient force, has made the city itself the ultimate creator of fashion. It is a conviction recently echoed by Grant who, reflecting on his relocation to

**10.2** *Martin Grant Paris*
installation, National Gallery of
Victoria, 2005–06

Photo: Helen Oliver-Skuse. Courtesy
National Gallery of Victoria, Melbourne

the city, stated: 'Paris has always been known, and hopefully always will be known, for its creativity' (Meagher 2008).

## The 2000s: Australians in New York

By 1999, the Australian Fashion Week schedule had expanded to include over forty-five designers from Australia, New Zealand and Asia. Aggressive marketing had seen the event host buyers from the world's retail elite, resulting in increased sales and greater exposure for antipodean designers – although, as the *International Herald Tribune* pointed out in 1998, lowered trade barriers and a low Australian dollar probably helped to make collections more appealing to foreign buyers. For the most part, domestic editorials continued to praise what they saw as an evolution in Australian design that was supported by government-sponsored initiatives such as the Melbourne Fashion Festival (1996– ),[5] the *Gang of Five* (2004, Paris) and *G'Day LA* (Australia Week 2006), which showcased contemporary Australian designers at home and abroad.

Promotion of original Australian design across all levels of the industry was also mirrored in the growing number of small retail boutiques in the inner city areas of the capital cities, which professed a mandate to support, nurture and cultivate local designers. In Melbourne, stores such as Alice Euphemia, Fat 52 and Robe Collective – all opening in the mid 1990s – advocated independent designers over mass-manufactured brands. Similar retailers, such as Blonde Venus in Brisbane, came of age the following decade and emerging designers opened their own flagship stores in Sydney.

Beyond generating international exposure, Australian Fashion Week also had an effect on how designers were positioned within the domestic market. National department stores now saw great financial benefit in investing in Australian labels, embracing home-grown talent as part of larger rebranding strategies. In particular, Myer Melbourne, under new managing director Dawn Robertson, waged a public fashion war with rival David Jones throughout 2004. Launching with a lavish open-air parade during lunch hour in central Sydney, Myer unveiled its new image as a high-fashion destination, and over the following months both stores attempted to sign up all of Australia's hottest designers to exclusive deals. David Jones claimed Akira, Collette Dinnigan, Sass & Bide and Willow, while Myer acquired TL Wood, Alex Perry, Tina Kalivas and New Zealander Karen Walker. In a considerable show of strength, Melbourne talent Toni Maticevski remained unaligned, his end reward being that he was stocked by both stores. This financial support served to increase levels of confidence and ambition among emerging designers. As Collette Dinnigan astutely acknowledged in 2002:

a changed fashion culture and mature domestic fashion industry have now produced a generation of young designers who are geared towards entering the global market, are media savvy, who know how to build up their profiles, set specific goals, aim to be stocked in this store or that store, to do a solo show at Australian Fashion Week and to take their collections to New York. (Demasi 2002)

Leading such changes were young designers Toni Maticevski, Sass & Bide, Ksubi, Willow and Josh Goot.

## Sass & Bide and Ksubi

Representative of the more commercial end of Australian design, successful duo Sarah-Jane Clarke and Heidi Middleton (Sass & Bide) and Sydney trio Dan Single, George Gorrow and Gareth Moody of Tsubi (now Ksubi) both started as cult denim brands. Following a similar trajectory, each label began as an underground phenomenon within Australia, headed to London and then ended up in New York, achieving enormous international success along the way.

Sass & Bide established their label in 1999 and within two years had become famous for creating a low-waisted stretch jean, notable for its two-inch zip. Presenting their first ready-to-wear collection, *Lady Punk*, at Australian Fashion Week in 2001 to positive reviews, they repositioned themselves again in 2002 by showing on-schedule at London Fashion Week. The collection – titled *Thumbelina* – was described by *Women's Wear Daily* (29 October 2003) as a not-too-pretty fusion of the old, beaten up and imperfect. This air of glamorous nonchalance was to form their signature aesthetic, and by the end of the following year Sass & Bide was stocked nationwide in David Jones and internationally in department stores in the United Kingdom and the United States.

In 2004, Sass & Bide was invited to show on-schedule in New York, becoming the first label of this generation to be invited to do so. Presenting a collection of denim jeans, slinky sequined tops and beaded mini-dresses, the collection earned praise in *Women's Wear Daily* (9 February 2004) for emitting an alluring rock'n'roll energy. Tapping into something quintessentially New York, Sass & Bide received further validation when style maverick Sarah Jessica Parker wore one of the label's outfits on the cult TV program *Sex in the City*. Since then, New York has had a central role in directing the label's growth and expansion into new markets.

Irreverent and ironic by comparison, the Ksubi label was a fusion of fashion, music and art established in 2000 as the creative expression of the founders' twenty-something lifestyles. Freely appropriating the language of pop culture, Ksubi exploited the relationship between art and product in its designs – an early T-shirt was knowingly emblazoned with the phrase (after Basquiat) 'royalty, heroism and the streets'. A master of self-promotion, Ksubi became known for its rebellious, headline-grabbing antics as much as for its clothing designs. In 2001, at the label's first Australian Fashion Week parade, Ksubi released 200 live rats on to the catwalk. This was followed by another stunt two years later where models were pushed off a boat in the middle of Sydney Harbour.

In 2002, Ksubi made its London debut by staging an installation in an abandoned Tube station. Picked up by Selfridges and adopted by the likes of Kate Moss, the label soon became a sought-after cult brand. Celebrity endorsement also helped to raise the label's profile, enabling it to disseminate its fashion-as-lifestyle philosophy through events, collaborations, installations and publications, and to expand its fashion vocabulary. In particular, Ksubi's design partnership with Jeremy Scott during New York Fashion Week 2006 gained the label rave reviews. Accessory collaborations with London-based designer Richard Nicoll and hip-hop artist Kayne West also delivered further success.

Although an international presence was vital to these labels, the commercial nature of their practices implied a different business strategy for market growth. As such, Sass & Bide and Ksubi capitalised on their notoriety in order to establish flagship retail outlets in capital cities within Australia and abroad. Sass & Bide's first store opened in Sydney in 2005, followed by boutiques in Melbourne and Brisbane, while Ksubi opened City of the Dead in Sydney followed by a store in Manhattan in 2006 and The Bombed Mache in Melbourne in 2007. Challenging formal retail design architecture, Ksubi's Melbourne store was built with an environmental ethos and cut-and-paste style, using up to 80 per cent salvaged cardboard and reusable refuse. Yet conceptually it also aimed to push the boundaries of retail experience by operating as an ongoing art installation that is subject to random interventions by the creative design team.

## Toni Maticevski

By contrast, ex-RMIT graduate Toni Maticevski established his demi-couture label in 1999. Greatly influenced by French haute couture designers such as Madame Grès, Madeleine Vionnet and Balenciaga, Maticevski's aesthetic cleverly contrasted fluid silhouettes against garments of disciplined construction. His approach saw silhouette as primary, and he placed importance on following a traditional design process to determine proportion and fit, remarking that 'my dresses are not resolved until I start draping them on a mannequin' (Zamatin 2005: 23–24). Like those of Martin Grant, Maticevski's garments had a sculptural quality that privileged the relationship between cloth and the body.

Upon graduation, Maticevski worked briefly for Donna Karan in New York before following this with two seasons at Cerruti Arte in Paris. However, despite job offers from each firm, he chose the creative freedom to develop his own handwriting and label from Australia. Like Collette Dinnigan, who expressed the 'need to get your roots here first', Maticevski focused on producing small ready-to-wear collections from his studio in outer suburban Melbourne.

Maticevski's discipline and unique take on cut and construction saw him win the Best New Young Designer award at the Melbourne Fashion Festival in 2002. In May of the same year, he presented a hand-sewn collection of twenty-five diaphanous, draped dresses titled Beautifully Bruised at Australian Fashion Week. The collection was a study of classical cutting and draping techniques, which revealed his ability to manipulate sheer fabrics by way of pleating and pintucking. It also established his signature look: intricately tailored gowns crafted from diaphanous chiffons, silks, satins and voiles, earning him substantial critical acclaim and consolidating his local reputation as the 'next big thing' (Zamatin 2005).

By 2005, an enthusiastic press was claiming Maticevski's clothes as 'dynamic ambassadors for Australian fashion at a time when international buyers and media turned to us hungry for new ideas' (Breen Burns 2005). In reality, however, he was only stocked in limited quantities by local department stores Myer and David Jones, and by fewer than ten leading boutiques globally. Despite participating in consecutive Australian Fashion Weeks, Maticevski had not been able to translate universally positive feedback to sufficient new export markets for his label. His demi-couture methods and the complexity of many of his designs determined that his collections did not easily translate to reproduction in large commercial quantities. This constraint has made Maticevski more financially dependent on a private clientele than on domestic retailers.

Like the previous generation of talented Australian designers, Maticevski first took collections to Paris in November 2004 and 2005, but quickly redirected his focus towards America, joining a younger movement spearheaded by fashion compatriots Sass & Bide. In 2005, he was invited as one of ten emerging fashion names to show at the UPS hub, Bryant Park, during New York Fashion Week. Presenting a thirty-piece collection of delicate silk, tulle eveningwear and safari-inspired separates, Maticevski received favourable editorials in the fashion bibles *Women's Wear Daily*, American *Vogue* and on the website <style.com>. The collection was typical of his demi-couture approach and highlighted his technical expertise. In particular, the *Dali Goddess Evening dress* (2007 spring/summer), which explored sculptural drape, employed 1930s bias-cut construction techniques, irregular panelling and asymmetrical form (see Figure 10.3).

**10.3** Toni Maticevski, *Dali Goddess Evening Dress*, Spring/Summer 2007

Photo: Courtesy National Gallery of Victoria

New York also helped Maticevski's position within the Australian market. In 2008 he was invited to create a high-end diffusion line for Myer, which was to be representative of his ethos and aesthetic but without the costly demi-couture finishes.

For emerging Australian designers like Maticevski, New York represented a balance between status and financial imperatives. The reality for the majority of high-end Australian labels was that the domestic market only made up about one-third of turnover, so international sales were essential to growth and profitability. As a leading fashion capital with a strong tradition of manufacturing, retailing and design, New York was soon seen as the place to do business – particularly for those at the more commercial end of the market. America's reputation for innovative but practical ready-to-wear fashion (in opposition to Paris couture), culture of high-end department store retail and high concentration of press agents, media and celebrities made it an important and lucrative destination.

## Josh Goot

Self-taught Josh Goot was another Australian to see New York as the entrance to the global market. Based in Sydney, Goot had a background in media and communications, but launched a streetwear collection under the name Platform before going on to establish his eponymous label in 2004.

Like Maticevski, Goot first gained attention by winning the Best New Young Designer award at the Melbourne Fashion Festival in 2005, presenting a minimalist collection of loosely structured jersey coordinates. That same year, he showed a sportswear-influenced collection of trenches, blazers, racer-back singlets, pencil skirts and pants at Australian Fashion Week, establishing his signature vocabulary of monochromatic colour, cotton jersey and athletic contours. When he started out, Goot's styling was a straightforward one of tailored comfort. He stated: 'I want clothes to be easy. I want fashion to be easy' (Meagher 2008).

Goot's disarmingly simple, easy-care garments were still directional enough to have great commercial appeal, particularly with the local industry and retailers. His pared-down silhouettes reflected a global trend towards minimalism as seen on the European catwalks, and he received orders from several important American buyers. Later that year, his clothing was featured on the July cover of *Women's Wear Daily* as emblematic of fashion's clean new aesthetic. Within another twelve months Goot had entered into a design partnership with Australian Wool Innovation,[6] which enabled him to develop unique fabrics for his ranges, and he was invited to design a capsule collection for local chain store Target. Prior to Goot, Target had commissioned ranges from Alice McCall, TL Wood, Tina Kalivas and international star Stella McCartney.

In 2006, Goot was invited to show during New York Fashion Week alongside Toni Maticevski at the UPS tent. He received a favourable review for his collection of body-conscious stretch outfits. The garments were seen to typify a laidback, sexy cool synonymous with his native Australia, but he was also cautioned to develop a more pointed design message (Phelps 2006). In identifying Goot's aesthetic of relaxed informality, the editorial iterated perceptions about Australian fashion that had antecedents in the postwar era, but also indicated why his work might have particular appeal for American clients.[7] Goot himself noted that 'my clothes really make sense in America. New York designers are brilliant at doing sportswear basics in incredibly refined ways' (Holgate 2006: 198) (see Figure 10.4).

Temporarily relocating to New York, Goot showed for two more seasons, acquiring leading retailers Colette (Paris), Browns Focus (London), Henri Bendel (New York) and Neiman Marcus (Los Angeles) as well as stocking in Myer at home. Yet surprisingly, although Goot had been labelled one to watch by *The Times* and his business had prospered in New York, he returned home determined to pursue London, stating it was a 'better incubator' for young designers. Goot's decision to reposition his label alongside the more cutting-edge fashions of London was perhaps indicative of a slight shift in marketing strategy. As yet another leading fashion city, London had gained a reputation in the mid 1980s for producing edgy and experimental designers. From Westwood to Galliano and McQueen during the 1990s, to the current collections of Christopher Kane and Louise Goldin, London Fashion Week promised an exciting launching pad for new creative talents.

Debuting in London in 2008, Goot expanded upon his signature silhouette. Moving away from figure-hugging jersey, he showed loose, layered and draped garments featuring psychedelic prints and vivid blocks of colour. Goot described the look as pragmatic modernism while *The Independent* suggested his clothes embodied a 'simplicity of the kind of elegant minimalism advocated by Calvin Klein, Helmut Lang and Raf Simons' (Cole 2008). As Australian designers travelled further afield, it seemed they also journeyed further from limiting cultural definitions. The populist

**10.4** Josh Goot, catwalk image of outfit, Spring/Summer 2007

Courtesy Josh Goot

depictions of otherness or exoticism that had accompanied earlier arrivals in Paris were now being replaced by assessments based on historical design traditions and merit.

## Willow

Melbourne's Kit Willow Podgornik was another designer with no formal fashion training who was able to use Australian Fashion Week as a platform for greater international success. With a background in commerce, marketing and design, she launched her luxury lingerie label in 2003. The collection of sheer, velvet-trimmed bras with jewelled chain straps met with an enthusiastic response and was picked up locally by David Jones and internationally by Browns, Selfridges and Harvey Nichols. Like Dinnigan before her, Podgornik soon expanded into clothing design with an aesthetic that was a fusion of luxury and careless elegance, reinforced by the use of opulent fabrics and glittering embellishments.

Enthusiasm from English buyers led Podgornik to present a collection at London Fashion Week in 2004. British *Vogue* called her the most exciting label to come out of Australia in years, and she received further plaudits in *Fashion Wire Daily*. Podgornik also brought a discipline to her ostensibly pretty garments by combining structural tailoring with loose volume. Describing her design process, she stated: 'I always begin playing with a dress on the form, then adding the hardware – incorporating zips, boning, panels' (Inchley 2006: 152). Many of her dresses featured built-in brassieres that moulded the torso and bodices that imitated corsetry foundations.

In 2005, Willow was invited along with Goot and Maticevski to present at New York Fashion Week. In the United States, her label's sexy, glamorous aesthetic had already found wide appeal with Hollywood celebrities. *People Magazine* named the label one of hottest in Los Angeles. Images of starlets Mischa Barton and Nicole Ritchie wearing Willow helped to circulate awareness, and by the end of the year Podgornik had attracted a total of sixty-three stockists, only twenty-four of them in Australia. Yet, despite her accelerated success, Podgornik also struggled financially. In many ways, it was a dilemma faced by the majority of emerging Australian designers who struggled to match increasing growth with limited resources. For Podgornik, the problem was caused by a high volume of international orders, which the small-scale nature of the label was ill-equipped to handle.

In 2006, Willow presented a third collection in New York. Relaxing the label's signature look for a softer silhouette, Podgornik paraded a series of silk shifts and draped dresses in a palette of white, gold, grey and stone. Her garments were described by the press as accomplished, possibly revealing the influence of her studies with a master draper in Paris at the Atelier Chardon fashion school. Podgornik countered: 'I haven't changed my designs for the American market. When you're exporting Australian product, what people want is that Australian spirit – relaxed, earthy and elegant' (Safe 2006: 16).

Willow's inroads into New York had the important effect of consolidating the label's position within the domestic market. Over the next two years, Podgornik produced a near sellout diffusion range for chain store Portmans and launched a high-end lingerie line for David Jones. Joining a growing number of local designers such as Kirrily Johnston, Sass & Bide, Ksubi and Yeojin Bae, Podgornik opened her own stand-alone boutiques in Sydney and Melbourne in 2008 and 2009.

## Conclusion

Since the 1990s, Australian fashion has shifted from a position of real and imagined geographic isolation to being just one of many scattered fashion industries, or centres of consumption within the global economy. During this time, Australian designers themselves have gone from a position of vernacular constraint to one of style plurality, represented by a plethora of cult brands, commercial labels and innovative high-end design. Symbolic of this evolution has been the literal voyaging undertaken by Australian designers to 'make it' in the prestigious fashion capitals of Paris, London or New York. Fundamentally, their experiences, impact and reception have been instrumental in determining reputation, opportunity and business practices at home and in changing the status and perceptions of Australian design abroad. Today, emerging Australian designers are being encouraged to look towards Asian markets for the convenience of similarity in seasons and increasing trade and investment ties. It will be interesting to see what the implications of further fashion destinations might bring.

## Notes

1   The term 'haute couture' describes made-to-measure, high quality, fashion design and construction. To practise, couturiers must belong to the Chambre Syndicale de la Couture, a governing organisation based in Paris. Couture houses must employ at least twenty people in their workshops and present at least fifty original designs twice yearly to the press, in Paris (*Dictionary of Fashion* 1998: 122).

2  Dinnigan's achievements are reflected in the number of Australian and International awards she has received; Australian Designer of the Year 1996, Louis Vuitton Business Award 1997, Fashion Group International Award for Excellence, 1988, Leading Women Entrepreneurs Paris, 2002, 'Australian Legends' series Australian postage stamp, 2005.

3  A Melbourne-based professional organisation that supported, nurtured and advocated for independent Australian design.

4  In 1987, Grant received the 'Ice Breakers' innovative young designer award organised by *Follow Me* magazine. In 1988 he was awarded the Cointreau Young Designer of the Year Award.

5  In 1996 the Victorian government established the Melbourne Fashion Festival (MFF) to create a public platform for profiling all levels of design, processing, manufacturing and retail. Importantly, the event also had a cultural focus on including exhibitions, parades and lectures and administering a lucrative New Young Designer Award.

6  Australian Wool Innovation also had design partners in Akira Isogawa, Jayson Brunsdon, Easton Pearson, Peter Morrissey and Tina Kalivas.

7  During the 1950s, the practicality and comfort of American styles were adopted by Australian women in acknowledgement of a shared lifestyle and climate.

## References

*The Age* (2004), 'From Nunawading to Naomi', 22 August.

Alderson, M. (2003), 'Far from the catwalk, the real rag trade at work', *The Age*, 11 October, p. 6.

Attard, M. (2005), 'Collette Dinnigan', *Sunday Profile*, 24 April, <www.abc.net.au/sundayprofile/stories/s1350407.htm>.

Breen Burns, J. (2005), 'Style eyes', *The Age*, 22 February, p. 14.

Breward, C. (2006), Preface in C. Breward and D. Gilbert (eds), *Fashion's World Cities*, Oxford: Berg, p. ix.

Cawthorne, Z. (2005), *Australia in Fashion: Six Great Designers*, Sydney: Australian Postal Corporation.

Cole, B. (2008), 'Wizard of Oz: the fashion world is cottoning on quick to Josh Goot's bold flowing knits', *The Independent*, 27 April, <www.independent.co.uk>.

Davenport, R. (2003), 'Artists and artist colonies: the fabrics and frocks of Easton Pearson', *Object*, 43, pp. 34–7.

Demasi, L. (2002), *Ladies Room: Stories behind some of Australia's Most Fascinating Women*, Sydney: Harper Collins.

*Dictionary of Fashion and Fashion Designers* (1998), London: Thames and Hudson.

Dinnigan, C. (2008), Quoted in *Talking Heads with Peter Thompson*, ABC TV, 3 March, <www.abc.net.au/tv/talkingheads/txt/s2178583.htm>.

Gilbert, D. (2006), 'From Paris to Shanghai: the changing geographies of fashion's world cities', in C. Breward and D. Gilbert (eds), *Fashion's World Cities*, Oxford: Berg, pp. 4–31.

Holgate, M. (2006), 'New in town', *Vogue* (US), December, p. 198.

Hume, M. (1999), 'The verdict', *The Australian*, 21 May, pp. 2–3.

—— (2000), 'To thine own selves be true', *The Australian*, *Fashion Extra*, 5 May, p. 2.

Inchley, N. (2006), 'Soft focus', *Vogue Australia*, June, p. 152.

Isogawa, A. (n.d.) <www.akira.com.au>

Joel, A. (1998), *Parade: The Story of Fashion in Australia*, Sydney: HarperCollins.

Kerwin, J. (1996), 'The lace maker', *Women's Wear Daily*, 18 June, n.p.

Maynard, M. (2000), 'The dress that saved Sydney: Australian fashion and the global arena', lecture presented at the Centre for Critical and Cultural Studies, University of Queensland, 18 May.

—— (2001), *Out of Line: Australian Women and Style*, Sydney: UNSW Press.

Meagher, D. (2008), *Fashion Speak,* Sydney: Random House.

Overington, C. (1999), 'Collette's state of lace', *The Age*, *News Extra*, 10 April, p. 3.

Phelps, N. (2006), Collection Review September 9, <www.style.com/fashionshows/review/S2007RTW-JGOOT> accessed 11/3/09

Plant, S. (2002), 'The Akira factor', *Herald Sun*, *Weekend*, 14 September, p. 11.

Rocamora, A. (2006), 'Paris capital de la mode: representing the fashion city in the media', in C. Breward and D. Gilbert (eds), *Fashion's World Cities*, Oxford: Berg, pp. 43–6.

Safe, G. (2006), 'Willow finds a good fit', *The Australian*, 1 December, p. 16.

Singer, R.J. (1998), 'Australia exploits cultural diversity', *International Herald Tribune*, 17 October, <www.iht.com>.

Somerville, K. (2005a), *Akira Isogawa: Printemps-Eté*, exhibition catalogue, Melbourne: National Gallery of Victoria.

—— (2005b), *Martin Grant, Paris*, exhibition catalogue, Melbourne: National Gallery of Victoria.

Steinhauer, J. (1998), 'An auspicious moment for Australian designers', *New York Times*, 9 June, p. 9.

Tulloch, L. (1996), 'Priscilla misses on individuality', *The Independent*, 21 May, <www.independent.co.uk>.

Upton Baker, K. (1993), 'The power of two', *Vogue Australia*, September, p. 185.

Zamatin, L. (2005), 'A star is born', *The Age*, *Sunday Life*, 29 April, pp. 23–4.

# CONTEMPORARY AVANT-GARDE

## CUTTING-EDGE DESIGN

*Bonnie English and Liliana Pomazan*

**11.1** Susan Dimasi and Chantal Kirby of MATERIALBYPRODUCT, *Woodgrain Trench & Dress*, 2008
Photo: Sue Grdunc. Courtesy MATERIALBYPRODUCT

**T**HE FRENCH TERM 'avant-garde' was used in the early twentieth century referencing new and innovative practice, and was particularly germane when it was used in the context of the visual and performing arts. Whether this term is still relevant in contemporary discourse is widely debated. Fashion historian Diana Crane (1997: 126) has analysed a wide range of uses of the term, and argues that it has been applied to three types of 'changes' in art: in the aesthetic content; in the social content; and in the norms surrounding the production and distribution of artworks. She also contends that, in terms of Modernist fashion, it was a practice that challenged aesthetic norms and traditions prevalent in the construction and design of Western clothing and that questioned, at times, political and social ideologies rising in prominence at a particular time (Crane 1997: 128). She cites, in particular, the work of the couturière Elsa Schiaparelli as falling into this rather 'purist' category.

Applying this analysis to contemporary fashion design, this chapter argues that avant-garde practice redefines what fashion can be, and the means by which it colludes with or seeks escape from the traditional or the accepted tenets of the industry at any particular time. In many cases, it can also escape the powers of the commercial market. Contemporary avant-garde designers, like their Modernist predecessors, have the courage to experiment, to go 'against the grain' – and in so doing they can transform fashion into a cultural entity.

It may seem presumptuous to suggest that today's designers are inadvertently preparing us for the future, challenging the very nature of current fashion practices. Perhaps their work poses more questions rather than supplying answers, or promotes momentous change rather than embracing the 'status quo'. Arguably, avant-garde designers attempt to alter and materialise a new perception of the face of fashion in aesthetic, technical or cultural terms by offering new ideas or concepts, extending or advancing new technologies, or underlining new concerns for the environment and humankind in their work. Sustainable design, for example, demands a more responsible design methodology that might consider waste minimalism in terms of pattern-making, seamless construction, closed-loop textile surface design and reusable off-cuts. As we know, new developments in fashion design can encompass drawing, pattern-making, cutting, sewing, construction and decorative techniques, but they can also involve distribution, sales and marketing, and promotional campaigns. In other words, avant-garde practice is not mutually exclusive, but rather embraces a plethora of possibilities.

## Leading avant-garde designers

This chapter discusses a number of leading avant-garde designers, each of whom has contributed in their own way to Australia's twenty-first century cutting-edge practice in fashion design. Among these practitioners are Susan Dimasi and Chantal Kirby[1] of the MATERIALBYPRODUCT (MBP) label, Denise Sprynskyj and Peter Boyd of the S!X label, Gwendolynne Burkin of her signature label Gweyndolynne and Romance Was Born designers Luke Sales and Anna Plunkett. In terms of environmental and sustainable design, Lisa Gorman of the Gorman label is leading the fray in terms of producing 'organic' fashion.

## MATERIALBYPRODUCT

MATERIALBYPRODUCT's design philosophy and concepts are based upon a simple credo: that their studio designs systems, not products (Pomazan 2005: 4). The realised 'product', or ensemble, is embedded in the theoretical and ideational elements of the systems. Therefore, the by-products of the systems comprise the collections. On one hand, this cerebral approach touches upon Roland Barthes' concepts of fashion systems or models; yet on the other, it facilitates a solution to an age-old sartorial problem – fabric wastage. According to Rissanen (2009), there are numerous historical precedents for a no-waste approach in the creation of clothing, dating back to the Classical period of Greece in AD1000.[2] He quotes Bernard Rudofsky,[3] who was among the first to formulate a critique of contemporary fashion-making within a context of historical methodologies. Sustainable design principles recognise textiles as a valuable resource and yet 15 per cent of fabric is wasted with the cutting and sewing of one single garment.

Melbourne designers Susan Dimasi and Chantal Kirby are well aware of Issey Miyake and Dai Fujiwara's solution, conceived as APOC (a piece of cloth) in 1998, in which a knitted or woven tube of fabric, with seams inside the tube to form cavities, was cut to create an entire wardrobe. As this system involved no sewing and no wasteful off-cuts, Miyake saw it as the answer to a global problem – providing an efficient and accessible method of production that could provide clothing for Third World countries. Yet, while it has been very successful in haute couture circles or as a performance piece, no profound development has emanated from the original idea. Similarly, Dimasi and Kirby's work also focuses on methods of pattern-making, reinforcing Rissanen's contention that the onus should be placed on the designer/pattern-maker and not the manufacturer to come up with plausible sustainable solutions. These young designers spend many hours positioning the pattern pieces on the fabric, considering both the positive and negative spaces within the piece of cloth. They explain that:

> The figure–ground relationship is carefully orchestrated and refined . . . and the result seems to resemble a very sophisticated jigsaw puzzle. Through this innovative technique, at least two garments are simultaneously cut from the one length of cloth, one from the positive pieces and one from the negative. Depending on the design, the 'anti' (negative garment or fabric frame made from off-cuts) may be patched with other fabrics to complete the garment, or they may be left open and worn over the classic (positive) garment, almost as an accessory, or used as a diffusion line called 'waste collation'. (Pomazan 2005: 4)

According to Dimasi, 'by defining our own ways of reproduction, we are trying to avoid "sameness".' The pattern pieces are 'punched out' of the cloth and a 'dot system' comprising running lines of fine white circles is printed or punched onto the surface; this then becomes part of the design language. Trim is used as a process of joining the pieces, with the neckline bound first, then the top shoulder, sleeve and seam leaving the trim to run out. The trim is never joined and runs in one continuous path, making the visible seam invisible. The MATERIALBYPRODUCT name is either embroidered or printed on the belt or down the back, with the woven selvage of the cloth becoming the base of the label. Interestingly, the designers attempt to limit the steps needed to produce a garment, thereby translating the haute couture process into a manufacturing one.

> When process informs design . . . chalk is used to mark-up the garments and, as in their Soft/Hard collection, the mark-ups are seen as drawings in their own right . . . Safety pins are used for tacking some open panels and gaps and this underlines the concept of impermanence. (Dimasi and Kirby 2008)

Couture 'excess' refers to beaded sections of the garments, where the beading becomes the accessory.

Having created a signature style, the notion of 'Australiana' or a sense of place inspired Dimasi and Kirby to utilise imitation materials such as the wood veneer often used in the houses or backyards of Italian immigrant communities. Dimasi, in particular, responds personally to this idea, creating a dialogue between the fabric and the environment. As well, they use 'nasty nylon' curtaining patterns printed on fabric or recycled curtains as part of the familiar domestic landscape, and photograph their models in doorways or in front of window curtains to consolidate this vernacular. In their latest collections, the MATERIALBYPRODUCT designers have produced garments that have often extended their drapery to the floor, creating a type of installation within a defined interior. This suggests that, in conceptual terms, the material can extend beyond the realm of fashion, beyond the body, into the physicality of another space. The designers visit Paris twice a year and learn from the Belgians, especially Margiela, and the Japanese designers Kawakubo and Undercover. They share with Victor & Rolf, as well as Miyake, the idea that the spatial concept of designing garments works from the inside out. Responding to the notion that their work rejects traditional practices, Dimasi quips: 'There's no point in taking European work back to the Europeans' (Dimasi and Kirby 2008).

The MBP designers were awarded the Victorian Premier's Design Award in both 2006 and 2008, at which time they also presented work to an international jury[4] for inclusion in a major international project for Barcelona's Fashion Week 2009, showcasing the world's best avant-garde fashion. The Catalan government, in collaboration with the Barcelona City Council, aims to position the Catalan capital as an international reference for avant-garde fashion and provide a platform for young, emerging and independent designers. This committee felt that MATERIALBYPRODUCT's profile and work corresponded well with the concept of the event, and the label's work was seen as a brand conceived within a global context. Demasi and Kirby participated in the Barcelona exhibition and workshop held in March 2009 and gained international attention.

## S!X

The Australian-based designers Denise Sprynskyj and Peter Boyd established their fashion design company S!X in 1992, after completing their Bachelor of Arts Fashion Design degrees at RMIT University in Melbourne. Sprynskyj and Boyd are dynamic, non-mainstream designers who won the *Herald Sun*'s Best New Designers Award in 1995 and 1997, and received the New Design Award at the inception of the Melbourne Fashion Festival in 1998. They have exhibited their works in many exhibitions, including the 1999 Japanese touring show entitled *50 Years of Japanese Lifestyle: Postwar Fashion and Design*. Sprynskyj and Boyd were awarded the Fashion category of the prestigious City of Hobart Art Prize Fashion 2000. They won this prize out of a field of fourteen short-listed entrants – prominent Australian fashion, textiles and footwear designers such as Nicola Finetti, Sara Thorn, Georgia Chapman and Sonya Pletes of *Vixen*, and Johanna Preston of Preston Zly. While their work has been continually highlighted in the industry and media over the past ten years, most recently in 2008, the S!X designers curated *Sculpted Packages* at the World Shibori Symposium, won the Premier's Design Award for Commercial Fashion, and are currently collaborating with Chioda Menswear to recycle and recut his menswear into womenswear.

Although it is unusual for fashion students to immediately establish a fashion business with their own label after graduation, it proved to be a highly successful move. They established an atelier-style studio in Melbourne and treat their workroom as part fashion think-tank and part production house, maintaining a healthy multidisciplinary interest in the arts. Boyd explains:

> We had the idea that we would bring in artists, other milliners, jewellers and possibly other designers. We based it more or less on the Japanese model that we have read so much about, like Issey Miyake who takes on so many different artists. So we wished to have this wonderful studio complex where things like this could happen. (Sprynskyj and Boyd 2004)

Their imagistic sources are many and varied, yet their approach to their materials, styles and products is notable for its visual cohesion and identifiable cut. At a glance, it is obvious that their layered works are conditioned and arbitrated by careful artistic considerations – both visual

**11.2** Denise Sprynskyj and
Peter Boyd of S!X, *Untitled*,
Autumn/Winter 2003

Photo: Lucas Dawson. Courtesy S!X

and tactile harmonies take priority. Influenced by Miyake, they treat their creations as 'wearable art' and their philosophy towards design is linked to 'art povera', a dominant 1980s Italian cultural ideology. While it might seem that their adoption of these two creative paradigms was most unusual, it came at a time when fabric manipulation, fibre art, performance art and installations were burgeoning in Melbourne. Melbourne's multicultural arts policy, its festival events, new exhibitions, theatre performances and active 'outsider' or 'bohemian' outgrowths provided a cauldron of exciting, hybridised opportunities.

When Sprynskyj and Boyd began their collaboration, Australia was in an economic recession and many clothing businesses were closing. Industry stalwarts during the 1990s included well-known mainstream fashion designers such as Trent Nathan, Carla Zampatti, Morrissey Edmiston, George Gross, and Harry Who and John Cavill. Yet both Sprynskyj and Boyd felt that fashion at the time seemed 'tired and very conservative' and believed that Australian fashion needed a fresh, new approach. In 2004, Boyd discussed his initial fascination with the emerging 'new breed' of Belgian designers:

> The Belgians came on to the scene and made everything antiquated, all fashion became totally different and the recession happened . . . It was a bleak time. That whole thing did affect the way we were working we had an abrupt change and sort of shelved how we had been taught at university – just shelved it for the moment. (Sprynskyj and Boyd 2004)

Immediately Sprynskyj and Boyd, emulating the Belgians, radically disregarded traditional tailoring and garment construction. Unlike most conventional Australian designers, Sprynskyj and Boyd rode the first wave of the deconstructionist design movement led by the Belgian designers, including Martin Margiela and Ann Demeulemeester. S!X's deconstructed garments, such as its jackets, often lack part of a sleeve, collar, parts of the outer shell or other seemingly essential garment elements. They began using vintage garments and worked with lots of odds and ends, not only because of monetary constraints but in keeping with a recycling aesthetic. Specifically, it was the use of these fabrics, in conjunction with their decorative techniques, that informed their collections – more so than the experience of their training days, when they designed on paper, toiled, tested and toiled again, then finally resolved the completed piece. Interestingly, out of diversity, through limitation of resources and the necessity for experimentation, these two perceptive fashion designers generated much more playful and unconventional creative outcomes.

After years of liaison with the Australian Wool Corporation in Victoria, they based their award-winning collection for the 1998 Melbourne Fashion Festival on the forms and colours of Bali and selected a fine and spongy Australian black wool, donated by the local Yarra Falls Company. Using this fabric, they added unusual printed decorative techniques drawn from elements of Balinese shadow puppets with lanterns and other Balinese iconography. They showed this novel collection in Greville Street, Prahran – one of Melbourne's bohemian centres. The models had their faces painted white and wore masks, which was most daring for the time. The impact of their work was overwhelming, and Melbourne fashion designer Jenny Bannister and Robert Buckingham, co-founders of the Fashion Design Council, fought for the duo to be presented with the festival award. What was immediately recognised was that, not only were the garments visually outstanding, but also the concept and methods of production were cutting-edge. They had effectively challenged normative modes and offered Melbourne fashion a new and exciting experience.

Arguably, the inspirations for their collections came from a multitude of sources. For example, in Paris in 1998, Sprynskyj and Boyd became fascinated with Greco-Roman mummies and the way perfumed petals, among other substances needed for their next life, were placed within particular folds of the funerary cloth. Another extraordinary finding was that the fabric had pockets already woven into the cloth. Emulating this process, they pressed and created their own pleated fabrics, added layered papers and then used petals within each layer. By becoming highly exploratory in their design process, they brainstormed different ways of approaching the process. Boyd wrote:

> S!X has an ongoing interest in the construction techniques of garments, hence the stripping back of jackets and trousers to reveal the structure and frame. We are constantly researching new techniques and we like to question the status quo, and quite often our garments spring from a recycled base or employ a quick print method via the photocopier. No doubt the trained textile designer would think this unorthodox.[5]

It is worthwhile noting that, although Sprynskyj and Boyd both appreciate the design revolution ignited by Japanese and Belgian designers, they have never wished to imitate them. Instead, they advocate dissecting and critiquing, rather than cloning the works of other designers. For Sprynskyj and Boyd, other designers' work acts more as a historical backdrop than as an overwhelming presence or influence. In her early student days, Sprynskyj was influenced by Europe's Cristóbal Balenciaga and the sharp cut of Christian Dior's creations. Boyd admired Thierry Mugler and Azzedine Alaïa for their masterly construction techniques in tailoring and fit. They both still maintain a great appreciation of the sculptural forms used by Issey Miyake and the complexity of the work of Rei Kawakubo of Comme des Garçons. In the *Tokyo Vogue* exhibition catalogue, the work of Sprynskyj and Boyd:

> reflects a strong Japanese aesthetic, akin to the deconstructivist nature of Comme des Garçons . . . Using abstract shapes to form a garment base, they experiment by manipulating the cloth and exploring new dyeing and printing techniques. Their garments are often made from old garments and incorporate the use of paper, emphasising their interest in recycling. (English 1999: 94)

In 1997, Sprynskyj and Boyd spent time in Japan learning about the ancient craft of *shibori*. Sprynskyj persuaded Boyd that they should combine this ancient technique with recycling, because at that time they were restricted to using flat cloth and *shibori* added a completely different tactile effect. For the first time, they began to add pole-wrapped fabric to the sleeves of a recycled garment, or to its lining body. They became more and more interested in what might be called a 'remix mentality', where centuries-old traditional cottage industry materials were combined with contemporary forms and silhouettes. Sprynskyj and Boyd 're-formed' the work through hand-pleating, hand-stitching, appliqué, embroidery, patchworking or tucking and foiling. Invariably, the reminders of the processes or techniques are left on the surface of the reconfigured garment and become an inherent part of the design. The bold *shibori* techniques of *arashi* and *nui* enhance the visual richness of Sprynskyj and Boyd's garments, often suggesting a 'kimono aesthetic'. Like the Japanese, Sprynskyj and Boyd's design processes are developmental – one thing leads to another, whether it is a technique, a fabric or an idea. They incessantly discuss and question their design procedures. Boyd says that:

> In starting a collection you know you are not starting from zero . . . as soon as you finish it . . . you already know the problems with it . . . what hasn't been resolved and that's usually a starting point for the next one. (Sprynskyj and Boyd 2004)

Seemingly, Sprynskyj and Boyd's thought processes run counter to accepted modes of Western inspiration for fashion design. Their influences can be verbal, visual and eidetic, and the resultant hybrid amalgamations give their designs a richness that goes well beyond any simple replication of pre-existing models and modes. They seek beauty in unexpected places, especially in Melbourne's Chapel Street, where the fractured images of advertisements, the collage of artworks and especially the vintage or reconstructed garments create a colourful and dynamic environment. They relish the tactile pleasures of the markets, fairs or department stores. They are individuals who run their hands over clothes racks, if only to get 'seismographic' readings and to feel the shape between the 'inner form' and the 'outer shell'. These experiences have inspired the designers, to use Boyd's term, to 'excavate' vintage jackets and coats for both sexes and reposition them into new contexts. These excavated tailored garments are cut up and restitched in ways that reveal and give new visual appeal to the clothes. This is no mere pastiche. Cut-up and recycled vintage wear (they enjoy the iconoclasm of cutting up other designers' clothing), remixed elements and diametrically opposed pieces are embraced; waistbands on necks and upside-down jackets are reincorporated in a heady 'sampling'-based aesthetic mix. Consequently, their sustainable designs are not for the faint-hearted: they are designed for those who are forward-thinking and appreciate a high level of design and craftsmanship.

When *Object* magazine was looking for four significant emerging artists from around Australia in 1997, editor Jim Logan chose S!X. He suggests the duality of Sprynskyj and Boyd's intentions – to be recognised both as a team of commercial designers and as makers of original art clothes:

> Their original items made from recycled clothes have a wonderful raw energy and, more remarkably, the commercial versions of these garments retained the punch of the prototype while attaining . . . a high degree of professional finish. (Logan 1997: 30)

In her article entitled 'Beyond nationality: the influence of Japan on Australian fashion and textile designers, 1975–2000', Margaret Riley writes:

> Often termed as 'deconstructive' critique of the techniques of tailoring and the gendered stereotyping of women's wear, the S!X design philosophy has more to say about 'reconstruction' than 'deconstruction'. Materials usually reserved for the inner construction of clothing, such as pocket linings, are brought to the surface and finishing techniques, such as over-locking and hidden seaming, are exposed. (English 1999: 50)

Clearly, the work of these two independent Melbourne designers forms close conceptual and aesthetic links between art, fashion design and textiles technology. Each link adds conceptual layers to the work itself, as seen in their ensemble entitled *Re-cut* (2001). *Re-cut* comprises a recycled man's shirt inserted with laser-cut polyester, a hand-painted organza square-tailed dress and a handbag made from a man's jacket. Edward Colless, of the Tasmanian School of Art, describes the garment:

> 'Recut', by the Design Group 'S!X', cleverly and humorously deconstructs op-shop wear, confronting the staid uniform of a corporate suited world with the lively, youthful and sexy inventions of contemporary urban street-wear. 'Recut' not only recycles clothing that seems to have fallen out of use. It dramatically re-cuts the masculine into the feminine. This work collides the old with the new, through boardroom with the nightclub, and male with female. (Colless 2001: 2)

Sprynskyj and Boyd have a commitment to artistic ideals and at every opportunity have placed their garments into the public arena. Their work has been exhibited in numerous international as well as national shows, including *Tokyo and Paris* in 2005, *Freestyle* in 2006 and Craft Victoria's *How You Make It* touring exhibition with The Tunnel Connection (five pieces) in 2007. They are now recognised as leading avant-garde designers in Australia. Sixteen years after the founding of S!X, Sprynskyj and Boyd maintain an indisputably fresh design integrity – they cater to individualistic tastes and refuse to fit into the realms of Australian fashion fads and ever-shifting trends. S!X's Boyd and Sprynskyj are welded to a purpose: one of designing and producing distinctive garments that not only embody their artistic ideals, but also maintain their unique creative integrity.

## Gwendolynne

In 1997, Gwendolynne Burkin founded her eponymous Gwendolynne high-end women's wear label. From the beginning, Burkin has been recognised as a designer who has produced some of the most elegant and sophisticated clothing lines in Australia. Her design aesthetic is based upon a bygone feminine model coupled with a contemporary sensibility. Burkin's artistic vision is inspired by the historical dress of the eighteenth to twentieth centuries – an artistic mix of design elements and silhouettes. Her work has been compared with that of British iconoclast Vivienne Westwood because of the designer's passion for referencing past elements of dress in her

**11.3** Gwendolynne Burkin
of Gwendolynne, catwalk
image of outfit, Winter 2001.
Millinery: Richard Nylon.
Melbourne Fashion Week,
February 2001

Photo: Brad Hick. Courtesy Gwendolynne

designs. However, unlike Westwood's 'tongue-in-cheek' parody of historical
dress, Burkin's designs are serious in nature rather than intended as a joke
(Nelson 2003). Her designs align more closely to the late twentieth-century
fashion designs of the irreverent couturier Karl Lagerfeld with his masterful
appropriations of the past for the House of Chanel. In a similar vein, Burkin's

made-to-measure ensembles and ready-to-wear collections are also a nod to the past but strongly resonate with the cool chic of the current 'zeitgeist'.

Burkin's garments are informed by the pattern components of historical dress: she finds the cut and construction of the clothing compelling. She plays with their proportions, dissects sections and then transforms them into unpredictably fresh and ultimately wearable styles. For example, she may reinterpret the bodice from a Victorian dress, creating it in crochet-lace sewn on to a totally sheer skintone top with demure three-quarter length sleeves which seem magically to sit perfectly on the arms. Yet the top is worn over stretch satin hotpants and accessorised with short white 1950s-inspired gloves, then topped off with a tiny Edwardian-inspired hat made from white crochet cotton, designed by avant-garde sculptural milliner Richard Nylon.[6] Burkin and Nylon are kindred spirits and, as they perfectly complement one another in their design practices, it is no wonder that their collaboration has lasted twelve years. In a 2007 press release, the self-effacing Nylon stated:

> Gwendolynne is one of the few Australian designers who is not afraid to use millinery in her collection shows. Gwendolynne's clothes are beautiful poetry. My hats are merely the punctuation. (Burkin 2003: para 5)

Burkin is a fine fashion designer, pattern-maker and machinist in her own right. While she learned the craft of dressmaking and tailoring from a young age, she later studied fashion at RMIT University in Melbourne. When Burkin begins her design process, she usually starts with fabrics selected from her large collection of eighteenth-century and 1940s sources. Burkin's design development often includes sketching of garments – or, alternatively, begins with fabric draping – allowing the drape to inform the design. She integrates disparate design elements and thus begins the design development process. She prefers to work instinctively and allows a design to evolve organically, as she is not fond of solely constraining herself to designing the collections entirely on paper:

> I love to . . . find a key fabric, work with that fabric . . . Then often in the pattern-making and design area, I might start with one key idea and then let it evolve. Like I might make a beautiful coat, and . . . I'll do the first pattern, and then while I'm making it, I'll go, 'The bottom of this coat would make a great skirt. And the top of this jacket will make a great short jacket . . .' (Burkin 2002: para 3)

Burkin's ensembles are embellished with meticulous detail, and this is apparent in every collection. The fit of her dresses and tailoring pieces is extremely well realised:

> Burkin's philosophy supports a tradition of meticulous fine dressmaking that goes back to the greatest of clothiers. She is closely involved at each stage of her work, from initial concept and pattern-making through to completion and presentation of a range – every article in the Gwendolynne range bears the stamp of the designer's hand. (Burkin 2003: para 13)

Apart from Nylon, Burkin often invites diverse artists to work with her on her fashion shows, such as musicians, performers and visual artists. She firmly believes that fashion is part of the artistic realm and therefore should not be viewed as separate. The overall stylistic effect has a sense of romanticism and theatricality which is central to Burkin's *oeuvre*. Inspiration for Burkin comes in many forms – for example, the old and outmoded language of nineteenth-century advertising is of great interest. She says:

> I was also drawn to the whimsical and witty nature of beauty antidotes and advertising from the past. A play on different periods where things become amusing because of language that is outdated. (Powerhouse Museum 2002: para 7)

Burkin is a conceptual designer and her shows not only function as advertising, but also become an artistic experience through the theatricality of performance. Through this theatrical experience, she narrates the stories behind the collections, thus giving her devotees a glimpse of the creative process of her practice.

## Romance Was Born

Anna Plunkett and Luke Sales of Romance Was Born are dynamic and irreverent fashion creators who imbue each of their collections with an extraordinary array of original, individual fashion pieces. Since founding their label, they delight in designing playful, witty pieces that poke fun at the fashion establishment. Their clothing fabrications oscillate between glitz and kitsch aesthetics; however, as with Burkin, a contemporary coolness always prevails in their collections. The overtly exaggerated decorative designs and 'arty' feel of the clothing have been the magical ingredients in their great success and have made this label highly sought after.

**11.4** Anna Plunkett and Luke Sales of Romance Was Born, *Untitled*, Garden of Eden collection, Winter 2007

Photo: Lucas Dawson. Courtesy Romance Was Born

Plunkett and Sales met as undergraduate students studying Fashion at East Sydney Technical College. They became best friends and gained notoriety upon graduating by rejecting an internship with superstar haute couturier John Galliano. The allure of designing their own fashion collections without restrictions was too strong for the pair to resist.

As 'true blue Aussies', they design and manufacture their clothing within the country, even though it is much more expensive than using offshore production. A great source of inspiration for the duo is their love of Australia's enigmatic characters, kitsch Australiana and the landscape, as seen in their Regional Australia Collection (2006). The backdrop of the photographic shoot is made up of a banner of tea towels imprinted with Australiana imagery, with models standing on cartons of iconic Victoria Bitter Beer, wearing tops knitted in old-fashioned doily designs and wearing painted sunglasses with odd enlarged eyes. They take great pleasure in incorporating the impious, the tacky and the ostentatious in their designs. This mode of presentation imbues the garments with signifiers exuding a happy, joyous spirit. This joyfulness may be seen in the Nocturnal Collection of 2007, in which models are photographed just 'hanging out' in the playground. The photographs are purposely naïve in execution to enhance the bright candy-coloured streetwear garments. The collection includes funky, club-type sportswear-inspired clothing juxtaposed with sparkling beads, studs and appliqués.

Young and full of energy and enthusiasm for their craft, Plunkett and Sales aim to keep their fashion practice dynamic by advocating change and continuous development. With a sense of this purpose, they instigated an important collaboration with eminent Australian artist Del Kathryn Barton. Barton's artworks are thought-provoking representations of the spiritual connections she sees between nature and human beings.[7] Her depictions of partially naked young females entwined with animals are haunting and melancholic. Barton's expressive drawing style harks back to the erotic and unsettling imagery of Austrian artist Egon Schiele. Barton was commissioned to design prints for fabrics for three collections. Her surreal images and Plunkett and Sales' aesthetic were a match made in heaven. The collections were highly successful, especially the 2008 collection entitled Garden of Eden, which was first exhibited at the Kaliman Gallery in Paddington and then at the National Design Centre, Federation Square (Melbourne), which showcases Australian design. This shared exhibition gave the two avant-garde and eclectic designers:

> [a] licence to explore their truly artisan capabilities unimpeded and the results were breathtaking. Like creative bowerbirds they assembled a fashion wonderland drawing together all that was beautiful with their stunning over-the-top embellished style. (Romance Was Born 2008: para 3)

Like a contemporary form of Baroque Art, it encourages the eyes to feast on a brimming array of dazzling design details, prints and boundless textural embellishments and materials. For Plunkett and Sales, 'more is definitely more!'

The success of Romance Was Born increases exponentially year by year, and in March 2009 Plunkett and Sales won the coveted Woolmark Designer Award at the L'Oréal Melbourne Fashion Festival for their collection entitled Yeti Magic. Why did these self-professed larrikin designers win this prestigious award? According to fashion lecturer Jo Cramer:

> It was a breath of fresh air perhaps. Daring and amusing, such risks probably should be applauded, for fear of them disappearing altogether. What would the implications have been if they didn't win? That the fashion establishment shunned such playful creativity? Australia is a very small fashion market and so most labels are fixated on making sales (out of necessity) which necessarily clips their creative wings. Boutique buyers can be very conservative. Love them or hate them, labels like RWB remind us what fashion is about – self-expression and even some fun. (Cramer 2009)

## Gorman

Whereas Plunkett and Sales are cutting-edge in terms of rigorous design conception and development, another group of designers who have emerged in recent years deal with the notion of sustainable design and ethical business practices. This movement, both locally and globally, focuses on socially, environmentally and economically sustainable fashion. The clothing is not necessarily new in terms of fashion pattern-cutting or construction, but it is radical in terms of the ethical processes employed for the realisation of their clothing collections, including sustainability issues. While many emerging designers and companies, such as Tiffany Treloar,[8] Anthea van Kopplen[9] and the Sussan Corporation[10] are taking up the baton to champion environmentally friendly and fair trade clothing practices, one designer stands out from the crowd: Lisa Gorman of Gorman. Gorman is Australia's pioneer in organic fashion production, and she is esteemed for her commitment to genuine 'green' fashion. In 2006, Gorman began the difficult task of systematically scrutinising every part of her company's practice:

> Gorman began the enormous and complex job of pulling her business up to her morals. She employed an environmental consultant and for nine months they thrashed out the meaning behind fashion's flippant 'green is the new black' approach to the issue. From the brand of electricity she uses in the offices of

Gorman and Gorman Organic, to the raw materials she uses in
her frocks, and on her shop walls, Gorman went green from the
ground up at a time when others, less than honest or thorough,
were slapping the cute slogan on their ads. (Breen Burns 2009: 22)

Gorman has painstakingly reorganised her company from the bottom up and
established a best-practice business, benchmarking ethical sustainability.
Her holistic approach to the enormous complexity associated with producing
eco-friendly fashion is exemplary. For example, within a short timeframe

**11.5** Lisa Gorman of Gorman,
Organic '04 collection, 2004

Photo: Ben Glezer. Courtesy Gorman

Gorman has added a sustainable fashion line called Gorman Organic and increased the use of certified organic and sustainable fabrics and yarns in the main collection. The printing process is done using environmentally friendly water-based printing and azo-free dyes, and the company has reduced garment-washed styles in its seasonal lines. Gorman has instigated a 90 per cent reduction in the use of garment packaging and changed to recyclable packaging such as LDPE quality polybags. Since 2007, five dollars from every Green & Serene T-shirt sale has gone to Friends of the Earth. And, since its launch in 2008, each time a customer rejects a shopping bag the company donates another 49 cents to this environmental group.

Sue Thomas, an author focusing on ethics and sustainable fashion practice, notes that Gorman's work is:

> ongoing in that she is a model to follow for other designers, striving to make her company and practice as sustainable as possible. She is dealing with the fact that design for sustainability can't be about absolutes yet. Gorman has a variety of other garments which don't fit into the organic line, yet the company is run to lessen their carbon footprint and the company use clever ways of marketing both their product and philosophy. (Thomas 2009)

The Gorman Organic collections consist of fashion 'basics' – for example, items such as hoodies, tank tops, T-shirts and pyjamas – constructed from yarns and fabrics that are certified organic in production or grown naturally in the wild. The core garments' designs are not trend-driven; the design impetus is to produce long-lasting, high-quality classic garments that may be worn until they wear out. In her first season, Gorman created a modern and simple collection consisting of top-grade organic fabrics, such as super-fine single-yarn cotton jersey and bamboo fabric.[11] Gorman's design aesthetic allows her clothing to stand apart from that of other companies offering similar apparel by incorporating a high level of pattern-drafting and detailing, giving the collections a point of difference in the marketplace. Therefore her clothing ranges are not only ethically sustainable, but are also well designed and conceived.

## Conclusion

Australian avant-garde fashion designers have extended the margins of both the industry and the marketplace. They have moved the boundaries by which we judge the difference between what is mundane, what is exceptional and what is visionary. They have attempted to find a balance between what is innovative, challenging and revolutionary, and what is commercially viable. Their work is sited at the crossroads of the theoretical and the practical, the junction between concept and reality; when they reach this intellectual turning point, it makes their work unique. Fostering impending change requires forthright actions, absolute conviction and an unfettered sense of free expression. What the future holds for fashion is undeniably in their hands.

## Notes

1  Chantal MacDonald has reverted to her maiden name, Chantal Kirby.
2  When the horizontal loom was introduced for weaving long lengths of fabric that could be wrapped around the body. Again in the Middle Ages, which signalled changes taking place in garment construction and finally during the eighteenth century, when mechanisation increased the speed of production.
3  Original publication dated 1947: 137–54.
4  An international jury met in Barcelona in December 2008 under the presidency of Barbara Franchin (EVE Director and ITS Project Supervisor, Italy) to select the designers to participate in the next 080 BARCELONA FASHION. This selection committee consisted of eleven experts who reflected the various components of the fashion sector: Vicki Beamon (creative director, Erickson-Beamon, UK), Jean-Luc Dupont (systeme D, France), Takeji Hirakawa (freelance journalist and fashion professor, Japan), Lutz Huelle (designer Lutz, France), Frederic Martin-Bernard (journalist, *Le Figaro* and *marie claire*, France), Jorgen Sailer (menswear designer, Dries Van Noten, Belgium), Llues Sans (Santa Eulalia, Spain), Robin Schuliz (head buyer, Maria Luisa, France), Ingrid Van Gerven (Department of Innovation, Universities and Enterprise of the Catalan government, Spain) and Vincent Vantomme (senior partner/recruiting, LinkUnlimited, Belgium).
5  Letter written by Peter Boyd to Bonnie English, 7 June 1999.
6  Milliner Richard Nylon and Gwendolynne Burkin have experienced a continual collaboration since her label began on 11 November 1997.
7  For example, image of . . . *she appeared as a lover might* . . . by Kathryn Del Barton, <www.artinvestmentguide.com/KathrynDelbarton/Del%20 Kathryn%20Barton.pdf>.
8  Tiffany Treloar, daughter of renowned fashion designer Prue Acton, is currently in the process of making her company sustainable. This process includes the use of green power, introducing organic materials into her collections, recycling and consulting with CSIRO scientist Ian Russell regarding appropriate dyeing and printing processes that have minimum impact upon the environment (Breen Burns 2009: 22).
9  Anthea van Kopplen of envelope.vk is a design innovator who has dedicated her small fashion business to providing the community with services in the

areas of research, design and development of socially and environmentally sustainable apparel.

10 Sussan Corporation (Australia's largest women's wear fashion retailer) has been dedicated to reducing its carbon footprint since 2007 in preparation for the introduction of an Emissions Trading Scheme in 2010. The corporation endeavours to become carbon neutral by 2012 by reducing greenhouse gas emissions through sourcing at least 20 per cent renewable energy and using recycled materials.

11 Gorman Official Website: <www.gorman.ws/default.aspx#/gorman/about_us-k/aboutus>.

# References

Attiwill, S. (2004), *A Matter of Time: 16th Tamworth Fibre Textile Buyer Biennial*, exhibition catalogue, Tamworth, NSW: Tamworth Regional Gallery.

Breen Burns, J. (2009), 'Designed not to wear out', *The Age*, 12 March, p. 22.

Burkin, G. (2002), interview by Powerhouse Museum, Powerhouse Museum, exhibition 12 April to 21 July, <www.powerhousemuseum.com/sourcingthemuse/int_gwendolynne_burkin.asp>.

—— (2003a), 'Reveries of innocence – Mercedes Australian Fashion Week', press release, Melbourne: Gwendolynne.

—— (2003b), 'Tribute to designer's ten year friendship – Richard Nylon & Gwendolynne Burkin', press release, Melbourne: Gwendolynne.

Colless, E. (2001), 'City of Hobart Art Prize: judges' statement', Hobart.

Cramer, J. (2009), interview by L. Pomazan, Melbourne, 8 April.

Crane, D. (1997), 'Postmodernism and the avant-garde: stylistic change in fashion design', *Modernism/Modernity*, 4(3), pp. 123–40.

Dimasi, S. and Kirby, C. (2008), interview by B. English, Melbourne, 29 August.

English, B. (ed.) (1999), *Griffith University's Tokyo Vogue: Japanese and Australian Fashion*, Brisbane: Griffith University, Queensland College of Art.

Logan, J. (1997), 'Spring flowers and summer showers', *Object Journal*, 4, pp. 29–30.

Nelson, K. (2003), 'Melbourne: Gwendolynne's feminine cool', *My Way*, 4 January, <http://fashion.myway.com/feature/id/ff%7C4576.html>.

Pomazan, L. (2005), *Punch Out: MATERIALBYPRODUCT*, Melbourne: 3 Deep Publishers.

—— (2006), 'MATERIALBYPRODUCT: fashion systems for the new millennium', paper presented to Unleashing Collections: Cloth, Costume and Culture conference, 24–26 March, Auckland.

Powerhouse Museum (2002), 'Label: Gwendolynne Burkin', Powerhouse Museum Exhibition, 12 April to 21 July, <www.powerhousemuseum.com/sourcingthemuse/des_gwendolynne.asp>.

Press, C. (2008), 'A fine romance', *Vogue Australia*, 53(5), May, pp. 107–10.

Riley, M. (1999), 'Beyond nationality: the influence of Japan on Australian fashion and textile designers, 1975–2000', in B. English (ed.), *Griffith University's Tokyo Vogue: Japanese and Australian fashion*, Brisbane: Griffith University, Queensland College of Art, pp. 48–60.

Rissanen, T. (2009), 'Fashion creation without fabric waste creation', <http://zerofabricwastefashion.blogspot.com>.

Romance Was Born (2009), 'Romance Was Born: the story', <www.romancewasborn.com/pdf/romance_was_born.pdf>.

Sprynskyj, D. and Boyd, P. (2004), S!X interview by L. Pomazan, Melbourne, 25 May.

Thomas, S. (2009), interview by L. Pomazan, Melbourne, 15 April.

# THE BUSINESS OF FASHION

*Jo-Anne Kellock*

**12.1** Country Road, *Untitled*, Winter 2009
Photographer Tesh Patel. Courtesy Country Road

**I**N AUSTRALIA TODAY, a successful fashion business is a 'tag' often attributed to high-end or high-profile designers and brands with broad youth appeal. Labels such as Akira, Sass & Bide and Ksubi are widely recognised. Creating a fashion label is a popular career choice, as is evidenced by the high proportion of new start-up businesses and an over-subscription to fashion design and technology courses (Green 2008). Contemporary Australian fashion designers have achieved international recognition and enjoy celebrity status. However, over the years others, too, have excelled at building fashion businesses, such as the Just Group, R.M. Williams and Rip Curl. These also have held a presence on the global stage, have stood the test of time and are regarded as successful.

But what is the definition of success? Is it determined by brand profile, designer status or profitability? Should the number of employees or duration of the business also be considered? There is no doubt that the business of fashion is highly competitive; it is filled with stimulation and there are many rewards. However, this does not always translate into company profits, nor does it necessarily guarantee a sustainable competitive advantage that will endure. The business of fashion, on the whole, is conducted in an unregulated environment and, although exciting, has a high risk of failure compared with other sectors. In the first twelve months of operation there is only a 68 per cent survival rate (TFIA 2008).

# The big picture

Undoubtedly, fashion is subject to the forces of the free market – at its best and worst. To thrive in the sector and build a successful fashion business requires a convergence of product innovation, critical success factors, favourable driving forces, strong management expertise, informed market intelligence, creative talent and adequate resources. As if that were not enough, there are also external forces to navigate, such as Australia's demography, climate extremes, liberalised trade policies and urban densities, and forces further afield such as the global economy, production centres, technology and international standards – all of which impact on the business of fashion.

Creative talent, marketing and networking ability are skills found in many success stories, and in the fashion business these skills are demonstrated by a company's attendance at fashion festivals, its sustained profile in magazines and, most importantly, its healthy sales figures.

**12.2** CJ Wilson factory, Johnston Street Fitzroy circa 1960 to 1965

Courtesy Council Textile and Fashion Industries of Australia Limited

Fashion is a valuable part of the Australian Textile Clothing and Footwear (TCF) sector, and its definition extends to encompass accessories and uniforms. It is a polarised and fragmented sector, made up of a small number of large businesses that control 50 per cent of the market; the remainder is made up of a large number of small to medium enterprises (SMEs). In the Business Innovative Capability Report of 2008, the average size of an Australian fashion business is 4.1 employees per management unit and these SMEs comprise 86 per cent of fashion businesses (Green 2008).

The fragmentation of the sector makes collaboration difficult. Although there have been various representative bodies in the Australian marketplace, the two most noteworthy are the Fashion Industries of Australia (FIA) and the TCF Council of Australia (TCFCA). In 1997 the FIA merged with the TCFCA to become the Council of Textile and Fashion Industries of Australia Limited (TFIA). This peak body today plays a strong advocacy and representative role in the TCF industry. The fluctuations in the exchange rate, the losses of skill and knowledge from an industry restructured within the last thirty years and the flooding of the market with imported products have all impacted on the ability of fashion businesses to operate competitively. In general, the TCF sector – fashion included – has not demonstrated an ability to cope well with radical change.

## Definition of a fashion business

Fashion businesses of all sizes are no longer as easily defined by their products or activities as they once were. They function differently, their activities ranging from traditional to various combinations of design, wholesale, retail, manufacture, importing and distribution. In its merchandising of current styles of clothing and accessories a fashion business can be difficult to categorise, especially in Australia, as the owners move up and down the supply chain seeking margins and economies of scale. Manufacturers have moved into retailing and some department stores now run quality assurance (QA) departments that resemble product development areas in manufacturing businesses. Agents have developed their own labels and many designers merchandise their own products.

All this reflects an industry under restructure; businesses have had to increase the value of their products, their number of product ranges, the frequency of sales, or the margins on their products, which they achieve by reducing costs. Some fashion businesses reduce their size while others are forced to increase management levels to cope with offshore production.

Generally speaking, the fashion industry is polarised in terms of size of business. The size of the fashion business can vary greatly from a publicly listed brand house such as Australia's largest fashion business, Pacific Brands, which has taken many years to evolve and currently employs approximately 9000 people, to the smallest fledgling design business at the other extreme which can consist of a one-person entity. Small to medium sized enterprises have recently been defined in Australia under the *Fair Work Act*, which came into force in July 2009, as those with fewer than fifteen employees, whereas in Europe SMEs are defined as having 50–100 employees. Significantly for smaller businesses in Australia, the market demands niche product in short runs, which puts pressure on profits and in turn increases the risk of failure. Many owner-operators resort to multi-tasking to save on costs, and often run out of steam or capital or both – hence the high failure rate of new fashion businesses. At the same time, larger businesses face similar hurdles – and when they move their production offshore, the business' knowledge and skill is often transferred along with the management of the process.

## Market analysis

A market analysis would determine that Australia is one of the world's most urbanised countries, with about 70 per cent of its population living in the ten largest cities. Most of the population is concentrated in coastal regions, mainly along the eastern seaboard and the south-eastern corner of the continent, where the bulk of Australian fashion businesses are located. Since World War II, Australia's lifestyle has reflected its mainly Western origins, but Australia is also a multicultural society that has been enriched by nearly five million settlers from almost 200 nations coming from all regions of the world. We know from overseas sizing studies that different ethnic groups possess different body characteristics. This, of course, further adds to the complexity of the product mix for fashion businesses.

One of the many challenges facing the Australian fashion industry is the ageing population and how best to design for the aspirational but deliver to the masses. With a median age of thirty-seven years and a greater propensity to shop less but spend more, the average consumer is not widely catered for. The Baby Boomer market has at last been confronted with this obstacle, which the industry has chosen to largely ignore. Instead, designing for the younger person continues to be the main focus of the industry.

Market categories are becoming more complex and less clearly defined. Although Australia is classed as one of the wealthiest countries in the world, fashion competes for its share of household expenditure, which has been declining steadily for the last twenty years. This could reflect a drop in the cost value of clothing, as the number of units consumed remains relatively unchanged.

## Anticipating change

While Australian fashion businesses can adopt new trends quite readily and embed them quickly into their product ranges, when it comes to the supply chain they do not tend to cope well with radical change. It would seem that they are better at digesting small adjustments over a longer period of time. This is aggravated by geographical isolation from global fashion centres and close proximity to the cheaper Asian manufacturing hubs. Since the 1980s, liberalisation of trade and economic policies has meant that Australian fashion businesses have had to adjust their supply chains to survive competitive price pressures from overseas manufacturers.

Until the global financial crisis, this trend was emerging globally with international lobbying for Free Trade Agreements. However, larger countries such as China and the United States have recently moved to protect their TCF industries through the use of non-tariff barriers, such as rebates to exporters and funding for home-grown projects. For many years, the Australian TCF sector enjoyed very favourable protection through quotas that restricted the flow of imports. The last quota was dismantled in 1993, followed in 2000 by the introduction of a 'phasedown' in the tariff schedule, which reduced the levy on imports – now projected to be 5 per cent for textiles by 2010 and for apparel by 2015. The longer 'phasedown' period for clothing reflected the higher percentage of protection needed for apparel, reflecting its history of difficult economic adjustment. Since the early 1980s, the TCF sector has received additional support in the form of grants to assist with the changes in policy, and in 2000 approximately $100 million per annum was allocated to the TCF sector (including fashion businesses that made a large proportion of their products locally) to encourage innovation and investment in new machinery and equipment.

While many of the fashion manufacturing firms have gone offshore, closed down or merged in the period of adjustment, there have been a number of survivors. Carla Zampatti, a high-end Australian designer recently recognised in the 2009 Queen's Birthday Honours List for her contribution to Australian fashion, has kept her manufacturing in Australia for twenty-seven years, proving that it is still possible to make garments in Australia and maintain a viable business. She was also named the 2009 Australian Fashion Designer of the Year.

Fashion retailers, on the other hand, are under pressure from discount stores and thus have been driven to make a lot of changes. Some of the big department stores in Australia, such as Myer, now have QA departments involved in product development. Other changes to the fashion industry have seen manufacturers move into wholesale and outsource components or complete articles in order to fulfil designer orders. Identified by government investigations into the industry as the 'design and merchandise model', this new-look model has been tagged and widely adopted by fashion businesses.

While price pressures have endured during the period of adjustment, this has subsequently led to innovation in range development and creative marketing campaigns. In recent years, some designers have supplemented their ranges by creating 'diffusion' brands for new luxury categories. For example, the designer Collette Dinnigan has presented lingerie as a diffusion line. Discount department stores such as Target are leveraging their brands on limited edition overseas designer offerings using labels such as Stella McCartney. As well, higher-end department store David Jones has run a strong marketing and promotion campaign for Australian designers over a five-year period, which has proven to be very successful.

## Contextualising the Australian market

External influences within the fashion industry are usually attributed to market forces and depend on brand positioning. These positions range from high-end design and low-volume categories to low-end design and high-volume categories. Since the start of the 1990s, Australia's modern society and culture have had to adjust to globalisation, liberalised trade and a unified world market. One of the biggest influences on the market has been the emergence of the European luxury brands and the associated industries occupying a pinnacle place in Australia's economy. International shows and the evolution of the internet, which has accelerated the adoption of trends and made the latest designs accessible to the smallest fashion businesses, have benefited the Australian consumer. Menswear luxury brand Zegna and womenswear label Armani are good examples of luxury brands that occupy an enviable position in the Australian fashion chain. L'Oréal is an example of an associated international brand that has had a major influence on Australian fashion through its support of the Melbourne Fashion Festival.

The notion of luxury has also broadened in that time to encompass a 'new luxury' phenomenon, low ticket items uniquely designed for higher price, greatly extending the categories that were once reserved for the elite in Australian society. This has broadened the consumption base to include the middle classes and created new opportunities for fashion design businesses in Australia. However, in today's global financial crisis, luxury is being redefined. According to Shaf Dewani, managing director of locally owned up-market womenswear retailer Paul & Joe (McIntyre 2009), 'the sometimes crass, mass stampede for luxury witnessed in the past decade is over for good and niche is back.' In the same article, Stancombe Research and Planning's Susan Stancombe adds that a new 'consumption etiquette' is emerging for luxury segments, which is all about going underground:

> There's a return to recessive logos, less ostentatious designs and more of the enduring timeless classicism that made luxury great. People will continue to buy luxury; they will just buy differently and more discreetly. Middling 'mass-tige' will disappear while true prestige and the value ends of the market will prosper.

Clearly, this suggests a new focus on designer fashion, consumers and sustainability, and could possibly create wonderful opportunities for Australia's design talent. Colin McDowell, well-known British costume historian and author, claimed in his address to the Australian fashion industry ten years ago that 'in the sixties there occurred a terrible rupture between the designer and consumer from which we have not recovered' (McDowell 1998). Undoubtedly, the rupture McDowell refers to coincides with the advent of ready-to-wear apparel after World War II, and the subsequent changes made to distribution channels in order to dispense ready-to-wear garments to the consumer. Gradually, with the development of much more sophisticated apparel marketing and brand advertising strategies, the role of advertising today has overshadowed the importance of technical knowledge and skill in construction and fit – so much so, in fact, that in naming the 'design and merchandise' model, the term 'fashion technology' was eliminated from the policy formation vocabulary and those working as technicians lost their voice within the fashion supply chain.

Historically, this shift away from technical skill and craftsmanship becomes evident when viewing the Yarra Park Costume Collection in Bulleen, Victoria. Loel Thomson, the conservator of this private collection, has organised 3000 garments into a social history of Australia since the late 1790s. What is most striking about the collection is the level of detail evident in the earliest garments, which were hand-stitched, yet displayed sophisticated styling. Sadly, the decline of technical skill becomes even more evident as the collection progresses through each decade.

Certainly, the invention of the sewing machine in the late 1880s was, at least in part, responsible for the shift. However, as work, home and social obligations also changed for modern, liberated Western women, so did the design, make and functional requirements of their clothing. Mass production, combined with the might of powerful brand advertising and changes to the merchandising of apparel, have changed the nature of the shopping experience for the average Australian consumer. For example, in many upmarket fashion outlets, garments are arranged according to colour, or collection coordinates, rather than size. With 'time-poor' limitations and a flood of imported products, the search for quality apparel that fits has become a challenge. This creates a new consumer paradigm and raises issues around sustainability for Australian fashion businesses.

Today in Australia, ready-to-wear unconstructed garments occupy the volume end of the market. At the other end of the market, high fashion dictates the trends, many of which still emanate from European fashion houses but are slowly being eroded by young Australian design talent. Fashion labels are often more likely to be differentiated by brand imagery associated with lifestyles and national advertising.

There is no doubt that the casualness of many of the successful Australian labels is driven in part by the climate and the lifestyle. In international terms, Country Road's White Hot summer collection of 2002 was an outstanding example of effective design, presentation and promotion. In the advertising photograph, the yellow glow around the man's face was not only a subtle reminder of the sun's glare, but its clever imagery also suggested warmth, comfort and clean living. Other good examples of the success of the Australian casual wear market include surfwear and swimwear brands such as Rip Curl and Seafolly. They market through 'value-adding' and/or association with individuals and events, which filters through to the low-cost ticket items in their ranges such as branded T-shirts.

The most popular fashion labels tend to be those that appeal to the younger generation, whose marketers can conduct special events, whose designers can create for movie, music or sports stars (charged with the responsibility of entertaining us), or whose sales staff are able to court business in elite international retail establishments. Labels such as Willow and Sass & Bide have braved the international scene early in their development and reaped the rewards for doing so. Fashion brand companies have also extended their margins by marketing additional product categories such as accessories and perfumes.

Arguably, the future lies somewhere between those designers who can merge fashion, sport and science into value-added products and others who can design to the principles of ethical, environmentally friendly and locally sourced ranges. As facile as this may sound, fashion forecasting or looking towards future needs and new product categories is more a science than an art, and requires in-depth market analysis.

## Current industry concerns

While there seems to be no shortage of design talent in Australia, the development of technology associated with garment construction has been eroded due to the unfortunate closure of many manufacturing businesses. Consequently, an inevitable outcome of this situation that confronts the industry is the large decline in the level of manufacturing employment over the past ten years. Employing over 100 000 workers in the late 1990s, the industry now employs 48 000. Thus, in turn, one of the biggest concerns facing the Australian fashion industry is the apparel manufacturing supply chain and, in particular, the reduced capacity to supply small orders (quantities of twenty or fewer copies per garment size) to small and medium enterprises.

Melbourne remains the apparel manufacturing capital of Australia, yet much production has moved offshore. Currently, Vietnamese outworkers in Australia mainly service short-run apparel productions; however, as the average age of current Vietnamese outworkers approaches fifty years, concern is growing about who will continue to perform this role. Located in close proximity to the Asian region, the global centre of apparel production, larger Australian fashion businesses have, by and large, found solutions in South-East Asia, predominantly China. However, as companies moved into niche markets, their equipment and labour requirements became more specialised. As manufacture moved offshore, much of the machinery went with it, leaving a machine production technology deficit in Australia.

Australia has been a strong proponent of Free Trade Agreements, having recently concluded negotiations with its ASEAN neighbours. The impact of this policy is debatable, although the trends are evident, and at this time the industry nervously awaits the next wave of tariff reductions scheduled for January 2010. Trade policy, in general, has had a huge negative impact on Australian apparel manufacture, but fashion retail has mostly benefited. Unable to compete with lower wages in emerging countries, much of the production has gone offshore or is hidden in outworker communities in the western suburbs of cities like Melbourne and Sydney. Australian politicians have for many years openly advocated the merits of a service economy and have failed to understand the importance of maintaining a proportion of manufacture within Australia, if for no other reason than to support product development and essential services.

Undoubtedly, garment manufacturing is labour-intensive. And labour is cheap in emerging countries, where low exchange rates can also provide an advantage. It could be argued that cost structures are simply transferred with outsourcing arrangements that require additional layers of management to supervise the process. While financial gains have been achieved in labour costs, many of the processes and much of the machinery used for garment construction in Australia have remained relatively unchanged for fifty years. Paradoxically, the Australian fashion industry is polarised, with a small number of big players who can afford the investment in new technology and can outperform a large number of under-resourced small businesses, which have neither the capital nor the skills to take advantage of the improvements. Hence there is an urgent need to address a 'high-tech', short-run manufacturing model for the Australian fashion industry.

Other concerns for the industry emerged as a result of the global economic downturn in 2009. A lack of resilience and falling profits, combined with late and cancelled deliveries, continued to put undue pressure on fashion businesses, particularly retailers. The sudden 30 per cent fall in the value of the Australian dollar in October 2008 against the US currency, for example, caught many importers by surprise. While all businesses are subject to internal tensions between staff, resources and management capability, in an economic downturn many have to lay off staff and freeze any growth plans. As well, financial restraints often lead to higher staff turnover, which is not conducive to the nurturing of a sustainable working environment. Undoubtedly, Australian designers are under constant time and resource pressures because of the small size of orders compared with their international counterparts and the new phenomenon of 'fast fashion', which has increased the time pressure burden even further. But this also has benefits, as these resilient designers have adapted by becoming extremely efficient and accustomed to working with fewer resources.

## Addressing the problem

In order to compete, the fashion industry has reoriented itself from a largely domestic manufacturing sector, seeking scale efficiencies, to a mixture of smaller local manufacturing activities augmented with significant design, niche marketing and local/import mix with a focus on maximising the returns on local value-added activities. Cue Design's popular womenswear brand manufactures 80 per cent of its products here in Australia, with the rest being sourced offshore. There are a relatively small number of large, well-known players that have a significant market presence, and a myriad of smaller businesses in Australia. There is also significant growth in small to medium design businesses, many of which are not strictly manufacturers but are part of the manufacturing supply chain and rely on domestic manufacturing to survive as a point of difference.

Over the past ten years, some on the manufacturing-specific side of the industry have successfully diversified their operations into the less traditional TCF areas, such as performance-based and industrial textiles offering increasingly sophisticated functional usage, and niche clothing and footwear areas where product differentiation and high value-adding are essential. There has also been a growing trend that has seen many manufacturers source more products offshore, focusing their activities on supply chain management and on specific areas where Australia is more competitive, such as innovative design, branding and market development, and customer service. As a result of this, while many manufacturing-specific areas have declined, these other areas have taken on increasing importance and focus, and have helped enhance the value of the remaining domestic manufacturing activities.

## Success stories

There are a number of Australian companies that have enjoyed long-term success by managing the impact of both internal and external pressures to varying degrees. They include the following.

### Pacific Brands

Starting business in 1893 manufacturing bicycle tyres, Pacific Brands has gone through many changes from the structure of its business to a 'product mix'. Today, Pacific Brands is a leading manager of Everyday Essential Brands in Australia and New Zealand, marketing some of the most recognised clothing, textile and footwear brands including Berlei, Bonds, Clarks (children's), Dunlop, Everlast, Grosby, Holeproof, Hush Puppies, King Gee, Mooks, Mossimo, Sheridan, Slazenger, Sleepmaker, Tontine and Yakka. In 1929, the company started in the shoes market, in 1937 in sporting goods, in 1960 in mattresses, in 1969 in underwear, and in 1985 they renamed the company Pacific Brands as a division of Pacific Dunlop. With this conglomeration of companies, the strength of the brand names increased.

Since 2001, Pacific Brands has acquired a number of influential companies, the first being Sara Lee Apparel Australia in 2001, Kolotex hosiery and Sachi women's footwear in 2003, Sheridan in 2005, Peri and Foam Products Australia (FPA) in 2006 and the Yakka Group and the streetwear division of Globe International in 2007. The company was listed on the Australian Stock Exchange in 2004. Generating over $2.1 billion of sales in the 2008 financial year and employing 9000 staff over a 300-brand portfolio, the company has implemented a new strategy to reduce debt. In February 2009, Pacific Brands announced it would close seven clothing factories in

**12.3** Hard Yakka Legends: Quarry. Designer: Wilson Everard

Photo: Wellcom. Courtesy Hard Yakka

Australia, which is costing the industry 1200 jobs and 650 additional jobs lost in non-manufacturing roles, including the administrative staff of the Hawthorn head office.

## Cue: 1968 to present

Cue began with just one family-owned store in Sydney's Strand Arcade in 1968. Its debut began in the swinging sixties and the label rolled out popular contemporary fashion designs, including its famous power suits of the 1980s and ready-to-wear smart casual collections of the 1990s. Today, Cue remains prominent in the wardrobes of women of all ages, as the company's designs have been embraced by generations of women. Cue remains Australian-owned by the original family, which has continued to expand its business to New Zealand. The company proudly boasts that most of its products are Australian made, and its claim to fame is churning out innovative contemporary design in its stores on a weekly basis.

## Brown Sugar: 1975 to present

Brown Sugar has been dressing Australian women since 1975. It started with a small store in Brighton, Melbourne. At first it was intended as a fashion boutique housing various labels and collections from well-known Australian designers, but the focus shifted and Brown Sugar quickly began to design and manufacture under its own label. The company is committed to good fit (available in half sizes), trend adaptability and timeless fashion. While Brown Sugar continues to expand and strengthen its business principles, all pattern-making, fit and quality assurance are conducted in-house. Brown Sugar prides itself in creating beautiful, feminine fashion.

## Rip Curl: 1969 to present

Two men – Doug Warbrick and Brian Singer – were determined to both surf and run a business so, with surfing their main priority, they introduced the Rip Curl brand. Rip Curl sponsored many of the best surfers in the world with its 'Number One' wetsuit and close involvement in the sport of surfing. Committed to the technology of its products, Rip Curl produced wetsuits for windsurfers, sailors and water skiers, as well as surfers. They are attractive and colourful, playful and fun. As the company grew, to minimise manufacturing costs by exporting to other continents, they decided to build on selling designs, ideas and technology made under the licence of the country where there was a market. In 1981, Rip Curl established its first corporate licensee in Southern California. Today there are nine stores within walking distance of one of America's most popular surf breaks. They market the adage that Rip Curl has never lost touch with the surf, and twenty-eight years on some of the company's offices worldwide still remain empty in search of a good wave!

## Seafolly: 1975 to present

Since 1975, Seafolly has continued to diversify across the broad international swimwear market. The label is currently stocked in fashion department stores and swimwear boutiques all over the world. The designs are innovative and fun, and epitomise the Australian beach culture. The product's success is due to the endorsement and sampling of staff members and their families, who enjoy testing the quality of the apparel accessories and lifestyle products. Seafolly has always remained privately owned and 100 per cent Australian made. In March 2003, Seafolly announced a partnership with Nike Inc. to design, manufacture, market and distribute Nike swimwear in Australia, New Zealand and Asia. The company's success is summarised by its motto: 'Seafolly is a style, a colour and a perfect fit for everybody.'

## Country Road

Starting out as a niche women's shirting business in 1974, in the 1980s and 1990s Country Road expanded its Australian store base and wholesale business and entered the US and Asian markets. Through brand development and product extension, it developed a 'superstore' concept, which meant that Australians could purchase womenswear, menswear, accessories and homewares from a single store. When the US venture failed in the 1990s, this impacted on the Australian company and ultimately its profitability. However, it recovered when the new investor, Woolworth Holdings Ltd, South Africa, purchased it in 1998 and began to rebuild the business with a new modern identity in 2004. Expanding into new product categories, Country Road has continued to flourish and regain its market position with sixty retail stores, an additional eighty concession outlets, and over 2000 employees in Australia and New Zealand. Since its creation, the Country Road brand has grown to become one of the best-known and highly regarded clothing and retailing brands in Australia. The brand enjoys 97 per cent recognition in Australia and is inextricably linked to an Australian lifestyle that is relaxed, stylish, modern and desirable.

Mainstream Fashion – Daywear Separates –
Peter Norton.

Mainstream Fashion – Casual Weekendwear –
Women's – East Side Clothing Company.

Mainstream Fashion – Casual Weekendwear –
Men's – Najee.

**12.4** Bicentennial portfolio,
*FIA Newsletter*

Courtesy Council of Textile and Fashion
Industries of Australia Limited

Mainstream Fashion – Daywear Dresses –
Stitches.

## Berkeley Apparel

Berkeley Apparel was founded in Melbourne by Joseph Cohen in 1907 as a men's suiting company, using tailoring skills and a philosophy based on quality and style. Originally with an emphasis on high-end manufacturing, the business has moved into importing high-value brands. In 1976, Berkeley acquired the licence for Pierre Cardin and in 1988 gained the licence for Nino Cerruti to supply to the Australian and New Zealand markets. The 1990s saw the launch of its own brand, Studio Italia, which offered Italian style and quality at an affordable price and went on to win the prestigious Fashion Industry Award (FIA) in 1994. In 2000 Berkeley supplied the Sydney Olympic Games with uniforms for the male athletes and officials. In 2002 it was the first Australian manufacturer to develop the 'washable' suit. Over the past two decades, Berkeley has changed from a manufacturer to a distributor, building a reputation for its stylish and innovative suits at affordable prices. With its hundredth birthday celebration in 2008, the company also commemorated the contributions by four generations of the Cohen family.

## Sportscraft

Sportscraft was founded by Wolf Bardas in 1914 under the name Sportsleigh. Originally a manufacturing business, it soon established a reputation for quality, consistent fit, fabric innovation and great value. In 1950, the name Sportscraft was registered and it soon became a household word and a true Australian fashion iconic brand. Like so many other successful womenswear businesses, the brand added menswear to its range in the early 1970s. Today Sportscraft has extended its range to include accessories, including ties, scarves, jewellery, handbags and shoes, and has twenty-seven stores nationally, stocked at Myer and David Jones through their concept stores.

## Future prospects

The future of Australia's fashion businesses will be influenced by the global economic downturn and the government's labour and environmental policies. Brands – in particular global brands – have performed increasingly important roles in our everyday lives. For the last twenty years, consumers have dictated a trend for complex customised products that not only fulfil a functional suitability but also satisfy an emotional aspiration. A need to belong, our sense of security and even our identification have become intrinsically interwoven with brand purchases.

The brand phenomenon has become so complex that companies have resorted to nuances to separate themselves from their competitors. Perhaps that complexity will be seen as an impediment for future generations, which will reject the restrictions of over-regulation. Global fashion brands that have attempted to tailor their products to appeal to the culture of individualism have suffered heavy losses because they have been unable to achieve economies of scale.

However, larger companies are usually in a position to afford the new technologies which, since the late 1990s, have slowly continued to work their way into the market. These technologies include body scanning, 3D avatars, digital imaging, garment rendering, radio frequency identification and automated garment development tools. As a result, the search continues for ways to best commercialise the new technologies for a mass market that has become accustomed to purchasing apparel through volume brand/label channels. Automated garment development technologies could provide solutions, but at this stage the technology is predominantly in the hands of researchers funded by government programs. Those companies that are taking up automated garment development technology are using parts that they can integrate into their existing structures.

Unfortunately, most of the technologies are cost prohibitive for small business; yet they are the ones in a position best able to customise a product for the individual. On the other hand, it is commercially unpalatable for large corporations who can afford the technology to deliver the level of service required for a truly customised product. It is not surprising, then, that some of the technologies have not been taken up as quickly as one would have expected. This is disappointing, because solutions could be found for better-fitting garments and bring relief to consumers in search of apparel that fits and most suits their physical features.

In April 2009, EU TCF industries met to discuss a new phase in developing automated garment development technology to overcome the problem of waste products associated with over-consumption. With an estimated cost of €21 billion in unsold waste product accumulating in the European marketplace, the environmental sustainability argument is gathering momentum and is likely to create renewed interest in this field. Individual designers have the ability to remake and reuse waste materials, a trend emerging from European benchmarks which will gradually accelerate, driven by a consumer sentiment that is becoming increasingly aware of global footprints and the safe use of chemicals.

The internet will continue to play an important role both in helping the industry to collaborate and as an information and trend-setting resource. It could also become the host for a national database that profiles the target market and allows retailers, designers and technicians to data-mine for base sizes and parameters in ranges and inventory levels. A new clothing size standard is also long overdue and needs to be developed in cooperation with Standards Australia. The industry is yet to debate what a new standard could look like. A policy framework may offer better solutions than 'a one size fits all' model.

Flexible, formal workplace training models that link education and industry offer solutions because they have the potential to foster a rapid exchange in technology. In a 2009 interview, federal Minister for Trade Simon Crean argued that those countries that will lead in the future are now investing heavily in training and infrastructure. The fashion industry would do well to heed his advice.

In conclusion, in order for government, industry bodies and educators to assist fashion businesses, the Australian fashion industry should participate in comprehensive research into the supply chain that re-profiles the industry. Old ways of measuring its performance are no longer a true reflection of its well-being. Throughout history, Australians have demonstrated a resilience and capacity to triumph over adversity. Through innovative product development, investment in new technologies, and the continuing merging of education and industry, opportunities will emerge.

## References

Crean, S. (2009), interview with F. Kelly, *Breakfast*, ABC Radio National, 20 May.

Green, R. (2008), TCF Review: *Building Innovative Capability Report*, Canberra: Department of Innovation, Industry, Science and Research.

McDowell, C. (1998), address to Business Seminar, Melbourne Fashion Festival, March.

McIntyre, P. (2009), 'Luxury retreats to a niche for the stealthy wealthy', *The Age*, 28 May, n.p.

Textile and Fashion Industries of Australia (TFIA) (2008), *TFIA Focus*, <www.tfia.com.au>.

# FASHION FRONTIERS

*Liliana Pomazan*

**13.1** Philips Design, *Bubelle*, 2006
Courtesy Philips Design

**I**N *Australian Fashion Unstitched*, fashion and textile designers, museum curators, academics, researchers, writers and business representatives have reflected on past achievements. This final chapter projects some new ideas about the future of the Australian fashion industry. In the first decade of the new millennium, a paradigm shift is becoming apparent with the rise of the independent fashion designer. Our new generation of designers do not feel thwarted by the attitudes of last century – the 'cultural cringe' that so many authors have written about – which assumed that fashion design in Europe, especially French and Belgian, American and Japanese, was superior to Australian design. Nor are the new designers slaves to the dictates of the trend-forecasting companies, such as Worth Global Style Network (WGSN) or Stylesight. Instead, their diversification in design, and their capacity for experimentation, innovation and design integrity will characterise their strengths and will propel them into the future. This chapter considers three future directions, all integral to the development of a stronger and sustainable fashion future: the rise of independent designer fashion; the development of ethical and sustainable fashion as part of the collective global conscience; and the embracing of new technologies.

## Independent designers

For emerging independent designers, the spirit of the time is one of optimism and dedication. They are not only producing fashion for the Australian lifestyle but are also aiming to showcase their work on an international level by participating in fashion on global terms. Looking back in history to the 1980s, when the market was saturated with collections that were far too derivative of international models, the Fashion Design Council of Australia (FDC) (Burton and Worth 1996), emerged as a guiding light, encouraging young designers, many of whom had come out of art schools, to step outside of the 'status quo' and to show their innovative creations in their fashion parade extravaganzas.

In 1983 the FDC, co-founded by Kate Durham and Robert Buckingham with the help of graphic designer Robert Pearce in Melbourne, gained a momentum that culminated in its *coup d'état* show entitled Fashion '89, which was presented in two venues to an audience of over 10 000 people. It allowed individual emerging designers, many of whom were relatively unknown and made up their garments in their 'back rooms', to bring out the revolutionary in themselves. Buckingham insisted that, right from the beginning, the parades were primarily about having fun, but they developed into dynamic, sophisticated and artistically pleasing multi-art 'cabarets' that combined great music, lighting, theatrical modelling and unique fashion. These were instrumental in putting Melbourne fashion on the map and encouraging the rise of the independent designer in Australia.

In the new millennium, it seems that a similar phenomenon is taking place. According to Jo Cramer (2009), fashion academic and designer, a new breed of designers is emerging:

> From a design perspective, the new generation of independent designers show a renewed interest in the craft of making, and are more confident to dismiss international trends in pursuit of their own creative expression. Australian fashion suffers still from the 'cultural cringe', with most big fashion brands here copying (almost stitch for stitch) overseas fashions, but this next generation offer more hope for this country finally finding its own identity. (Cramer 8 April, 2009)

Embedded in the rise of the independent designer is the return of the artisan, with quality achieved through high levels of craftsmanship evident in their garments. Veteran designer Katie Pye (2009) comments on the global 'cultural meltdown' and states:

> if people could become 'makers' again, they would have the pleasure or self-fulfilment of making garments themselves . . . achieving camaraderie, enjoyment and a sense of achievement in their studio-based practice.

From what the design academies are saying, a larger percentage of students are genuinely recognising and understanding the importance of the craft of design and the craft of making as integral to the design process. Karen Webster (2009), currently Director of Melbourne's L'Oréal Fashion Festival, argues that this is not just happening in fashion but also:

> . . . in all arenas, so you're seeing across creative industries there is a return of the artisan, an appreciation of bespoke methods are being realised in arenas including industrial design, food design, architecture, interior design. This is a significant aesthetic and cultural shift signifying a distinct design movement that contrasts to quick response, fast product that has filled our shelves for many years. I believe it is a counter shift to mass-production and homogenised product and highlights a true appreciation for the craft of making, something's taken someone time to create and it's been a well considered design process. (Webster 2 June 2009)

Arguably, this type of paradigm shift occurs for many reasons, but progressive fashion education plays a primary role, encouraging students to express themselves through experimentation, to develop high-level skills and to create innovative and dynamic clothing. Pluralistic design has dominated fashion trends from the 1990s, whether it is expressed in DIY streetwear, art-as-fashion, high-end made-to-measure, new or vintage, recycled or reconstructed designer collections. With the rise of the independent designers with their own particular sensibilities and interests, new fashion styling will cater to the demands of the discerning and ever more sophisticated fashion consumers who expect individualised, forward-thinking garments and want choice.

Reporting on Rosemont Australian Fashion Week 2009, *Vogue Australia* advocated East Sydney TAFE student Dion Lee as one of the top ten designers to watch out for in the next few years, as the strength of his conceptual approach to design was clear from his Spring/Summer 2009–10 collection showing. Lee had previously won the 2008 coveted Fashion Graduate of the Year award with his highlight pieces, which featured sophisticated origami folds, cutout work and bold, Balmain-inspired large-shouldered garments. *Vogue Australia* referenced other emerging designers who 'searched well beyond the mainstream' to design their collections, namely Geoffrey J. Finch of Antipodium, Therese Rawsthorne, Konstantina Mittas, Anna Plunkett and Luke Sales of Romance Was Born, Kym Ellery of Ellery, Jade Sarita

Arnott of Arnsdorf, Ben Pollitt of Friedrich Gray, Karla Spetic, Gary Bigeni, Dhini Pararajasingham of Dhini, and Monika Tvanek and Ingrid Verner of TV (*Vogue Australia* July 2009). These designers are a few among dozens who boldly adhere to their vision and the belief that their work is as good as any on the global stage. Webster (2009) relates that she discovered, much to her dismay, that in the mid 1990s it was impossible to conceive of a viable independent fashion sector in Melbourne. However, she realises that in 2009 this is now a real possibility, as the independent fashion scene is dynamic and emerging as a design *tour de force*:

> In the last fifteen years we've seen this shift, with major events like the Melbourne Fashion Festival providing a platform for the showcasing of independent fashion. Alongside this we have seen the rise of the independent retailer such as Alice Euphemia, the series of Fat stores and Milly Sleeping in Carlton which have really supported the local designers. Additional to this you also have the department stores now battling it out against each other; jostling for the premium position to discover the 'hot new thing'. Department stores are helping to support a lot of those designers in the early stages of their careers. (Webster 2 June 2009)

Fashion weeks, such as Rosemont Australian Fashion Week, L'Oréal Melbourne Fashion Festival, the Mercedes Fashion Festival in Sydney and the Brisbane and Perth Fashion Festivals will continue to showcase Australian design talent and further facilitate international sales opportunities. Unlike the Fashion Design Council, which had to find funding to stage its fashion parades, a much-improved infrastructure now exists that platforms these fashion festivals. Government funding and corporate sponsorship now bolster these international events, which encompass associated business seminars, conferences, international fashion presenters and tourism promotions.

Simon Lock (ABC Online), founder and managing director of Australian Fashion Week in Sydney since 1995, says that the industry-only event now attracts 150 overseas buyers, who include prestigious buyers from exclusive stores like Barneys, Harrods and Lane Crawford. He emphasises that Spring/ Summer collections are very important to the Australian designers' year, representing about 70 per cent of their business by the time the collections are launched in-store in August. Fashion exports are worth about $240 million (2006) to the economy every year, and this event generates around $100 million in wholesale orders with the help of Austrade, the government's export agency. Whereas Europe and North America have been the key traditional markets for local designers, according to Lock: 'The future now for the Australian designers is Asia and the big markets of Hong Kong and China' (ABC Online 2009a).

While fashion remains a niche industry in Australia, international sales are growing by more than 10 per cent a year, and Australian Fashion Week attempts to show a balance of established and New Wave designers. Emerging designers who will attract a whole new generation of fashion buyers looking for something innovative include Anna Thomas, Melanie Cutfield and Nevenka, as well as Jayson Brunsdon, who has built a business spanning Britain, the United States, the United Arab Emirates and most recently Singapore (2008). Brunsdon also believes that Asia is the new frontier for Australian fashion designers, due to its large population. Lock insists that the growing international interest in Australian fashion is tantamount to the way the Australian fashion scene is perceived overseas.

## Globalisation and sustainability issues

The global environmental movement has gained momentum over the last decade, and this shift towards a concerted effort to save the planet from the ravages of the textile and fashion industry's carbon footprint is also becoming a central focus for Australia's fashion industry. General consensus indicates that taking some action – however small to begin with – will make a considerable contribution to curbing the environmental damage currently occurring, and will also help to rectify poor labour practices evident in a number of areas of the production and retail processes within the textile and fashion industry. Sue Thomas, author on ethics and sustainable fashion practice, notes that:

> Australia's proximity to Asia and China means the percolation of responsible conscious design practice will benefit the local and offshore supply chain. Designers are attuned to the zeitgeist of the ethical consumer who is disturbed by human and animal rights abuses and a lack of social justice. As designers, they are looking to support the supply chain stakeholders – including the consumer – to make responsible choices. (Thomas 25 June 2009)

Australian design historian and environmentalist Tony Fry (2009), in his book entitled *Design Futuring: Sustainability, Ethics and New Practice*, calls for greater designer responsibility, redirective practice and conscientious consumption. He argues:

> there is an overwhelming imperative to create a powerful futuring counterforce which embraces the fact that the fundamental change upon which our future depends, the change towards sustainment, cannot occur without design. (Fry 2009: 58)

He explains redirected practice as:

> akin to a new kind of [design] leadership, underpinned by a combination of creating new (and gathering old) knowledge directed at advancing means of sustainability while also politically contesting the unsustainable status quo. (Fry 2009: 57)

In the fashion industry, new designers are reconsidering traditional practices of pattern-making, cutting and construction methods, and use of waste materials. Also, as part of the design process, they are redesigning original or classic garments in ways that defy categorisation, forcing the fashion audience to critically assess accepted sartorial norms and practices.

**13.2** Lisa Gorman and Nest Architects, *Ship-Shop*, 2008

Photo: Jesse Marlow. Courtesy Gorman

In terms of business practices, larger corporate groups, such as Sportsgirl, are actually now establishing a sustainable strategy within all of their business and readdressing the fundamental strategies they employ in the commercial, designer and customer sectors of their business. Like Marks & Spencer, they are aiming to improve their performances systematically and gradually over a designated period of time. According to Webster, Sportsgirl works differently from the others:

> Sportsgirl has commissioned innovative designers such as Romance Was Born to create capsule collections by placing significant orders with them. The designers produce these orders within their own production capacity managing the process directly themselves. Target who have also supported independent designers including Yeojin Bae, TL Wood and Gail Sorronda in the past few years with their 'Designers for Target' collections work in a different framework. The designers work collaboratively with the buying and production teams to develop the prototypes and then Target take full responsibility to produce the collections utilising their production and manufacturing network. (Webster 25 May 2004)

This presents the dilemma currently faced by the fashion design industry, which the director of the Council of Textile and Fashion Industries of Australia Limited (TFIA), Jo-Ann Kellock, endorses:

> Undeniably, the fashion industry's sustainability is tempered by Australia's ability to supply designers with a local industry infrastructure and skilled labour. The future of the Australian fashion industry on the surface looks positive because of the growing pool of design talent and Australia's rising ability to market itself. However, locally made products will continue to be an issue unless the industry can . . . find skilled sample machinists – the need is critical now and will continue to grow. (Kellock 27 May 2009)

While Kellock acknowledges that Anna Plunkett and Luke Sales of Romance Was Born are among a small percentage of designers who are able to produce their designs within Australia, using their own resources, there are many other designers who have limited choices and have turned to offshore production:

> At the moment things looks potentially dire. The market for fashion (especially innovative fashion) is comparatively small in Australia, and the impending recession coupled with the removal

of remaining tariffs could strike the already struggling industry a near-fatal blow. Cheaper production prices in Asia are pushing the last of local manufacturing offshore, but many higher end labels cite the lack of local skill as their main reason for reluctantly moving to offshore production. We are losing our skill base. If we've lost our manufacturing base, our manufacturing expertise, and our resources, and we haven't built up factories, to produce locally will become harder and harder and even if people want to return now to Australian manufacturing, it would take a major investment to set it up. (Kellock 27 May 2009)

Arguably, the challenges regarding the sustainability practices facing Australian designers over the next decade are immensely daunting and reflect similar conditions across the planet. According to international sources, moving proactively towards improving environmental performance across the textile and fashion industry's supply chain is a must, including sustainable design, fibres and fabrics and maximising reuse, recycling and end-of-life management of textiles and clothing as well as the laundering of clothes (UK Government 2009). If history has taught us anything, it is that out of great constraints and restrictions have come great inventions and ideas. From this perspective, with the highly individual and exceptional design talent in Australia, the future must be bright.

## Future textile and fashion technologies: 'smart fashions'

At the opposite end of the spectrum is the exciting and awe-inspiring work of artists, designers and scientists working with far-future technology in their practices, producing prototypes that gives us a hint of the possibilities of how technology may shape clothes in the near to distant future. The radical shift in investigating and exploring the potential of 'what a garment is and what a garment can be' has continued in the work of the renowned avant-garde Parisian fashion designer Hussein Chalayan. His Airplane Dress (Spring/Summer collection 2000) heralded the future of technologically based fashion for the new millennium. This dress, realised from the same material used in aircraft construction, changed shape by the use of a remote control. Chalayan's designs have been informed by technology and inspired by architectural theories and science. When asked to describe the evolution of his work for a recent interview, Chalayan responded: 'My work has become more and more cross disciplinary . . . to express my ideas' (*Designboom* 2009 para 1). His *oeuvre* can better be classified as 'fashion architecture', as the intellectual principles of fashion and architecture are seen as parallel practices because they both create environments 'defined through spatial awareness – the structures they create are based on volume, function, proportion, and material' (Museum of Contemporary Art, Los Angeles 2006). Furthermore:

> Thanks to technological advances, the practices of fashion and architecture have never been so intertwined: pleating, seaming, folding, and draping are now part of our architectural vocabulary and garments of sophisticated structural complexity are making their way down the runways and onto the streets. These two creative principles have been, and continue to be, driving forces in our society. (Italian Cultural Institute of Los Angeles 2006, para 2)

Many diverse and innovative Australian fashions have largely depended upon the quality and characteristics of the textiles themselves to give full realisation to the designer's vision and to contribute to a lexicon of what we considered modernity in fashion. However, over recent years there has been a crossover between interdisciplinary fields, including art, textiles, design, science and technology, to produce interactive textiles and 'smart fashions'.

In our twenty-first-century world, the textile and fashion industry is now used to terms related to far-future technologies or nanotechnology. In recent years, the breadth of the range of textiles for fashion purposes has become extraordinary: nanotechnology has further propelled research and development of traditional and recently developed fabrics into the stratosphere of never-ending possibilities. Terms such as 'smart fabrics', 'intelligent textiles', 'e-textiles', 'interactive textiles' and 'smart fashion' multiply every day and are rapidly becoming part of the vocabulary of the textile and fashion industry. Many companies, globally and locally,[1] are working on seemingly surreal scenarios and ideas projecting mainstream society into the realm of far-future technological innovation. Nanotechnology expert Carl Masens from the University of Technology, Sydney states that: 'Nanotechnology will impact on our lives in ways we can only imagine' (CSIRO 12 Sept 2008 a: para. 2). Nanotechnology has fuelled the collective imagination of what may be possible within the coming decades.

Far-future innovation depends upon multidisciplinary collaborations, and it is now common to have pioneering and groundbreaking prototypes designed by a number of partners or research probes teams, including scientists, computer analysts, electrochemistry and electronics specialists, textile and fibre engineers, textile, fashion, industrial, interior and architectural designers, economists and future trend forecasters. These probes teams have set up new multidisciplinary systems by the very nature of their shared design process: here the most important techniques that form part of the group design engagement come from visual thinking and 'thinking through doing':

> Research probes mobilise users' tacit knowledge about their beliefs, aspirations and desires, providing a deeper level of knowledge and insight into what might be the catalysts and drivers of future consumer wearable technology. (Central Saint Martins College of Art and Design 14 June 2009)

Teams will experiment and invent prototypes using traditional current technologies with far future applications and potentialities. Nanotechnology is a burgeoning field in a potentially endless spread of disparate areas – which, of course, include the textile and fashion field of research. Nanotechnology's huge leap in the advance of what is possible in order to make our lives better is uncontainable and lends to an optimistic view of the possible applications for the textile and fashion industry.

Australia's Commonwealth Scientific and Industrial Research Organisation (CSIRO) is one of the leaders in the field of nanotechnology in textiles, and has numerous clusters of researchers working within the rapidly increasing field of 'smart fabrics', 'interactive textiles' and flexible wearable systems. CSIRO nurtures local alliances in nanotechnology and is involved in research and development hubs and research networks with most Australian university research and development groups. Globally:

> Australia is well positioned to take the lead in textiles innovation, due to its strong production base, good technology base and established infrastructure (manufacturing, marketing, distribution, quality control). In Australia, technology supply to the industry is led by CSIRO Textile & Fibre Technology, the leading domestic technology supplier to sectors such as wool, cotton, leather and technical textiles at the fibre, yarn, fabric and garment levels. (CSIRO 12 Sept 2008 b: paras 2–3)

In the future, opportunities for nanotechnology in the textile and fashion industry will most likely be in product innovation, not process innovation. This groundbreaking technology will be used to create new fabrics and also enhance the properties of existing materials. Available nanotechnology innovations in clothing that are currently available include: fabrics that are stain, wrinkle and liquid resistant; garments that absorb body odours; garments that emit deodorant by slow release; clothing that changes colour with change in light and with external or body heat; and garments made from superfine merino wool knit for skin tear prevention. Further intensive explorations in the field include new blended fabrics with carbon nanotubes (CNTs), to be used in sportswear, mountain clothing and military uniforms. For example, composite fabrics with CNTs or interweaving with extruded CNT fibres will introduce higher conductivity and capacitive, as well as high, strength (CSIRO 2009b: para. 1). Textiles will be improved in the areas of ultra-violet blocking, durability, breathability, flexibility, recyclability, colour retention, self-repair, and so on.

Research and development also address aesthetic qualities, such as luminosity of fabric, and the creation of synthetic fabrics with the properties of natural fibres by using surface coating (CSIRO 2009b: para. 8). Added to the long list of projects are electronics embedded into fabrics to make them more durable and stable and to enable them to survive the process of regular machine washing. This is the brainchild of Dr Mark Looney and Mr Peter Waters at the CSIRO (Geelong, Victoria). The scientists have invented a way of 'seamlessly' integrating conducting polymers into the structure of textiles or existing garments. According to the CSIRO:

> Textiles produced by the new process have potential to incorporate an array of communication devices, and act as sensors for temperature, strain, pressure, humidity, and chemical biosensing. These might also be used as barriers to electromagnetic radiation, as anti-static treatments, and for heating and cooling. Garments and other products manufactured from these textiles could make daily life easier, healthier, safer and more comfortable. (CSIRO 12 September 2008: para. 2)

Artists and designers have utilised technology to create hybrid fabrics and garments. The possibilities within the field are ever-expanding and awe-inspiring in their nature. Three of the leaders in their fields are Donna Franklin, Lucy McRae for Phillips and Leah Heiss. Refreshingly, these designers look towards fashion's possible future, rather than to the past.

Donna Franklin's *Fibre Reactive Hybrid Dress* (2004–08) was produced in silk organza, perspex and wood and transformed by the mycelium and fruiting bodies of the fungus *Pycnoporus coccineus* (Australian Orange Bracket Fungus). Franklin, a contemporary textile artist, held an artist-in-residency position from 2003 to 2004 at the University of Western Australia's celebrated SymbioticA, the centre of excellence in biological arts. She collaborated with the team to 'grow a dress' rather than sew a dress. While working on this project, Franklin posed the following research question: 'Imagine a fabric that grows ... a garment that forms itself without a single stitch' (Australian Government n.d.). Colleague Gary Cass is researching fashion created from wine (Franklin and Cass n.d.), and Franklin teamed up with him and Alan Mullett from the University of Western Australia to author *Micro'be'*, an arts project that uses science to convert wine into a cellulose product. Franklin and Cass experimented with new biological textile techniques that they invented with futuristic dressmaking in mind:

> Instead of lifeless weaving machines producing the textile, living microbes will ferment a garment. It smells like red wine and feels like sludge when wet, but the cotton-like cellulose dress fits snugly as a second skin. The material is very delicate, comprising micro-fibrils of cellulose. The colouration of the fabric will depend on the wine used, red wine – red fabric, white wine or beer – a translucent material. A fermented garment will not only rupture the meaning of traditional interactions with body and clothing, but will also examine the practicalities and cultural implications of commercialisation. (Australia's Cultural Portal 13 Jun 2009)

Exploring other new and exciting possibilities around architectural body forms and trans-disciplinary design for the future definition of garments, is Australian Lucy McRae.[2] McRae's work involves an artistic collaboration called 'Lucyandbart' that explores 'low-tech' methods of re-shaping the human silhouette (McRae 12 May 2009). Quite specifically, she describes herself as a 'Body Architect', as her work explores the intersection of fashion, architecture and the human body. At the innovative Philips Design in Eindhoven, the Netherlands, McRae worked on the body's reaction to, and interaction with, the environment. As a member of the the Probes team, McRae had worked with many designers, engineers, garment technologists and lighting specialists in a program which explores far future design. With Clive van Heerden as the Director of the project and Jack Mama as the Creative Director, the Probes team developed 'provocations' from advanced concept through to prototype. Van Heerden has been working and pioneering wearable technology concepts since the 1990s and continues to expand the scope of technological applications on and around the human body. Part of the program's initiative is to provoke discussions, create scenarios and gain feedback from people in order to understand what future needs may be. The team identifies future trends before they become submerged in mainstream society. McRae explains:

> If a technology has no human need, then technology will die. The Probes team develops projects and provocative scenarios to try to understand human need and necessity. My work at Philips has taught me that innovation and successful implementation of technology happens in markets that require such technological applications. 'Sensing' textiles in the medical world will be the first to be mass produced as wearable technology applications, simply because there is a need. What happens next is that the youth culture 'hack' these body garments and turn them into something which they can identify with. This will be one area of development that will shift wearable technology from a purely *haute couture* 'art' level to something worn by the masses. (McRae 9 June 2009)

The Skin Probe project, made up of McRae and a team of fifteen designers and technologists, developed two 'Soft Technology' garments to identify future possibilities for high technology materials and electronic textile development in the areas of skin and emotional sensing. These outfits, entitled Bubelle and Frisson (2006), explore emotive technology and show how the body and the near environment can use pattern and colour change to interact with, and predict, the emotional state of the wearers. Bubelle, also known as the 'Blushing Dress', has a bubble silhouette and the material is illuminated by circular patterns that simulate real time regarding the wearer's emotions – whether the wearer is aroused, excited or anxious – and these are projected in the atmospheric space around her body. The Frisson garment explores the possibilities of a shivering textile, in which a constellation of tiny LED hairs light up across the body as someone blows into the palm of the wearer's hand. The Frisson is an interactive body suit with hundreds of LEDs meticulously soldered on to copper wires attached to the fabric. In essence, the Bubelle and Frisson are designed to measure skin signals that trigger light emissions through biometric sensing technology. Aiming to address 'sensitive' technology:

> These garments were developed as part of the SKIN research project, which challenges the notion that our lives are automatically better because they are more digital. It looks at more 'analog' phenomena like emotional sensing and explores technologies that are 'sensitive' rather than 'intelligent'. (Regine 2006 para 2)

**13.3** Philips Design, *Frisson*,
2006

Courtesy Philips Design

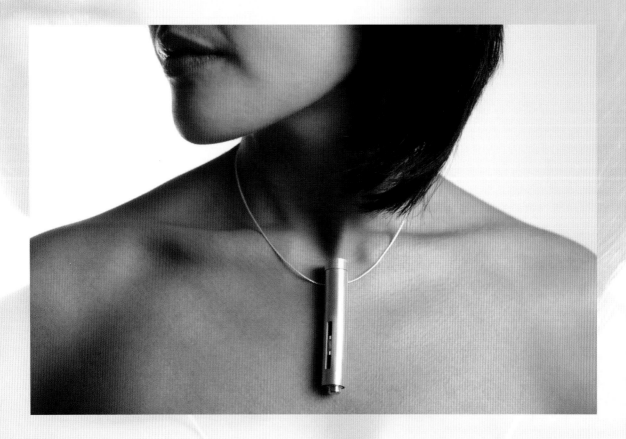

**13.4** Leah Heiss, *The Diabetes Neckpiece,* 2007–08

Photo: Narelle Sheean. Courtesy Leah Heiss

Acknowledged widely for its very successful, technologically far advanced outfits, Skin Probe was awarded the prestigious Red Dot Design's 'Best of the Best Award'[3] from a pool of 879 design entries from forty-seven countries. Excitement, play, fantasy as well as serious design brainstorming drive the Skin Probe team's work.

Another project for the Philips Design team involves electronic implants, or rather emotional tattoos that change, depending on the feelings of the wearer. The team researched and examined the growing trend of permanent body adornment and modification such as tattoos, piercing, implants and scarring. In indigenous cultures, in particular, tattoos and physical mutilation are among the oldest forms of personal expression and identity formation. In modern times, subcultures have used tattoos as a form of self-representation, a visual language communicating personality and status. One outcome of this project has been The Electronic Tattoo film, which Philips describes as the film that expresses 'the visual power of sensitive technology applied to the human body' (Philips 2009) through the interaction between two lovers.

Working at the forefront of future technological applications for jewellery is Leah Heiss. Heiss is a Melbourne-based artist, designer and academic whose research, practice and teaching merge jewellery, design, nanotechnologies and spatial investigation. Her central aim is to enhance the emotional relationships between people through emerging technologies, specifically nanotechnologies. Her most recent work focuses on the benefits of new technology to enhance health through the wearing of jewellery for the needle-free delivery of insulin and the wearing of body vessels for water purification. Heiss's designs have been exhibited widely, and she has presented her work at conferences and festivals both locally and globally.

Prior to her work incorporating nanotechnology, Heiss designed and produced a collection of 'enabled apparel' entitled Ether Beat. The garments were electronically enhanced so that they were able to 'sense, process, transmit and receive the ECG wavelength' (Heiss 2006: para. 1). This range of prototypes, produced in pairs, comprised singlets (*Under Beat*) that contained ECG electrode sensors and processing equipment, which could be connected to two outerwear garments: a blouse (*Ether Beat*) and a scarf (*Ether Scarf*). The blouse and scarf housed signal-processing equipment, small vibration motors and radio transceivers. The heartbeat wavelength from your 'remote friend/lover/relative' can be received through a vibration in the garment (Freeman-Greene 2007). Heiss speculates whether the wearing of these 'intelligent clothes' could encourage physiological and emotional empathy.

Heiss's extraordinary vision was realised when, from the initial stages, she incorporated technology into the design process. The prototypes were successful because of the integration of design development and process rather than just an incorporation of electronic pathways, processing equipment and battery power to existing garments. Heiss used a diverse range of materials, including high-density foam, silk organza, silver, solenoids, Arduino microprocessors, electronics and optic fibre. The Inner project was developed during the ANAT reSkin Wearable Technologies Laboratory[4] in early 2007. Heiss stated that the project:

> deals with issues of intrapersonal understanding – focusing on foibles, oddities, idiosyncrasies and eccentricities that may allude to emotional states. The garment senses a nervous habit – in this case touching the sternum – through the sensitive gingko brooch at the neck. This information is transmuted into an internal output: softly activating solenoids which tap against the ribcage, and an external output: subtle pulsating optic fibre along the stomach. (Heiss 2007: para. 1)

In 2008, Heiss completed the first highly competitive artist-in-residency offered by Nanotechnology Victoria. This residency assisted Heiss in the realisation of several interlinked 'subtle technology' projects. The key 'wellness jewellery' pieces with therapeutic properties include the Diabetes Neckpiece and Patch Rings, which allow transdermal patches (NanoMAPs) to be applied to the skin, enabling pain-free delivery of insulin to the body (O'Dwyer 2008). NanoMAPs, developed by Nanotechnology Victoria, are small (10 × 2 mm) circular discs which have an array of micro-needles on their surface delivering insulin, replacing the often painful traditional syringe. In sociological terms, Heiss asks 'how we might "enable" our favourite jewellery/artefacts with functionality above and beyond the aesthetic' (Heiss 2008: para. 2).

Another noteworthy ongoing project is the 'Carrying Wellness' neckpiece and water vessel initiated in 2007. The neckpiece and water vessel carry mesoporous iron oxide ($Fe_2O_3$), which can remove arsenic and other contaminants from water. The vessel and neckpiece are designed for people in transit in countries where arsenic is prevalent in drinking water, such as India and Bangladesh (ABC Online 2009b). The Carrying Wellness neckpiece is used in conjunction with a water vessel with filtration components to ensure that the purified water is safe to drink.[5] Heiss explains:

> My work puts me in a unique space artistically. I engage directly with the research and development of new technologies in a highly commercial and competitive arena. This allows me to make simultaneously emotionally sensitive and technically advanced projects, particularly when dealing directly with the body through jewellery and garments. (Heiss 2009c)

Presently being developed is another of Heiss' projects, entitled *Polarise* (2008–09). The *Polarise* project is a 'dynamic' installation of blown-glass vessels containing magnetic liquid. The elements react to the presence of a magnetic field: '*Polarise* suggests how our jewellery and personal artefacts may respond to unseen energies surrounding us' (Heiss 2009a: para. 1). These highly innovative and unique pieces have received public recognition nationally and internationally.

## Conclusion

These collaborations between experts in disparate fields work towards broadening horizons and setting new goals to sustain a buoyant textile and fashion industry. The highly exploratory and experimental innovations of design teams and laboratories, fuelled by the visions and experiments of artists, designers and scientists utilising new technologies, challenge the notions of how technology may shape clothes in the future – of 'what a garment is and what a garment can be'. The boundaries are imaginatively blurred and the aim is to explore and expand not only the functional and aesthetic requirements of clothing, but how to aim to fulfil consumers' desires for intelligent, sensitive and emotional garments. A continuing series of textile and fashion projects investigates highly innovative technologies, which enhance our relationship with the planet and the people on it. Australia occupies a unique position, both geographically and creatively, in the Southern Hemisphere, which provides a dynamic environment of ideas for global researchers at the forefront of investigation into wearable technology practices.

## Notes

1  Internationally, there are many companies (some of the leaders in this development include Sensatex, DuPont, ADA, Foster-Miller, Santa Fe Science and Technology, SOFTswitch and International Fashion Machines, among others) developing interactive textile products for use in a wide range of applications. See <www.plastemart.com/upload/Literature/Conductive-polymers-produce-smart-interactive-textiles-SMITs.asp>.

2  Lucy McRae trained as a classical ballerina and is an Interior Design graduate from RMIT University, Melbourne.

3  The international jury for the Red Dot Design competition based its decisions for choosing the best concepts of the year on the degree of innovation, realisation, aesthetic quality, functionality and of course usefulness, human interface, ergonomics and, not least, emotional content (<www.techpin.com/philips-design-skin-probe-wins-best-of-the-best-award>).

4  reSkin: in Summer 2007, the symposium intertwined the practices of media arts and sound design, textile and weaving, jewellery, object and fashion design to produce the reSkin Wearable Technology Lab. This collaborative project of ANAT, the Australian National University School of Art, the Centre for New Media Arts (CNMA) and Craft Australia places jewellers and fashion designers with new media artists in an intensive three-week research and development lab (see <reskin.anat.org.au/about>).

5  Both the Carrying Wellness and Diabetes projects were exhibited as part of an exhibition at RMIT Gallery entitled *Liminal* in November 2008, then showcased in in.tangible.scape.s in Belgium and the Levitas exhibition at Gallery Forty-five downstairs in March 2009.

# References

ABC Online (2009a), 'One-on-one: Simon Lock', *The Shallow End*, ABC TV, 13 June, <www.abc.net.au/news/arts/theshallowend/200705/s1911584.htm>.

—— (2009b), 'Designing the future: medical jewellery', *The New Inventors*, ABC TV, 25 June, <www.abc.net.au/tv/newinventors/txt/s2416729.htm>.

*Australia's Cultural Portal* (2009), 'Australia's smart fashions: interactive textiles and cyber-jewellery', 13 June, <www.cultureandrecreation.gov.au/articles/fashion/smart>.

Burton, S. and Worth, W. (eds and dir.) (1996), *Fashion Design Council: Revolt into Style*, Melbourne: Keno Eye Pictures.

Central Saint Martins College of Art and Design (2009), 14 June 2009. <www.csm.arts.ac.uk/docs>.

Commonwealth Scientific and Industrial Research Organisation (CSIRO) (2008), 'Integrating electronics into smart textiles', 12 September, <www.csiro.au/science/ps133.html>.

—— (2009a), 'Nanohouse brings nanotechnology home', 22 March 2009, <www.csiro.au/files/mediaRelease/mr2003/Prnanohouse.htm>.

—— (2009b), 'Textiles: creating fibre solutions', <www.csiro.au/science/Textiles.html>.

Cramer, J. (2009), interview by L. Pomazan, 8 April.

*Designboom* (2009), 'hussein chalayan', 13 May, <www.designboom.com/eng/interview/chalayan.html>.

Freeman-Greene, S. (2007), 'Band of hope', *The Age*, 3 November, <www.theage.com.au/news/arts/band-of hope/2007/11/02/1193619117811.html?page=fullpage>.

Fry, T. (2009), *Design Futuring: Sustainability, Ethics and New Practices*, Sydney: UNSW Press.

Heiss, L. (2006), *Ether Beat 2006*, <www.elasticfield.com/ether.htm>.

—— (2007), *Carrying Wellness: September 2007–present*, <www.elasticfield.com/wellness.htm>.

—— (2008), *2008 Diabetes*, <www.elasticfield.com/diabetes.htm>.

—— (2009a), *Polarise 2008–2009*, <www.elasticfield.com/polarise.htm>.

—— (2009b), *Inner 2007*, <www.elasticfield.com/inner.htm>.

—— (2009c), interview by L. Pomazan, 23 June.

Italian Cultural Institute of Los Angeles (2006), *Skin and Bones: Parallel Practices in Fashion and Architecture*, 21 March, <www.iicusa.org>.

Kellock, J. (2009), interview by L. Pomazan, 27 May.

McRae, L. (2009), interview by L. Pomazan, 12 May.

Museum of Contemporary Art, Los Angeles (2006), *Skin and Bones: Parallel Practices in Fashion and Architecture*, 19 November, <www.moca.org/museum/exhibitiondetail.php?id=370>.

O'Dwyer, E. (2008), 'Ring of life', *Sydney Morning Herald*, 25 August, <www.smh.com.au/news/innovations/ring-of-life/2008/08/25/1219516362612.html>.

Philips (2009), 'SKIN:Tattoo' 27 May, <www.design.philips.com/philips/sites/philipsdesign/probes/projects/tattoo/index.page>.

Pye, K. (2009), interview by B. English, 14 May.

Regine (2006), 'Lucy McRae's talk at NEXT', *We Make Money Not Art*, 4 December, <www.we-make-money-not-art.com/archives/2006/12/lucy-mcraes-tal.php>.

Thomas, S. (2009), interview by L. Pomazan, 25 June.

UK Government, *Sustainable Clothing Action Plan*, launched at London Fashion Week, 20 February, <www.defra.gov.uk/news/2009/090220a.htm>.

*Vogue Australia* (2009), 'Talent time', July, pp. 50–55.

Webster, K. (2004), interview by L. Pomazan, 25 May.

—— (2009), interview by L. Pomazan, 2 June.

# List of illustrations

Gwendolynne, Nicola Finetti, Akira Isogawa and Vixen, 2002. Photographer Jean-Francois Lanzarone. Courtesy Powerhouse Museum, Sydney.

**8.1** Hotel Bondi Swim, bikini with 'LOCAL' embroidery, 2008. Photographer Derek Henderson. Courtesy Hotel Bondi Swim Pty Ltd.

**8.2** Watersun, strappy maillot, 1966. Photographer John Waddy. Courtesy *Vogue Australia*, The Condé Nast Publications.

**8.3** Robin Garland, dart-shaped, front-tied bikinis, 1973. Courtesy *Vogue Australia*, The Condé Nast Publications.

**8.4** Seafolly catalogue, 1989–90. Photographer Grant Mathison. Courtesy Seafolly.

**8.5** Zimmermann bikinis, 2007. Photographer Simon Lekias. Courtesy Zimmermann.

**9.1** *Prue Acton in London*, 1967. © Newspix/News Ltd/3rdParty Managed Reproduction Supply Rights. Courtesy Newspix.

**9.2** Lucas, Melbourne 1934–68. *Fashion Book*, 1961, Autumn (Pierre Cardin reproduced in Australia by Lucas). National Gallery of Victoria, Melbourne. Gift of Mrs Margaret Price, 1980 (D206–1980). Courtesy National Gallery of Victoria.

**9.3** *Dress with Sunglasses Designed by Carla Zampatti for Polaroid*, 1974. Photo: Zampatti Bicentennial Wool Collection. Courtesy Carla Zampatti.

**9.4** Jenny Bannister and Ken Gensrich, *Medieval Stud Dress and Belt*, 1980. Leather, metal studs. National Gallery of Victoria, Melbourne. Purchased 1985 (CT18A-1985; CT18B-1985). Courtesy Jenny Bannister and Ken Gensrich.

**9.5** Sara Thorn & Bruce Slorach, ABYSS, *Jacket and Kilt*, 1985, screen-printed cotton. Melbourne 1985–92. Sara Thorn (designer) born Australia 1961 and Bruce Slorach (designer) born Australia 1961. National Gallery of Victoria, Melbourne. Presented by the National Gallery Women's Association, 1995. Courtesy Sara Thorn.

**10.1** Akira Isogawa, catwalk image of outfit, Spring/Summer 08/09. National Gallery of Victoria, Melbourne. Courtesy Akira Isogawa.

**10.2** *Martin Grant Paris* installation, National Gallery of Victoria
(9 December 2005 – 7 May 2006). Photographer Helen Oliver-Skuse.
Courtesy National Gallery of Victoria, Melbourne.

**10.3** Toni Maticevski, *Dali Goddess Evening Dress*, Spring/Summer 2007.
Collection: National Gallery of Victoria. Photo: Courtesy National Gallery of
Victoria, Melbourne.

**10.4** Josh Goot, catwalk image of outfit, Spring/Summer 2007. *Image: First
View*. Courtesy Josh Goot.

**11.1** Susan Dimasi and Chantal Kirby of MATERIALBYPRODUCT,
*Woodgrain Trench & Dress*, 2008. Photographer Sue Grdunc. Courtesy
MATERIALBYPRODUCT.

**11.2** Denise Sprynskyj and Peter Boyd of S!X, *Untitled*, Autumn/Winter
2003. Photographer Lucas Dawson. Courtesy S!X.

**11.3** Gwendolynne Burkin of Gwendolynne, catwalk image of outfit,
Winter 2001. Millinery: Richard Nylon. Melbourne Fashion Week, February
2001. Photographer Brad Hick. Courtesy Gwendolynne.

**11.4** Anna Plunkett and Luke Sales of Romance Was Born, *Untitled*, Garden
of Eden collection, Winter 2007. Photographer Lucas Dawson. Courtesy
Romance Was Born.

**11.5** Lisa Gorman of Gorman, Organic '04 collection, 2004. Photographer
Ben Glezer. Courtesy Gorman.

**12.1** Country Road, *Untitled*, Winter 2009. Photographer Tesh Patel.
Courtesy Country Road.

**12.2** CJ Wilson Factory, Johnston Street, Fitzroy, circa 1960 to 1965.
Courtesy Council of Textile and Fashion Industries of Australia Limited.

**12.3** Hard Yakka Legends: Quarry. Designer: Wilson Everard.
Photographer Wellcom. Courtesy Hard Yakka.

**12.4** Bicentennial portfolio, *FIA Newsletter*. Courtesy Council of Textile and
Fashion Industries of Australia Limited.

**13.1** Philips Design, *Bubelle*, 2006. Courtesy Philips Design.

**13.2** Lisa Gorman and Nest Architects, *Ship-Shop*, 2008. Photographer Jesse Marlow. Courtesy Gorman.

**13.3** Philips Design, *Frisson*, 2006. Courtesy Philips Design.

**13.4** Leah Heiss, *The Diabetes Neckpiece*, 2007–08. Photographer Narelle Sheean. Courtesy Leah Heiss.

# Index